INTRODUCTION TO
HISTORICAL LINGUISTICS

INTRODUCTION TO
HISTORICAL LINGUISTICS

ANTHONY ARLOTTO, *Harvard University*

HOUGHTON MIFFLIN COMPANY · BOSTON

NEW YORK · ATLANTA · GENEVA, ILL. · DALLAS · PALO ALTO

Printed in the U.S.A.

Library of Congress Catalog Card Number: 79-170967

ISBN: 0-395-12615-0

For my mother,
To the memory of my father,
and
For Thorkild and Katryna Jacobsen,
with respect and gratitude.

Contents

Illustrations

Preface

In view of the proliferation of linguistic publications within the past decade, the appearance of a new textbook requires justification. The discipline of historical linguistics has been in existence for more than a century and a half, and the amount of writing on the topic is more than enough to fill a lifetime or two with enjoyable and informative reading. Unfortunately, most of this material is available only to the initiated linguist and the polyglot; the English-speaking beginner has no more than a few rather dated elementary textbooks (or chapters) which can introduce him to the intellectual curiosities and patterned structures which occupy and delight the historical linguist.

This book is intended to be the principal text for a first course in historical linguistics, although it is hoped that it will also prove useful as background reading for courses in the histories of particular languages or the comparative philology of specific language groups. It does not presuppose any training in general linguistics; the appendices may be used or ignored depending on the individual student's background. Likewise, if one has objections to specific theories, such as classical American phonemics or transformational grammar, the sections dealing with these may be safely left out without impairing the continuity of the rest of the book.

Although it would be impossible to acknowledge all those whose scholarship is incorporated in this book, there are some individuals whose direct involvement merits specific mention. For many ideas and examples, I have relied heavily on the lectures and writings of my teacher, Calvert Watkins. Bruce Boling and Sheila Houle read the original draft and made many useful suggestions. Ives Goddard helped with the data from American Indian languages. Sandra Chung supplied the Polynesian sets in Chapter 7, and Dr. Frank Siebert generously allowed me to use his Algonquian data and maps in Chapter 15. Susan Norwood and Charles Bradshaw helped in compiling the bibliographies and checking individual forms. I am especially indebted to Morton Bloomfield for reading the entire manuscript and for continued encouragement and guidance.

Janet Hinkley, secretary to the Department of Linguistics, unselfishly gave her rare free moments to typing the manuscript. Victoria Turner of Houghton Mifflin helped in all aspects of this project with patience, understanding, intelligence, and generosity.

Anthony Thomas Arlotto
Winthrop House

1

The Scope of Comparative and Historical Linguistics

Linguistics is an academic field devoted to studying the various aspects of human language and, to some extent, the interaction of human language with other areas of human culture and behavior. It can be defined simply as "the science of language" because it attempts to gather data concerning a range of phenomena, to observe the patterns which underlie those phenomena, and to express the observed regularities by means of formal rules. To draw a parallel with the natural sciences, we can trace the formulation of Boyle's law. By observing the behavior of gases, Boyle was able to extract the simple formula that the pressure divided by the volume was a constant. In terms of ordinary mathematical notation he was able to express this as:

$$\frac{P}{V} = C$$

Now in a very important way, linguistics differs from the natural sciences in its ability to conduct controlled experiments. We cannot isolate a speaker in a laboratory and perform experiments to determine exactly what is happening when he speaks. Even if we did do this for a limited time, our results would be of doubtful validity, since various non-linguistic factors, such as previous associations, social opinions, and range of experience, would affect the outcome. The only apparent way to achieve the rigor of the laboratory science would be to isolate a number of infants from birth and carefully control all contact with language under widely varying conditions for each of the several children. To say the least, such experiments would be unethical.

Some of the scientific problems continually faced by linguists are shared by ecologists, who find that they must deal with total natural systems and cannot find all the answers by controlled experiments in laboratories. Like linguists, they must go out and observe the data in the natural environment, formulate hypotheses, and test them in methodologically imperfect, but nonetheless fruitful, ways in order to reach scientifically valid conclusions.

Like other scientific areas, linguistics can be divided into several subfields. The most abstract of these is *theoretical linguistics,* which borders on the areas of applied mathematics and applied logic. The theoretical linguist formulates and studies the abstract models and conventions used to express the regularities observed in human language. He is also interested in those elements or rules which are common to all languages and which are known as *linguistic universals.*

The second large division of linguistics is that which is generally called *descriptive.* As the name implies, the descriptive linguist is one whose task it is to describe particular languages; broadly speaking, these must account for the sounds of the language, the parts of speech, and how one puts together words to form sentences. We call the completed descriptions of languages *grammars.* The descriptive linguist may write a grammar of his own language, or he may choose to work on another language by eliciting information from a native speaker. He will collect words and sentences and will ask his informant direct questions about the language, such as whether or not a certain phrase sounds "natural."

Finally, we might mention that numerous scholars consider themselves to be doing interdisciplinary work involving linguistics and at least one other field. In recent years, we have witnessed the remarkable rise of these combined disciplines. For example, one who wishes to work extensively on the relationship between language and psychological phenomena such as perception, learning, or thought is called a "psycholinguist." In a similar vein, there are also sociolinguists, anthropological linguists, and mathematical linguists.

Since a descriptive linguist analyzes a language as it exists at a given point in time, his study is said to be *synchronic* ("with time"). Opposed to this is the study of a language at different points on the time dimension, called *diachronic* ("through time") investigation, and this is the area we will deal with in this book. The starting point of such a study is the clearly observed fact that *languages change in time.* The speech of a given generation is never quite identical to that of its parents or to that of its children. Of course, the differences between adjoining generations are slight and for the most part will go unnoticed. However, given a time span of centuries or millennia, minute differences will have a cumulative effect and often a given language will acquire a very new form. Its resemblance to the earlier stage will appear only after investigation.

For example, the following passage was translated from the Bible (Matthew 9:1–2) into English at three different points in time:

Old English Tenth century	Ða astah hē on scyp, and oferseglode, and cōm on his ceastre. Ða brohton hig hym ǣnne laman, on bedde licgende.
Early New English (Tyndale, 1526)	And he entred into the shippe: and passed over and cam into his awne cite. And lo they brought unto him a man sicke off the palsey lyinge in his bed.
New English Bible, 1970	So he got into the boat and crossed over, and came to his own town. And now some men brought a paralyzed man lying on a bed.

The last translation we read with no difficulty, since it is written in the language we use today. The middle one may look a bit unfamiliar, still it can be understood by a twentieth-century reader. But the first appears so strange, so far removed from present-day English, that in order to understand it, one would have to study Old English much as one studies a foreign language. In many senses, though, all three of the cited passages represent the same language. From the first to the last, there has been an unbroken tradition of individuals learning the language called English in childhood, and then passing on what was essentially the same language to the next generation.

If we take even an informal look at the Old English passage given above, we can note differences between it and the New English translation. These differences are representative of the *changes* which English has undergone in some thousand years.

The very first letter (Ð) is strange to us, because we no longer use it in our writing system, but it is simply the Old English way of writing the sound of *th* as in *thin*. The first word is a conjunction meaning 'then'. The second word is completely gone from the language; it is the past tense of the verb *astigan* 'to go up'. The next phrase should be recognizable, for it means 'on ship'. Note the spelling of the word *scyp;* we presume that at one time this word was pronounced something like *skip*. In terms of language change, what this tells us is that at some point in time, English speakers stopped saying *sk* and in its place began to say the sound we write *sh*. We know that this had already happened by the Early Modern English period because of the spelling in the second passage. One of the most striking differences between the Old and New English passages is the fact that the Old English subject pronouns (*hē* and *hig*) often follow the verb (here, the first verb of the series), whereas New English subjects almost always precede their verbs. In the very last phrase of the passage, we find the word order *on bed lying* (*on bedde licgende*), in which the participle follows the prepositional phrase. The New English order is just the opposite.

The items we have just noted are English examples of what is known as *language change*. In later chapters we will examine the different kinds of change, see what patterns can be observed throughout a given language, and try to express them in a formal linguistic way. The changes that languages undergo in the course of time are the data for historical linguistics. The historical linguist views human language as a dynamic, ever-changing phenomenon, stable insofar as it allows communication between speakers at given or nearby points of time, but ever changing as it reflects changing speech habits, as it is subject to internal and external factors, and as it adapts to new situations of the speech community.

In his most elementary work, the historical linguist takes two stages of a given language, both of which presumably have been studied by means of grammatical analysis. Then he tries to express in some formal way the changes that the language has undergone in passing from one stage to the other. He might, for example, take as his data the grammars of Old and New English or the grammars of Old and Modern French. Diagrammatically, we might look at the data this way:

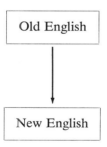

Each stage of the language is described by a grammar as being some relatively coherent system of elements; there are also rules for combining these elements to form sentences.[1] In the

---

[1] For our purposes, the terms "elements" and "rules" are to be taken in their broadest sense. Thus, some of the elements of English are its words, such as *red* and *house*. There is also a rule of English grammar which tells us that an adjective (generally) stands before the noun it modifies, e.g.,

shift from the older to the newer stage, some of these elements are dropped and new ones appear; some rules are deleted while others are added; and elements and rules can undergo various modifications. In other words, the historical linguist shows how one grammar develops into another over a period of time.

At the basis of historical linguistics lies the fact, shown by empirical evidence, that language change does not take place in a totally haphazard fashion. Rather, language changes occur in patterns which can be expressed in terms of a formal notation. The foundation of all modern linguistics, the fact that human language is amenable to scientific analysis, was first shown and accepted on the basis of data drawn from observations of language change.

Now that we have a rough idea of what historical linguistics is, let us see where the *comparative* part of our study comes in. We can state, on the basis of all previous observations, that, given enough time, a language will change. Now we might ask whether or not all languages change in the same way. While some of the same tendencies and processes have been observed in widely separated and structurally different languages, it appears that at some point the history of each language must be treated separately and described according to its own development. What this means is that when a langauge is spoken over a very wide area it will indeed change. but the changes found in one place may be different from those encountered in another. Thus, we often have a situation where a single old language will appear in several different forms at a later stage.

To illustrate what we mean, let us consider a hypothetical case. In a particular geographical area, we find the speakers of language A. Now the region inhabited by these people is bounded by the sea on two sides, by mountains on another side, and by a large river on the fourth side.

---

red house. There are similar elements in French: *rouge* 'red' and *maison* 'house'. However, the corresponding rule of French grammar is different from that of English in that in French an adjective generally *follows* the noun it modifies, e.g., *maison rouge* 'red house'.

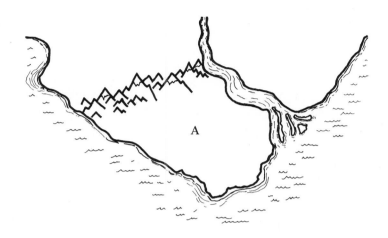

Due to certain circumstances, say a famine, or political division, or even imperialist ambitions, two large segments of the population migrate away from the original homeland. One group moves beyond the mountains and the other group finally is able to ford the forbidding river and settle on the other side. We now have three geographical areas in which language A is spoken.

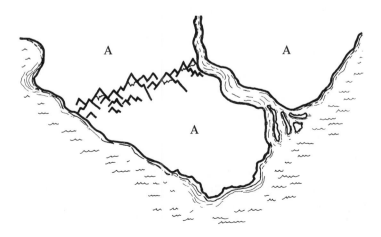

Suppose further, that, as time goes on, communication between the areas diminishes. An occasional caravan or touring
troupe may go from one region to the next, but there is no
large-scale contact among the speakers of the three territories.
What will happen, then, is that language A will change in one
way in the original homeland, in another way in the land
beyond the mountains, and in yet a third way in the area
across the river. In about a thousand years, then, the people
who live in the three regions will each be speaking a language
which is different from the other two.

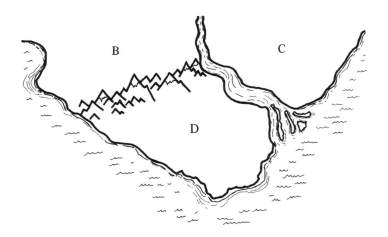

The three new languages will probably still show some
similarities, but will not be mutually intelligible. A well-
known example of this is the case of Latin and its derivatives,
the modern Romance languages.

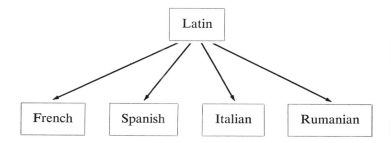

This is a historically visible case of a single language which underwent different changes in different geographical regions. When a sufficient number of changes had taken place, it became possible to speak of separate languages in the later stage.

We are fortunate in having Latin, the "ancestor" of the Romance languages, written down or *attested* in large numbers of documents. However, it is more often the situation that we observe obviously related languages with no recorded ancestor. Such is the case of the Germanic languages. We have English, German, Dutch, the Scandinavian languages, and several others, which appear to be related in much the same way, though not to the same degree, as the Romance languages. Yet we have no one attested language in which all of these might have their origin. But this does not cause the historical linguist to abandon the task of describing the history and relationships of the Germanic languages. Rather, he posits the

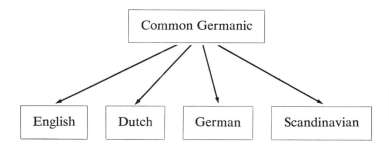

existence of an unattested ancestor to explain the similarities. This language is usually called by the name of the language group, preceded by the word *common*. In the case under discussion, the linguist asserts that there once was a language termed "Common Germanic" which, unfortunately, was not preserved in written documents.

By comparing the languages which are attested, the historical linguist tries to determine which elements are common to all. He adds to this his knowledge of the general principles of language change and seeks, as far as possible, to describe the structure of the common language. He is then able to discuss the different changes in the attested languages by tracing their development from his sketch of the common language. The process of discovering and describing the elements and rules of the common language is known as *reconstruction*. And the method by which this is done in most cases is called the *comparative method,* since it involves comparing different language systems.

This, then, is a broad outline of what historical and comparative linguistics are all about. In the following chapters, we will take up the various processes of language change, the problems of reconstruction, and the groupings of languages into families with a common ancestor.

2

Philology and Field Work

The first step in any linguistic research is the actual collection of the data which will be subject to analysis and interpretation. The linguist has four obvious sources of material: his own speech, the speech of others who speak his language, the speech of people who speak foreign languages, and written records. Every speaker or writer is the product and representative of a *speech community,* a group of people who speak the same language with more or less minor variations which are due to geographical, social, occupational, or other factors.

Some linguists may be surprised that a chapter in any modern textbook should unite such seemingly diverse topics as philology and field work. To many, the two are diametrically opposed methods of operation. Philology conjures up images of old, nearsighted (and probably German) professors leaning over ancient documents, consulting dusty reference works, and producing ten pages of commentary for each line of text in the manuscript. Field work invokes the picture of a young linguist sprinting about the countryside, armed only with tape recorder and notebook, tracking down the last five speakers of some about-to-be-extinguished language, and eliciting from them endless series of paradigms and folktales.

The principal differences between these two approaches lie in the nature and availability of the sources and in the methods of evaluating the data. The field worker is blessed by being able to pose direct questions to his informants about their language and culture, but he is handicapped because his data are generally limited to a single point in time. Quite the reverse is true for the philologist. Since he cannot ask native speakers of dead languages for information not found in his texts, he must often infer what is unseen from what is seen. However, from the point of view of history, he has a definite advantage in that he may very well have texts from different time periods. Instead of hypothesizing what a language may have looked like several centuries or millennia ago, he will have definite evidence recorded in his documents.

The methods of the philologist and the field worker may indeed differ, but their goals are the same—good, reliable facts about specific languages, including word lists and glosses, original texts with their translations, and notes or comments about relevant cultural, historical, and geographical facts. To the historical linguist, both philologists and field workers are indispensable for the same reason: they provide the data on which he bases his theories about the history of specific languages and the history of language in general.

In most cases, an historical linguist will himself be a good philologist and/or field worker. Being in such a position enables him to go back and check his sources for possible omissions, mistranscriptions, inconsistencies or other errors. Needless to say, the linguist who considers himself a philologist or field worker is also expected to have the highest standards of quality associated with these disciplines; he will be familiar with the scholarly literature, as well as the relevant facts of the cultural setting from which his data emanate.

WRITING SYSTEMS

Since the field worker assembles data by his own hand and can pose direct questions, he does not face the problems of the philologist in dealing with assorted writing systems or *orthographies* and trying to determine the value (phonetic and semantic) of particular graphic signs and words. The field worker may choose to write in a widely accepted system of symbols such as the International Phonetic Alphabet, or in one conventionally used by the scholars in his particular field (for example, there is an alphabet which is generally known and employed by American Indianists). He may even devise a new system which he feels is adequate for writing down a given language. In any event, he must be certain that his readers know exactly what are the values of the various phonetic symbols.

As might be expected, the system of writing used in any particular document is one of the first hurdles that the philologist/linguist must overcome in gathering data for further research. A good number of the languages presently spoken use the Latin alphabet with perhaps minor modifications such as additional signs (as in the French use of accents) or different phonetic values for certain letters (as in Turkish, where the letter *c* is always pronounced like the *g* in *George*). There are also several other alphabets in widespread usage, such as Cyrillic, the system for writing Russian, several other Slavic languages, and various unrelated languages in the geographical confines of the Soviet Union, such as the Turkic language Uzbek or the Iranian language Tajik. The Arabic alphabet is used for Arabic and Persian, and was formerly used for a number of other languages, including Turkish and Indonesian. Even today, not all languages of the world are written in alphabets; some use different writing systems. A very brief survey of writing will highlight some of the difficulties encountered in the inital stages of understanding written texts.

All human orthography is an attempt to set down visually the flow of spoken words. The primacy of a spoken over a written language is so obvious as to be hardly worthy of mention. We all learn to speak our own language well before we learn to write, and there were and are many peoples of the world who never learn to write or whose languages have no writing systems; but all men, by definition, speak a perfectly formed language.

The first stage in putting spoken words in visual form is the method of simply drawing pictures which resemble the concrete objects that words refer to. The crudest attempts at picture writing differ radically from mere picture painting because in writing there is a sequence of ideas; one picture follows another in the same order as one word follows another in the flow of a spoken sentence. Thus, in Sumerian, the ancient language of Mesopotamia, the picture ▱ represented a foot; or in the earliest stages of Chinese, the sign 馬 represented a horse. In both cases, the sign is a picture of a concrete object; it gives information about what the word means, but tells nothing about how it might be pronounced. With the spread of literacy, even if severely limited to a priestly or scholarly class, the pictures tend to become simpler, if only to save time in writing. Later on, they will become more stylized, and the actual parallel with reality becomes more difficult to see. Thus, the Chinese sign for "horse" eventually came to be written 馬 . As time goes on, the stylized pictures undoubtedly undergo a further development in that they become standardized so that all persons literate in a given language will write and understand the same signs. In China during the third century B.C., the first Emperor of the Ch'in Dynasty personally decreed the standardization of the writing system throughout his domain. The chosen standard forms were, of course, those of his native province.

The first significant jump from picture writing to a more manageable system comes when the picture is no longer taken for its value as an image of some particular object, but is taken for its value as representing a sound or a group of sounds. The first case of a picture's undergoing such a transformation occurred in Sumer. It appears that a scribe was trying to write the expression *Enlil-ti* 'Enlil (an important Sumerian god), the lifegiver'. Perhaps the scribe forgot the sign for 'lifegiver', perhaps there was none, or perhaps he was in a hurry. In any event, after writing the sign for Enlil, he wrote the sign for arrow ⤳ , which is also pronounced *ti*. On being read aloud, this would be understood by his readers as meaning 'lifegiver', especially given the fact that "Enlil, the lifegiver" was a common phrase.

Another extremely important factor in the move from pictorial to phonetic representation was the need to write down proper names. It is relatively easy to design a picture-sign for the word *city,* but how detailed would a picture have to be in order to distinguish one city from another? Therefore, the second phonetically written word we have is the name of the ancient Sumerian city Girsu. The scribe attempting to put this name in writing, simply put together the sign *gir* ⟨⟩ , meaning 'knife', with the sign *su* ⟨⟩ 'meat'. The new formation had nothing to do with either meat or knives, but merely used the signs as a means of writing particular syllables.

An advance such as this gives rise to the type of orthography known as the *syllabary.* In contrast to an alphabet, where each sign represents a single sound (or phoneme), each sign in a syllabary stands for a whole syllable or group of sounds. Many ancient languages were written in syllabaries, and perhaps the most famous syllabaries in current usage are the Japanese. A partial table of the Japanese Katakana syllabary will illustrate the principle:

ラ	ra	マ	ma	ナ	na
リ	ri	ミ	mi	ニ	ni
ル	ru	ム	mu	ヌ	nu
レ	re	メ	me	ネ	ne
ロ	ro	モ	mo	ノ	no

A glance at the Katakana writing of two foreign words will show how it compares with an alphabet:

マ リ ナ

ma - ri - na = 'marina' (place for keeping boats)

リ マ

ri - ma   = Lima (capital of Peru)

The next step in the development of writing systems is the shift from syllabaries to alphabets, which is taken when the syllable is broken down into its component sound parts. A further degree of economy is achieved here because fewer signs are necessary in the system, and they can be used in more combinations. For example, consider the following signs of an ancient Cuneiform ("wedge-shaped") syllabary and their equivalents in the Latin alphabet:

Cuneiform	Latin	Cuneiform	Latin
	ba		ka
	ab		ak
	an		la
	na		al

We see that in Cuneiform writing, we need eight signs, whereas in the Latin alphabet we need only five to express the same number of sounds. If the above list were expanded to include all vowels and consonants, the numbers of signs actually saved would be increased dramatically.

So the first step in a philological investigation of written documents is the understanding of the writing system. In the history of archeology it has happened and probably will again happen that someone will discover documents written in an orthography which has been completely forgotten and resists immediate interpretation. In such a case, the philologist must engage in a process known as *decipherment* to determine the sound and semantic values of the written symbols. In the case of the previously unknown Egyptian hieroglyphics, scholars were fortunate enough to find the Rosetta Stone, a tablet which gave the hieroglyphics together with a later form of Egyptian writing and Greek. When no such happy discovery is made, the philologist must patiently bring to bear his knowledge of possibly related scripts and languages. He makes educated guesses as to the content of the documents; he looks for the occurrence of known proper names; and he works with probabilities involving sheer mathematical distribution of signs. Some writing systems, such as the pre-Columbian Mayan of Mexico or the Khitan of the tenth and eleventh centuries in northern China, continue to resist all attempts at decipherment.

EDITING WRITTEN DOCUMENTS

The most important data used in the development of the principles and methods of historical linguistics have come from *philology*. By philology, we mean that discipline which concerns itself with the interpretation of written documents within their cultural context. For a time, historical linguistics was known as "comparative philology," since it basically involved no more than comparing the ancient written languages. In fact, the first to insist that he was doing something fundamentally different from the ordinary philologist was the German Indo-Europeanist August Schleicher (1821–1868), who devised the family tree model to express genetic relationships among languages (p. 41). Schleicher made it clear that he wanted to be known not as a *philolog*, but as a *glottiker*, a term we might well translate from German as 'linguist'. While the tasks of the linguist and that of the philologist are not identical, it nonetheless remains true that solid philological investigation is a necessary prelude to describing the histories of languages with written traditions.

At the present time, the philologist makes his principal contribution to historical linguistics by editing written documents. The term *documents* includes all texts which have been set down in stone or on clay tablets, parchment, paper, or other physical objects. The philologist gathers texts relative to a

Example of Edited Old Uighur Text

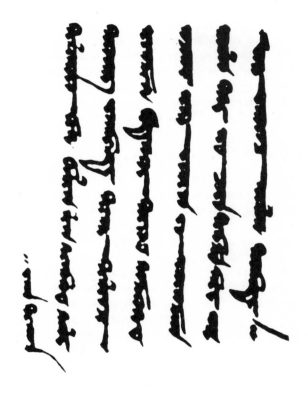

TRANSLITERATION

20.   .   y'n'   tβq̈'č
21. tylyntyn   pyš   p'lyq̈lyq   synkq̈w   s'ly
22. twtwnk   y'nkyrdy   twyrk   tylynč'
23. 'βyrmyš   pwdystβ   t'ytw   s'mtsw
24. ' 'č'ry   nynk   ywryqyn   'wq̈ytm'q̈
25. ' 'tlq   tsy   'yn   čwyn   tykm'   k'βy   nwm
26. *p*ytyk   yytynč   'wylwš   twyk'dy . .

TRANSLATION

20–26   Again, Singqu Sali Tutung of Bishbaliq translated
from the language of the Tawgach into the language
of the Turks the Kavya Book *tsy 'yn čwyn* called
[in Turkic] *The Description of the Life of the
Bodhisattva, the Great T'ang Tripitaka Master.* The
seventh chapter is finished.

NOTES

1. Bishbaliq was an important city in medieval Central Asia.
It was located on the trade route in Dzungaria, somewhat
south of the Altai mountains near present-day Urumchi.

2. Tawgach = Chinese. Tawgach was the name of a dynasty
which ruled in northern China from A.D. 386 to 535.

3. Kavya. The meaning and etymology of this word are completely unknown.

particular area of his expertise and interest. He knows well
the culture which produced the documents, the writing system, and the language itself. He then proceeds to prepare a
critical edition of the text for the use of those who might find
the information contained therein helpful for their own
studies. Depending on the subject matter of the text, students
of many disciplines, such as history, government, literature,
religion, or philosophy, will have need of the edited version.
Needless to say, the actual content may not be of crucial importance to the linguist, who is interested not so much in what
is being said, as in the written language in which it is being
said.

The structure of a good critical edition of an ancient text
may be described as follows. If at all possible, a photographic
copy of the document itself is included; this enables others to
look back to the original source if any questions about the
editor's interpretation should arise. A text written in a relatively unknown, difficult script is generally transcribed or
transliterated into the Latin alphabet in accordance with accepted norms. (Most philological areas have conventional
systems of transcription.) Then the text is translated into
English (or some other modern language, depending on the
nationality of the editor).

The translation is accompanied by notes which ordinarily
deal with difficulties the editor encountered when interpreting
particular sections of the text. For example, he might comment on unusual spellings, point out allusions to other writings, or identify persons, places, and items mentioned. In the
notes he will also discuss how he came to decide on his interpretation of previously unknown words, usually by present-
ing similar words from related or neighboring languages. He
will also consider variants which might appear in other extant
manuscripts, if any, of the same text.

Besides the text itself, perhaps the most interesting part of
a critical edition is the general introduction. Here the editor
tells what is known of the history of the document, where it
was discovered, how it has been preserved, and whether or
not it has been previously studied. He would presumably also

call attention to related documents that may have already been edited. Other items in the introduction are the editor's opinions and evidence regarding the author, date of composition, and possible later copyists of the document. Of crucial importance for the historical linguist, of course, would be the date of composition, the period of time which the language of the document is supposed to represent.

A *bibliography* is usually appended. This is a list of all the books or articles mentioned in the edition, as well as other works which the author consulted in preparing his text for publication.

Some manuscripts are provided with a *colophon,* a short paragraph, usually at the end, which gives data relevant to the author and/or the date of composition. Sometimes we are able to date a manuscript quite precisely because information given in the colophon relates the date of the manuscript to one which is already known. Thus, for example, the colophon at the end of an Old Uighur manuscript of Manichean provenience reads:

Mani burqan . . .	barduqinta	kin	biš
Mani Lord	his-going	after	five

	yüz	artuqi	äki otuzunč	yilga
	hundred	and	twenty-two	in-year

'five hundred and twenty-two years after the going (death) of Lord Mani'.

We know from other, unrelated historical sources that Mani, the founder of Manicheism, died in A.D. 274; we can therefore confidently date this document in A.D. 796.

If at all possible, a critical edition should be provided with a list of all the words and grammatical morphemes which appear in the text together with English equivalents or explanations. Such a listing is called a *concordance* or *glossary* or *index verborum.* Accompanying each word there should also be an indication of the exact line or lines in the text where the given form occurs. In recent years, computers have proved to be invaluable aids in compiling concordances for many documents. Previously, each word together with a sufficient amount of context had to be copied on a separate slip of paper and then alphabetized by hand. This time-consuming process has been replaced, and now it is necessary to go through the text only once by punching it on cards. The cards are then fed into one of the many extant concordance programs, and an excellent concordance is available in a matter of minutes. It is assumed, of course, that before the text is punched, it will have been analyzed by an experienced philologist who will have made certain decisions regarding variant readings and boundaries between words and morphemes.

CONTINUUM OF LANGUAGES IN TIME AND SPACE

When we use the names of modern languages such as Dutch and German or of older languages such as Latin and Old French, we tend to think of them as self-contained, easily definable units. In fact, however, the temporal and spatial boundaries of a "language" are often quite elusive and not nearly so clearly marked as we might think at first glance. The phenomenon of human language usually exists in what we may look upon as a space-time continuum. Let us consider the time element first. Languages are constantly changing, and there are no really sharp breaks in their continuity between one point in time and another. Yet, linguists find it convenient and even necessary to speak of languages at different points in their history *as if* they were completely different entities. Thus, we speak of Old English, Middle English, and New English. There was no precise date when Old English became Middle English or when Middle English became New English. Terms such as these are at best handy reference tools which enable us to refer to a language as it existed at approximately such and such a time. The same could be said even in those cases when the *name* used to refer to the language has changed. Thus, there is no specific date when Latin became Old French or Old Italian or Old Spanish. There was simply a continuing evolution of Latin in three separate geographical regions. Spanish, French, and Italian are all simply later forms of Latin.

When we turn to the space dimension we often find a similar situation. Speakers of various languages do not group themselves so neatly as political boundaries would indicate. Over a geographical area that contains two or more closely related "languages" there is most often a *gradual* shift from one to the other. Thus, suppose we were to go on a journey from Lisbon to Madrid or from Amsterdam to Berlin, and were to stop in every village to note the local speech. We would not find an exact point at which Portuguese is replaced by Spanish or Dutch becomes German. The native speech of the last town on the Portuguese border would be very similar to that of the first town on the Spanish side. The political boundary which divides the two would be the determining factor as to which language is learned in the schools. But in the spoken language, the local dialects gradually blend into one another, thus forming a space continuum.[1]

Historical linguists have generally concentrated on the standard or written languages (usually the language of the capital or great cultural center), because the standard language has written records going back centuries and because before the invention of the tape recorder, our nonstandard dialect records are indeed scarce. But, it is very interesting, and often helpful for our task, to look at the variations of language in space; that is, the more or less slight differences in a language as it is spoken in different geographical regions. We refer to these different variations of major languages as *dialects,* and the individual who collects the data and plots the dialects on maps is called a *dialect geographer.* We shall

---

[1] Of course, this situation does not hold across boundaries where languages are unrelated or only distantly related. Thus, there is no gradual blending of German into Polish at the German-Polish border, or of English into Spanish at the Mexican-American border. Isolated pockets of speakers may be found on either side of the political boundary, but there is no continuum of slight changes from one dialect into another, as is the case with Dutch and German or Spanish and Portuguese.

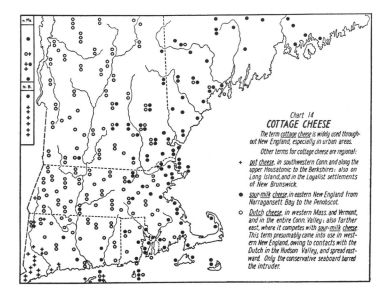

Chart 14
COTTAGE CHEESE
The term *cottage cheese* is widely used through-
out New England, especially in urban areas.

Other terms for cottage cheese are regional:

+ *pot cheese*, in southwestern Conn. and along the
upper Housatonic to the Berkshires; also on
Long Island, and in the Loyalist settlements
of New Brunswick.

• *sour-milk cheese*, in eastern New England from
Narragansett Bay to the Penobscot.

○ *Dutch cheese*, in western Mass. and Vermont,
and in the entire Conn. Valley; also farther
east, where it competes with *sour-milk cheese.*
This term presumably came into use in western New England, owing to contacts with the
Dutch in the Hudson Valley, and spread east-
ward. Only the conservative seaboard barred
the intruder.

not go into details about the aims and methods of the dialect
geographer, but merely point out some of the more relevant
aspects of his terminology and work.

The dialect geographer sets for himself the task of describing the distribution of linguistic forms over a specified geographical area. The forms selected for study may be phonological (different pronunciations of words), syntactic (different constructions in use), or lexical (different names for the
same or similar objects). The dialect geographer prepares
maps which note where specific forms are found and may
comment on the origin of the distribution. Where a boundary
exists between two different usages, he draws a line on his
map called an *isogloss*. Bundles of isoglosses are then felt to
mark off significant dialect regions. As examples, we can look
at the following two maps from the *Handbook of the Linguistic Geography of New England*. One shows the places where
different words for *cottage cheese* are used, and the other presents the isogloss lines for various aspects of New England
pronunciation. On the western end of the second map, we

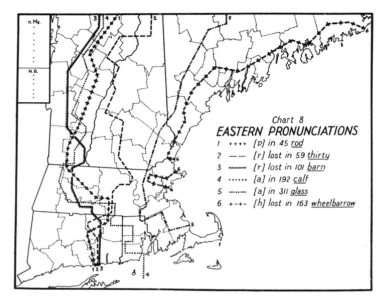

Chart 8
EASTERN PRONUNCIATIONS
1 ++++ [ɒ] in 45 _rod_
2 — — [r] lost in 59 _thirty_
3 ⸺ [r] lost in 101 _barn_
4 ······ [a] in 192 _calf_
5 —·— [a] in 311 _glass_
6 +-+- [h] lost in 163 _wheelbarrow_

can note a number of isoglosses running very close together; these mark off the significant dialect boundary of Eastern New England speech.

Historical linguists often shy away from the material presented by dialect geography, simply because its great number of slightly different forms seem to defy rational analysis. In the early stages of historical linguistic work, this is probably necessary: and it is best to stick to the standard language represented in the written sources. However, local, unwritten dialects, often preserve _relic_ or _intermediate_ forms, which may substantiate the historical linguist's hypotheses about the development of the standard language. In addition, dialect maps may be helpful to him in showing the spread of particular changes.

ETYMOLOGY

Perhaps the first question posed by people interested in language was, "Why does this word mean what it does?" The ancient Greeks considered the question and tried to investigate it by a science they called *etymology* (from *etumon* 'true meaning of a word' plus *-ology* 'study of'). Lacking any true or precise idea of linguistic history, their investigations were basically limited to deriving Greek words from other Greek words. This is, of course, quite simple in the case of obvious compounds. Thus in New English we can derive the word *football* from *foot* and *ball,* and show that the object is so called because it is a *ball* that is used in a game where it is kicked by the *foot.* This type of etymology we call a *synchronic etymology* in that it involves deriving words from other words existing in the language at the same time.

Unfortunately, synchronic etymology works only for words such as compounds or derivatives (*driver* from the verb *drive* plus the agent suffix *-er*). When we get down to simple forms, which are not formed from other extant roots, we must consider *diachronic etymology,* or the history of a word through time, how it was pronounced, and what it meant to previous speakers. An etymology is, essentially, the history of a single linguistic form.

Throughout the history of linguistic studies, philosophers and grammarians have sought etymologies, mostly with no systematic method of determining if the proposed etymology represented real historical fact or was simply a fanciful invention of the author. We know, and shall see later in this book, that words will change both in sound and meaning in the course of time. The situation not recognized by the early etymologists was that such changes are not completely haphazard, and that there are ways of finding and proving etymologies. By the eighteenth century, etymologizing had apparently become so popular a sport with no guidelines or restraints that Voltaire was said to have remarked: "Etymology is the science in which the vowels count for nothing and the consonants for very little."

Nowadays, the science of etymology is very serious business, and the burden of proof for any specific etymology rests on the person who proposes it. One should bear in mind the dictum of Meillet that *not every word has the right to an etymology.* The history of many words is obscure, or riddled with question marks, or open to several possible interpretations, or else completely lost. The good etymologist recognizes this and has no hesitation in ending his researches by saying "further origin unknown."

Theoretically, when we give any part of the history of a word, we are giving its etymology, that is, we can set an arbitrary limit on how far back in time we wish to go in determining previous forms and meanings of a word. Thus, we can trace a New English word back to Middle English, or further to Old English, or even further, to Common Germanic, or perhaps ultimately back to Common Indo-European (assuming, of course, that the given word has a provable Indo-European etymology). When we trace a word back as far as we can go, we are said to be giving its complete etymology.

FOR FURTHER STUDY

The only way to really appreciate good philological work is to examine ancient texts edited by outstanding scholars in particular areas. If you know an ancient language, look up some edited documents in the journals and monographs and see how authors attack and explain the problems they encounter. For the beginning field worker, Samarin's *Field Linguistics* is full of helpful hints and suggestions for eliciting and organizing new information from a native speaker. It is basically a guide for avoiding known pitfalls and making the most profitable use of time spent in the field.

Two of the most noted descriptions of writing and its history are Gelb's *A Study of Writing* and Diringer's *Writing.* These books contain examples of various writing systems, as well as detailed histories of their evolution from one to another. Parts of Pedersen's *Discovery of Language* deal with the many writing systems that have been used by Indo-European peoples. If you come across some unknown script you would like to decipher, first read about how others have done it and save yourself some time. Chadwick's *Decipher-*

ment of Linear B describes how a young Englishman, who was neither a professional linguist nor a philologist, "cracked" the script used in the Peloponnesus by making bold assumptions and disregarding previously held dogmas. If you can read French, try Thomsen's *Les inscriptions de l'Orkhon déchifrées,* a tale of loving patience and dedication (as well as good luck in playing hunches) that led to the understanding of the Ancient Turkic runic script found in Mongolia. Even if you don't plan on following in their footsteps, both Chadwick and Thomsen make exciting reading, like a mystery story, as pieces of the puzzle are put together.

Many linguists were and are suspicious of written records of oral data made by linguistically untrained individuals, such as travelers and missionaries. For the proper interpretation of such materials and their integration with the linguist's own work, one should consult Goddard's "Philological Approaches to the Study of Native North American Languages: Documents and Documentation."

For a look at how one attempts to determine the pronunciation of a "dead" language such as Latin, there is W. Sidney Allen's excellent little book *Vox Latina.*

3

Genetic Classification
of Languages

Considering the wide variety of languages in the world, whenever two or more of them showed certain similarities, students of language were irresistibly tempted to put them together in some sort of group or class. As a result, the history of linguistics is filled with attempts to classify languages according to various schemata; the criteria for putting a particular language in one or another group are just as varied.

TYPOLOGICAL CLASSIFICATION

Since the early nineteenth century, one of the most frequently recurring schemes for grouping languages has been the so-called typological classification. Basically, this system groups together languages which share "important" features or appear to have similar grammars. The classification by type is done without regard to the history or geographical location of the languages involved.

Perhaps the most famous and persistent scheme for typological classification was that devised by A. W. Schlegel in 1818. Schlegel's system was based on the number of meaningful elements (*morphemes*) which could be present in a word and the modifications these might undergo. If there was only one element of basic meaning per word, then the language was *isolative*. If there was more than one, but these were kept apart from one another and underwent no modification of form, the language was *agglutinative*. If, on the other hand, there were several meaningful elements, but these were in some way fused together or were modified in different contexts, then the language was *inflective*. Diagrammatically, we might represent Schlegel's classification scheme as follows:

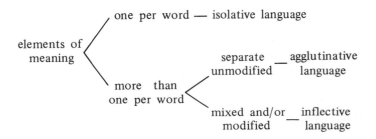

Illustrations drawn from the languages traditionally used to demonstrate this classification will make it more intelligible. Chinese is considered to be an isolative language; consider the following sentence:

t'a   dau   nar   ch'ü

he   to   where   go

'Where is he going?'

We see that in this sentence each word is separate from the others and each contains only one element of meaning.

Turkish is generally taken as an agglutinative language, as can be seen in the sentence:

šehir-ler-e   gid-iyor-um

city-*plural*-to   go-*present*-I

'I am going to the cities.'

Each of the two words in the above sentence contains three elements of meaning, but these elements are clearly distinct and identifiable.

Finally, Latin is often cited as an example of an inflective language. Consider the following sentence:

serv-*īs*   libr-*ōs*   d-*ō*

slave-*plural*+to   book-*plural*+accusative   give-*present*+I

'I give the books to the slaves.'

Each of the words in the Latin sentence contains three elements of meaning, but can be broken down into only two parts. The ending -*īs* contains the elements *plural* and 'to' and cannot be further analyzed; similar statements could be made for the endings -*ōs* and -*ō*.

Since the time of Schlegel, there have been numerous additional attempts to revise and redefine this system of classification.[1] Perhaps the most notable addition was the recognition of a class of *polysynthetic* languages which was intended to include certain native languages of the Americas in which subjects, objects, and other grammatical items are fused onto the verb stem and appear to form a single word. In the twentieth century, Sapir tried to devise an extremely elaborate typological classification of the Schlegel variety. This is presented in Chapter 6 of his book *Language*. Still later, Greenberg tried to devise typological schema for individual parts of a grammar using various indices of important features to indicate typological similarities.

In general, attempts to classify whole languages under typological schemes have been clumsy. No language, it appears, falls exclusively into one group. Chinese does have certain suffixes, and Turkish roots and suffixes do undergo changes when combined. Besides, the very definition of the term *word* is open to debate. Despite the twentieth-century revision and refinement of criteria for typological classification, it is still very much uncharted territory, and membership in one or

[1] In addition to the attempts at mere classification, there was a tendency to postulate an order of historical priority or development from one type to another. Thus, some stated that *all* languages begin at an isolative stage, then move on to an agglutinative stage, and finally reach an inflective stage. In this scheme of things, inflective languages such as Latin or Greek (or Indo-European languages in general) were seen as the world's most advanced or most developed languages, whatever that means. It is interesting to note that such opinions were formulated by individuals who spoke Indo-European languages. Statements of language development might be quite different if made by Turks or Chinese.

another group seems to depend at least partially on the whim of the linguist as to what is considered important.

LINGUISTIC UNIVERSALS

Much fruitful work remains to be done in comparative linguistics beyond attempts to pigeonhole complete languages in typologically based groups. One of the more important and fruitful goals is the search for linguistic universals. To give a simple definitions, *universals* are the linguistic elements or rules that are found in all languages of the world. Reflect for a moment on your intuitive notions when you begin to study a new foreign language, say Cambodian. Although you may think you know absolutely nothing about Cambodian, you will expect, among other things, to find consonants and vowels, nouns and verbs, a way of forming questions and imperatives.

With good reason you expect to find these items; they are found in all languages, and in your expectation you were unconsciously expressing beliefs about what a language has to have in order to be a language. You would be surprised indeed if any language you began to study had no way of asking questions! Things such as these are linguistic universals; they are found in every language and are thus of no value in helping us to put languages in groups.

Recently a great deal of research has been conducted by the transformational grammarians and their philosophical and psychological associates to determine universals of a more abstract nature. This type of research could be especially beneficial in furthering knowledge about the general nature of language and perhaps also of how it reflects human thought processes. For example, in no language of the world does it appear possible to have a passive sentence with a reflexive pronoun as the subject. Thus, while we can say *Susan bit herself,* we cannot say *Herself was bit by Susan.* The restriction or constraint which seems to be operating here is one that forbids reversing the position of subject and object (by means of passivizing the verb) when they both refer to the same person or thing. Transformational grammarians have dubbed this restriction the *cross-over principle;* it appears to be operative in all the world's languages, and so it is a linguistic universal.

The two approaches mentioned, typological classification and the search for universals, are methods of comparing languages. We now turn to that which is of greatest interest to us, namely the use of comparison and classification in order to extract historical information about the language or languages studied.

THEORETICAL OBSERVATIONS

Genetic classification is intended to yield material relevant to the history of languages. This classification is based not on the simple discovery of similar features in two or more languages, but rather on recurring correspondences between non-universal elements of language. The explanation for the correspondences thus found is not sought in the philosophical or psychological constraints on human speech, but rather in the facts of human history. In other words, the observed similarities and correspondences are accounted for by positing a definite contact of languages at some point in time past.

In order to understand more fully what are the theoretical bases of our historical-comparative studies, we will have to turn our attention to certain general linguistic facts. Language is a symbolic system in which certain sounds and combinations of sounds are used as symbols of, or stand for, certain concepts or relations in the mind of the speaker. For the most part, there is no natural or necessary link between a thing or idea and its name. In modern times, this idea was expressed most clearly by the Swiss linguist, Ferdinand de Saussure.

Saussure used a circle diagram to illustrate his point:

The whole circle is referred to as the *linguistic sign.* The top part represents the object or concept itself, that which is meant, and is called the *signified.* The bottom part, the group of sounds which stand for the object within a given language, is called the *signifier.* The important point to be made here is that there is no necessary or natural connection between the two parts. In other words, the *linguistic sign is arbitrary.* The arbitrariness is most obvious when we consider the simple fact of the existence of various languages in the world. Given the signified ( ), the signifier would be *chien* for a Frenchman, *hund* for a German, *köpek* for a Turk, *goŭ* for a Chinese, and so on.

This arbitrariness extends even to words which are considered as being *imitative* or *onomatopoeic,* that is, words which we suppose to imitate the sounds of natural things. We need merely note that English speakers reproduce the barking of a dog as *bow-wow,* whereas Japanese hear a dog saying *won-won* and Turkish dogs bark by pronouncing the syllables *hav-hav.*

If there is no natural or philosophical connection between the thing and its name, why then do words mean what they do? Since the time of Plato there has been speculation on the origin of language involving the questions of how and why man first learned to speak and how words came to mean what they do. Most of this speculation has turned out to be of no scientific import, and nowadays serious linguists leave the question aside.[2]

The only explanation for the connection between the signified and the signifier is that a particular linguistic tradition linked them together at some point in time. The reason why particular combinations of sounds represent particular objects or ideas is that they represented those things for a preceding generation. As far back as we can go in the history of man, we find that the reason one group speaks a particular

---

[2] Recent research into animal communication systems may shed some light on the nature and structure of prelanguage methods of "talking."

language is because they learned it from another group, usually a preceding generation of the same community. Thus, as far as we know, every language of the world has an equally long history. When we speak of a language as being very "old," usually one of two things is meant:

1. The language has old *written* records.
2. The language has not undergone extensive changes from its earliest written records up to the present.

The fact that we have English records dating back to the seventh century and Albanian only from the fourteenth century does not mean that English is really older than Albanian. Presumably there were Albanians speaking their language during the seventh century, even though nobody bothered to write it down.

So then, we can look upon historical linguistics as a study which describes the changes and developments of traditions that connect sounds with meaning.

CONCRETE OBSERVATIONS

Consider the following sets of names for the numbers from one to five in the following five languages:

	A	B	C	D	E
1.	eins	een	bir	i	ichi
2.	zwei	twee	iki	er	ni
3.	drei	drie	üč	san	san
4.	vier	vier	dört	sə	shi
5.	fünf	vijf	beš	wu	go

From this data, the first observation we make is that the names of the numbers are not linguistic universals; different linguistic traditions (or different languages) have arbitrarily chosen different groups of sounds to stand for numbers.

Look now at only the first three sets. Immediately, one can notice that sets A and B are more like each other than they are like C. In fact, they are remarkably similar. Once the resemblance has been noticed, the problem remains to explain it. Granted the arbitrariness of the linguistic sign, how is it possible that out of all conceivable sounds a human being can make, two languages have chosen such similar sounds in order to represent the first five numerals? Examination of other words in the two languages will result in discovering such a large number of similar cases that we can safely rule out the possibility of pure chance. For example, the numerals from six to ten in the same languages are:

		A	B
	6.	sechs	zes
	7.	sieben	zeven
	8.	acht	acht
	9.	neun	negen
	10.	zehn	tien

In passing we might also note that in some cases where the sounds differ, we find regular correspondences between the two languages. Where in language B we have a *t* at the beginning of a word, there is a *z* in language A. Or an initial *s-* in language A corresponds to an initial *z-* in language B.

If we rule out simple chance, then, why should languages A and B look like each other and yet different from language C? We have already said that a language at any given point in time is the result of a tradition extending indefinitely far back into the past. The only possible conclusion we can draw from the data presented is that the tradition which resulted in language A and that which resulted in language B were, at some time in the past, in contact. Speaking very conservatively for the moment, we can safely assume that the number names in language A and those in language B are offshoots of the same tradition. Even if we look at the numbers from six to ten in language C, we can note no remarkable similarities to either A or B:

6.	altĭ
7.	yedi
8.	sekiz
9.	dokuz
10.	on

Language A is German, language B is Dutch, and language C is Turkish. After our discussion of the German and Dutch numerals, we concluded that at some point in time the traditions which produced these numerals were the same. The same could be said of the Chinese (language D) and Japanese (language E) numerals. But suppose we move beyond mere correspondences of individual words or sets of words and look at grammatical constructions in these languages. For example, the sentence *This is a book:*

Chinese:	jei	shr	i	ben	shu
	this	is	one	(classifier)[3]	book

Japanese:	kore	wa	hon	desu
	this	(subject particle)[4]	book	is

[3] Under certain conditions, such as when following a numeral, each Chinese noun must be preceded by a so-called "classifier." A classifier is a word which tells what "class" of nouns a given word belongs to; these classes are often formed on the bases of considerations like physical shape. Thus the word for 'table', *jwodz,* and the word for 'paper', *jr,* both have the classifier *jang,* which is used for flat objects. In the example given here we have the noun *shu,* which takes the classifier *ben,* which might be translated something like 'volume'. Thus, a very literal rendering of the phrase *i ben shu* would be 'one volume book'. This Chinese usage has been considered similar to the English situation in a limited number of expressions such as "ten head of cattle."

[4] The particle *wa* in Japanese indicates that the preceding word is the subject of the sentence.

We see that Chinese and Japanese have vastly different grammatical systems, both in word order and in the use of items such as grammatical particles and classifiers.

Let us look at the same sentence in Dutch and German:

Dutch:	dit	is	een	boek
	this	is	a	book
German:	dies	ist	ein	Buch
	this	is	a	book

We see here that the similarities which we noticed in comparing individual words extends to the syntax of the languages involved since they have identical grammatical constructions.

Thus, although we may find many words in Japanese which might be very similar to Chinese (at least in its ancient form),[5] we do not put Chinese and Japanese into the same language family. A much simpler explanation is that the Japanese borrowed the words in question from the Chinese. (Borrowing will be discussed in detail in Chapter 12.)

The relationship between Dutch and German is quite different. Since the similarities are so great and pervade every level of the grammar of both languages, the question of borrowing cannot be seriously entertained. Instead, we come to the conclusion that Dutch and German were once the same language. This implies, then, that the similarities between Dutch and German are not due to contacts between two different languages, as is the case with Chinese and Japanese, but are due to their relation to a common ancestor.

COMMON LANGUAGES

It has been said that historical linguistics is based on a fact and on a hypothesis. The fact is that certain languages

---

[5] The Ancient Chinese forms from which both Modern Chinese and Japanese derive are: *iet* 'one', *ńźi* 'two', *sam* 'three', *si* 'four', and *nguo* 'five'.

show such remarkable similarities to each other that these similarities could not be due to chance or borrowing. The hypothesis is that these were once the same language. We call this ancestor language a *common language.*

The concept of the common language was introduced into modern scholarship by Sir William Jones, a British judge in India. Jones had studied a wide variety of languages, and in 1786 he delivered his famous *Third Anniversary Discourse,* which reads in part:

> The Sanskrit language, whatever be its antiquity, is of a wonderful structure; more perfect than the Greek, more copious than the Latin, and more exquisitely refined than either, yet bearing to both of them a stronger affinity, both in the roots of verbs and in the forms of grammar, than could possibly have been produced by accident; so strong indeed, that no philologer could examine them all three, without believing them to have sprung from some common source, which, perhaps, no longer exists: there is a similar reason, though not quite so forcible, for supposing that both the Gothic and the Celtic, though blended with a very different idiom, had the same origin with the Sanskrit; and the Old Persian might be added to the same family.

Sir William's statement added at least two significant advances to the understanding of language development. First was the idea of languages developing along parallel lines instead of in series. Before his time there had been attempts to derive one known language from another, often with ludicrous results. Thus, one might have tried to show how Latin was derived from Greek or Greek derived from Sanskrit in some kind of linear order:

What Sir William proposes is that the three languages all

evolved more or less independently from a common ancestor. In which case, our diagram would look like this:

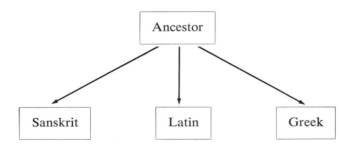

The second fact is that the ancestor "might no longer exist." What Sir William meant, obviously, was that the ancestor might not be attested, or written down. The assumption that such an unattested ancestor might have existed without leaving written records led to the great nineteenth-century investigations into the relationships of the Indo-European languages and the attempts to reconstruct their ancestor. Basically, the concept of the unrecorded common ancestor freed language students from having to explain everything in language history exclusively by what is found in written documents, and later it was shown that unattested forms were readily inferable and verifiable on the evidence of written records. And so for the past century and a half, linguists have collected data on many of the world's languages. They have compared these languages and extracted the similarities and recurring correspondences in attempts to prove common origins.

When the evidence that two languages were once the same becomes conclusive, we then speak of these two languages as being *genetically related.* Another way of phrasing the same fact is to say that they belong to the same *language family.* Note that when we group languages genetically, our claim is purely a historical one and does not necessarily imply that the attested languages resemble each other to any particularly definable degree (though in the case of German and Dutch the resemblances are patent). In the course of time, the given languages will have changed; the amount of change will be dependent on various factors, not all of which are clearly understood at the moment. Some of the more obvious ones are length of time involved, degree of geographical separation, and the amount of contact with other cultures.

Often, the similarities between two languages which attest their common origin will not be at all obvious at first glance. Or, on the other side of the coin, large amounts of borrowing may get in the way of correct conclusions. However, by a rigorous application of the criteria and methods of historical-comparative linguistics, it is often possible to say whether two or more languages are genetically related.

FAMILY TREES

The most popular diagram for expressing genetic relationships is the **family tree,** a device created by August Schleicher, a nineteenth-century German linguist. A tree diagram consists of a parent language as a starting point with branches showing the daughter languages and the particular affinities among them.

We assume that the end points (languages B, C, D, and E) represent historically attested languages, which the linguist believes to be genetically related. The language of which they are descendants is posited as language A, and is reconstructed as far as possible. The time span is represented by the line connecting A with its daughters. When we wish to speak of a form intermediate between the stage of language A and that of language B, we refer to it as *pre-B*.

Now it sometimes happens that two (or more) of the languages within a given family share certain features which set them apart as a group from the other members of the same family. This leads us to believe that these two languages underwent a common period of development not shared by the others. Suppose that languages D and E in the above diagram form just such a group. We indicate this by positing an additional language, language X, which stands midway between the ultimate ancestor (A) and the two attested languages which are more closely related to each other than to the rest of the family.

A language such as language X is called an *intermediate common language*. It is common because it has more than one descendant, and it is intermediate because it occupies a position between the attested languages and the oldest reconstructable common language. Problems of subgrouping languages within a family are among the most intricate in historical linguistics since they involve minute attention to detail and sophisticated evaluation of large amounts of positive and negative evidence. Examples of tree diagrams for various language families, including many intermediate common languages, will be found in Chapters 4 and 8.

The family tree diagram often has been criticized for not showing *all* the facts about relationships among languages. The criticism is somewhat justified, since the tree diagram seems to portray a simplistic view of languages breaking off from one another with no further contact. Thus, a partial tree of the Romance languages might look like this:

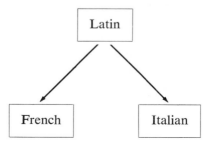

Obviously, the tree diagram does not show later contacts between the three languages, though it is known that many Italian words were borrowed by the French at the time of the Renaissance, and in more recent times, French words have entered Italian. Likewise both French and Italian have borrowed from classical Latin.

If we understand its limitations, the family tree model is still a very useful device for displaying genetic relationships. It shows that many languages may have developed from one, and shows that, despite outside influences, the essential parts of language are transmitted from generation to generation in an unbroken sequence.

LANGUAGE ISOLATES

Finally, we might mention the case of the linguistic orphan. When we have a language which appears to have no "relatives," either living or preserved in records, it is called a *language isolate*. The most famous of these is Basque, which is spoken in northern Spain and southern France. Obviously, we are greatly limited in describing the history of a language isolate since we lack our best tool, namely, comparison with related languages. We are, in fact, forced to rely exclusively on data internal to the language and the only method at our disposal is that of internal reconstruction (see Chaper 7). Of course, even language isolates may have certain dialectical variations and could be compared in an attempt to establish an earlier stage of the language.

FOR FURTHER STUDY

Studies on the abstract principles underlying the theory of genetic relationships are not numerous. Most of the more interesting work is embedded in concrete studies of specific language families. Mention should be made of the excellent little book by Meillet, *La méthode comparative en linguistique historique*. If your French isn't good enough to read this work in the original there is a translation by Ford with the

English title *The Comparative Method in Historical Linguistics.* Several other short articles by Meillet are also of great interest:

"Le problème de la parenté des langues"
"Les parentés de langues"
"Sur le sens linguistique de l'unité latine"
"Le vocabulaire dans le question des parentés de langues"
"Introduction à la classification des langues."

One article by Benveniste, "La classification des langues," gives a survey of opinions regarding genetic and other relationships among languages. Mary Haas's excellent little book, *The Prehistory of Languages,* also treats theoretical questions of language relationships. An article by Watkins, "Italo-Celtic Revisited," presents quite clearly the abstract principles underlying the concept of genetic subgrouping and intermediate common languages.

Those interested in typological classifications should consult Chapter 6 of Sapir's *Language* and Greenberg's article "A Quantitative Approach to the Morphological Typology of Language."

4

Language Families

As we noted in the previous chapter, for historical purposes, the most fruitful classification of languages is the genetic classification. As soon as linguists know of the existence of a language, there are attempts to put it in one or another family. In the initial stages of study, such a classification is tentative, pending complete evaluation of the available data and the actual writing of a comparative grammar which presents the detailed analysis of correspondences and so demonstrates or proves genetic relationships.

In some cases, genetic classification is agreed upon by all the scholars in a field. In others, there are still large-scale debates conducted in the journals and at academic conferences as to whether or not the relationship of one language to another has been proved. Note that a negative proof is impossible. We simply cannot demonstrate that two or more languages are *not* related. Additional evidence or future refinement of linguistic techniques may always reveal new aspects of language which must be considered. Instead, our conclusion must be either that a sufficient body of evidence has been built up to show a relationship exists or merely that such a relationship has not been proved.

What follows is essentially a list of major language families of the world together with representative languages of those families. The groupings presented in this chapter represent what appears to be a general consensus among the scholars in any given field. They do not represent all views, in that some might prefer smaller or larger families, and it is impossible to give a detailed discussion of these views in an elementary textbook.

LANGUAGE FAMILIES OF EUROPE AND THE MIDEAST

INDO-EUROPEAN

The language family which has been the subject of the most intensive study is the Indo-European. This group includes most of the languages of Europe as well as those of Iran and India. In this chapter we shall not consider Indo-European, but shall return to examine it in greater detail in Chapter 8. For the location of other European languages mentioned below, see the Indo-European map on page 106.

SEMITIC

Next to Indo-European, probably the most studied group of languages in the world is the Semitic family. The great quantity of studies is due both to a native linguistic tradition (principally Arabic and Hebrew) and to European interest, motivated primarily by Biblical studies. Semitic falls into three main branches: Northwest, Northeast, and Southwest. The Northeast group is known through a single ancient, historically significant language, Akkadian, which includes both Babylonian and Assyrian dialects, and was spoken in Mesopotamia during the several millennia before the beginning of the Christian era. The Northwest group includes several languages of the eastern Mediterranean area; the most important of these is Hebrew, of which we have records dating back to the second millennium B.C. By the second century B.C., Hebrew had ceased to be a spoken language, and in Palestine it was replaced by a related language, Aramaic. Of course, scholars continued to read and write in Hebrew, and in the twentieth century it has been completely revived as the national language of Israel. The most important member of the Southwest group is Arabic, whose extensive records date back to the sixth century A.D. The Southwest group also includes some of the languages of Ethiopia, such as Amharic and the liturgical language Ge'ēz.

HAMITO-SEMITIC

Many scholars now consider the Semitic languages to be but one branch of a larger group which is named the Hamito-Semitic family (see proposed family tree on p. 48). The other four branches of this proposed family are Berber, Cushitic, Chad, and Egyptian. The Berber languages are spoken in isolated pockets scattered throughout North Africa and the Sahara Desert; perhaps Tuareg is the best-known Berber language. Somewhat south of Egypt along the Red Sea coast of Africa and further south, we find the Cushitic languages; among these are Bogo, Tambaru, Somali, and Galla. In an area to the west and south of Lake Chad, we find the languages belonging to the Chad branch. Undoubtedly, the most important of these is Hausa, which is learned by many West Africans as a second language since it is widely used as a medium for trade among speakers of many different languages. Some other Chad languages are Ngala, Gabin, and Mandara. The Egyptian branch of the family consists of Ancient Egyptian and its descendent, Coptic, which is still used as the liturgical language of the Coptic Church.

SUMERIAN

Within what is now Semitic territory, there once existed a language isolate called Sumerian. The Sumerians founded their great civilization in Mesopotamia in the fourth millennium B.C., long before the coming of the Akkadians. Sumerian is especially interesting because documents written in Sumerian, dating back to the third millennium B.C., are the oldest records we have of any language.

FINNO-UGRIC

Within Europe itself, there are several languages which do not belong to the Indo-European family. The most important of these are Hungarian and Finnish, which together with

Proposed Family Tree of the Hamito-Semitic Languages

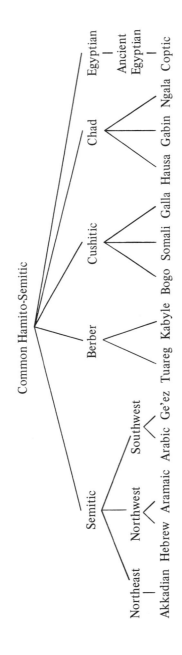

Note: Not all members of the family are included.

Estonian and Lappish belong to the Finno-Ugric or Uralic family. Uralic also includes a number of languages still spoken in the Soviet Union such as Cheremis, Samoyed, and Ob Ugric.

ALTAIC

In the southeast corner of Europe and continuing on into Asia Minor we find the Turkish language, which belongs to the Altaic family. Altaic has three main branches: Turkic, Mongolian, and Tunguz. Turkic is by far the most widespread group and has the largest number of speakers; in addition to Turkish, this branch includes a number of Central Asian languages such as Uzbek, Kazakh, and Kirgiz. Our first records of Turkic date back to the seventh century; the largest number of early documents are written in a Central Asian dialect known as Old Uighur. (See pp. 18-19 for an example.) The Mongol branch covers Khalkha, the official language of the Mongolian Peoples Republic, and certain other relatively minor languages of the Soviet Union and China such as Buriat, Dagur, and Khorchin. One well-known language of the Tunguz branch is Manchu, which was the native language of the last Chinese dynasty. Other languages in the same group are Evenki and Goldi, and these are spoken by scattered tribes in northern Siberia. Most Altaicists now hold that Korean is also a member of the Altaic family, but a separate branch from the three already given.

In earlier times of less critical methods, some scholars spoke of a Ural-Altaic family of languages. Nowadays, it is generally held that the genetic relationship between the Uralic and the Altaic families is unproved, and linguists speak of them as two separate families.

BASQUE

One other noted non-Indo-European language still extant in Europe is Basque, which is spoken in the Pyrenees in southern France and northern Spain. Basque remains a language isolate, and its conjectured relationships to other ancient or modern languages has not been proved.

NORTHERN AND SOUTHERN CAUCASIAN

In the mountainous Caucasus region of the Soviet Union there is a bewildering variety of languages spoken in a relatively small area. Some of these are clearly classifiable into known language families, such as Indo-European (Ossetic, an Iranian language, and Armenian) or Turkic (Karachay and Balkar). Others, however, fall principally into two separate groups: the Northern Caucasian and the Southern Caucasian language families. The Northern group contains languages such as Lezgian and Circassian, and the Southern family encompasses, among others, Georgian, Laz, and Mingrelian.

LANGUAGE FAMILIES OF ASIA

SINO-TIBETAN

In East Asia, the most important language family is the Sino-Tibetan. This group has two main branches, the Tibeto-Burman and the Sinitic. Of the former branch, the most important languages are Tibetan, attested from the seventh century, and Burmese. There are also several minor languages such as Lolo and Kachin. The Sinitic group includes most of the Chinese languages, which for political and cultural reasons are often referred to as "dialects."

Chinese has been written down since about 1300 B.C. in the form of characters or logograms. Each symbol originally stood for a single word and later for a syllable. The Chinese have also been remarkably interested in the phonology of their own language, and lexicography became a highly developed art, beginning in the centuries before Christ. Through the careful use of ingenious native devices such as rhyming dictionaries and rhyme tables, it is possible to reconstruct the phonology of various earlier periods of Chinese. The stages

Major Language Groups of Asia

Key to map of Asia

Dravidian
Sino-Tibetan
Vietnamese
Tai
Mon-Khmer
Altaic and Korean
Malayo-Polynesian

Japanese
Ainu
Semitic

Indo-European
Iranian
Indic

Familiar Languages

1. Arabic
2. Hebrew
3. Persian
4. Hindi
5. Bengali
6. Tamil
7. Telegu
8. Uzbek
9. Tibetan
10. Chinese
11. Burmese
12. Thai
13. Malay
14. Dayak
15. Tagalog

which have been most investigated include Archaic or Old Chinese, which is dated around 500 B.C., Ancient or Middle Chinese of approximately A.D. 600, and Ancient Mandarin, the language of northern China in the thirteenth century.

The contemporary Sinitic languages are usually grouped into six main divisions; several of these are widely known. Cantonese is spoken in Canton and Hong Kong; the Min dialects, spoken mostly in Fukien province, include the Amoy dialect as well as Taiwanese. The Wu dialects have the Shanghai language as their most important representative. Finally, there are the Mandarin dialects. They resemble one another rather closely, and after a shorter or longer period of time depending on an individual's own abilities, a speaker of one Mandarin dialect may make himself understood in another. The Mandarin languages are further subdivided into three main groups: the Northern is exemplified in the language of Peking, which is the standard of all China; the Southwestern group includes the Szechuan dialect; Southeastern Mandarin is represented by the language of Nanking.

In addition to the Tibeto-Burman and Sinitic languages, some scholars consider Yenissei Ostyak (spoken along the Yenissei River in central Siberia) to be a member of the Sino-Tibetan. Our documents about this language are extremely limited, and studies on it are few; thus, nothing definite can be said at this time. Yenissei Ostyak is considered to be a language isolate by some authorities, and so is often listed as a Paleo-Asiatic language (see below, p. 55).

Within China itself, among the few remaining pre-Sinitic languages we have the Miao-Yao family, spoken by scattered remnants of what once undoubtedly was a widespread and flourishing family. Ainu, the language of the aboriginal inhabitants of Japan, and Japanese are two languages whose linguistic relationships to each other as well as to established families are very much in doubt. There are some who consider them to be related to Korean and the Altaic languages in a wider family which would be called "North Asiatic" (see proposed family tree on facing page).

Proposed Family Tree for the North Asiatic Family

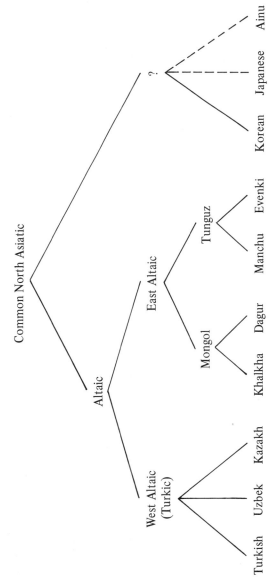

Note: Not all descendant languages are included; broken lines indicate less certain relationships. ? indicates a suspected, but as yet unproven and unnamed, intermediate common language.

TAI

In Southeast Asia, the most widespread family is Tai. In addition to Thai (Siamese, the standard language of Thailand), Laotian and several languages spoken in southern China belong to this group. Previously, some linguists had classified the Tai languages with the Sino-Tibetan family. It has, however, been shown that many of the proposed similarities were due to borrowings and not genetic relationship. Most contemporary scholars reject the notion of a genetic connection.

MON-KHMER

Other families in Southeast Asia include the Mon-Khmer family, which has two noteworthy representatives: Mon, spoken in Burma and Thailand, and Khmer, or Cambodian, the official language of Cambodia. Vietnamese, or Annamite, presents peculiar problems in genetic classification because it seems to share similarities with almost all its neighbors. Nothing conclusive has been shown, but there are claims which link it with Thai, Sino-Tibetan, Mon-Khmer, and even Malayo-Polynesian.

DRAVIDIAN

The majority of the people in India speak one or another Indo-European language, more specifically, one or another descendent of Sanskrit, as we shall see in Chapter 8. However, in the southern part of the country, there are numerous representatives of a still flourishing, pre-Indo-European group, called the Dravidian family. The most noteworthy members of this group are Tamil, Telegu, and Malayalam.

MALAY-POLYNESIAN

Further to the east and south, we have the very widespread Malayo-Polynesian family, which includes most of the languages in the islands of the Pacific and Indian oceans. Just off the east coast of Africa is the island of Madagascar (Malagasy Republic), where the principle language spoken is Malagasy, a member of this family. Malagasy is part of the Malayan branch, which also includes Bahasa Indonesia, the standard language of Indonesia, as well as various other languages spoken in the Indonesian archipelago, such as Javanese and Sundanese. Also belonging to the Malayan branch are Malay, the official language of Malaysia, and numerous languages spoken on the various Philippine Islands, including Tagalog, one of the official languages of the Philippines. The Polynesian branch of the family encompasses the languages of many of the Pacific Islands, from Maori in New Zealand through Samoan, Fijian, and Hawaiian.

AUSTRALIAN AND PAPUAN

The native languages of Australia all appear to belong to a single Australian family. However, on the much smaller island of New Guinea, there is a tremendous variety of spoken tongues. Most of these are poorly described, but even given what little is known, there have been few attempts at genetic classification. Some scholars are inclined to regard the whole island as containing a very large number of language families and language isolates, each spoken by no more than a few villages. The languages are collectively known as Papuan, a term intended to be a mere geographic description.

PALEO-ASIATIC

In the northern part of eastern Siberia there are several languages, each spoken by a small group, which seem to bear no relationship to any others or to each other. For convenience, these are usually called the Paleo-Asiatic, Paleo-Siberian, or Hyperborean languages, and include Chukchee, Yukaghir, Gilyak, and sometimes Yenissei Ostyak.[1]

---

[1] We noted above (p. 52) that some scholars consider Yenissei Ostyak to be a Sino-Tibetan language.

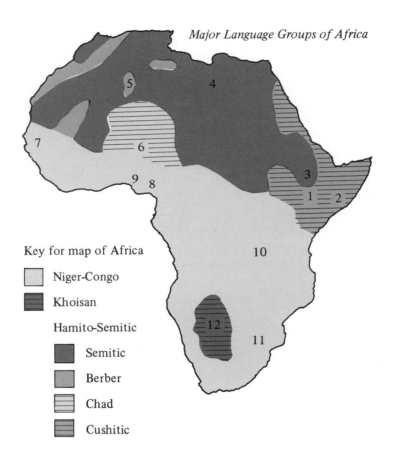

Major Language Groups of Africa

Key for map of Africa

Niger-Congo

Khoisan

Hamito-Semitic

Semitic

Berber

Chad

Cushitic

Familiar Languages

1. Gulla	5. Tuareg	9. Yoruba
2. Somali	6. Hausa	10. Swahili
3. Amharic	7. Wolof	11. Zulu
4. Arabic	8. Ibo	12. Bushman

LANGUAGE FAMILIES OF AFRICA

NIGER-CONGO AND KHOISAN

Besides certain Hamito-Semitic languages mentioned above, it appears that most of the languages of Black Africa can be classified into one of two families: Niger-Congo and Khoisan. Niger-Congo is divided into six main branches; the three most important of these are the West Atlantic, the Kwa, and the Benue-Congo. As representative of the West Atlantic group, we might mention the Wolof language of Senegal or the Fulani language of northern Nigeria. The Kwa group includes a number of prominent West African languages such as Gã, the official language of Ghana; Yoruba and Igbo, which are spoken in southern Nigeria; and Ewe, a language of Togo and parts of Ghana. In addition to certain languages such as Kambari and Mbembe, the Benue-Congo group counts the Bantu languages as a separate subbranch. These are spread throughout Africa beginning slightly north of the equator and continuing south to the tip of the continent; the two most known of the Bantu languages are Swahili and Zulu.

In areas scattered throughout the southern part if Africa, we find the Khoisan languages, which include Hottentot and Bushman branches. These languages are especially noteworthy from the phonetic point of view because they include clicks as ordinary members of the consonant class. Certain other African languages such as Zulu (a Bantu language) also have clicks; but these are phonetic borrowings from Khoisan.

LANGUAGE FAMILIES OF THE AMERICAS

NORTH AMERICAN INDIAN

At the present moment the principal languages spoken in the New World are English, Spanish, Portuguese, and French, all Indo-European languages brought to the Americas within the past five hundred years. Before then, the lands of the Western

Hemisphere were inhabited by groups of people speaking many different languages, which are ordinarily subsumed under the purely geographical heading of American Indian languages. Some of these have undoubtedly disappeared with no records whatsoever; others are attested in the writings of early missionaries and travelers; still others have been subjected to rigorous linguistic description within the past century. The living use of almost all of these languages has been on the decline; no more than a handful show any vitality, because most are not being learned well by younger generations. In childhood many young Indians learn a European language, and often never acquire an adult command of their parents' tongue. In listing the geographical distributions of these indigenous languages, linguists are generally describing the situation that prevailed on the eve of the coming of the Europeans.

ESKIMO-ALEUT AND ATHABASCAN

In the extreme north, around the shores of the Arctic Ocean (in Alaska, Canada, Greenland, and the tip of Siberia), we find the Eskimo languages, which are generally linked to the native language of the Aleutian Islands in an Eskimo-Aleut family. Just south of Eskimo-Aleut in the Pacific Northwest (Alaska, northwest Canada, and California) we have a number of languages belonging to the Athabascan family, in which we find languages such as Beaver and Chipewyan. A separate branch of Athabascan is Apachean, found in the United States Southwest; these languages, the most important member of which is Navaho, are still widely spoken. Athabascan is often linked with two other languages of the Canadian Pacific Coast, Haida and Tlingit, to form a larger family which is known as Na-Dene.

ALGONQUIAN

Spread throughout central Canada, the Great Lakes region, and the eastern seaboard of North America as far south as

Key to map of America North of Mexico

Eskimo-Aleut	Penutian	Caddoan
Algonquian	Salishan	Haida and Tlingit
Iroquoian	Uto-Aztecan	Uninhabited or insufficient early data
Athabascan	Hokan	
Souian	Muskogean	

Language Isolates

1. Yuchi
2. Tonkawa
3. Karankawa
4. Zuñi
5. Kutenai
6. Beothuk

Familiar Languages

7. Delaware
8. Mohawk
9. Erie
10. Ojibwa
11. Choctaw
12. Osage

13. Crow
14. Arapaho
15. Comanche
16. Shoshonee
17. Navaho
18. Beaver

North Carolina is one of the most important of all American language families, Algonquian. Micmac, Abnaki, Delaware, and other Eastern Algonquian languages are found along the coast; Ojibwa, Cree, and various other languages are found in the Great Lakes region. To the same family belong certain languages of the Western Plains, such as Arapaho and Cheyenne. As a result of relatively recent field work, it has been shown that two languages of California, Wiyot and Yurok, are related, though distantly, to Algonquian. This discovery has led to the positing a larger family, called Algic. The following family tree shows part of the Algic group:

Partial family tree of the Algic languages

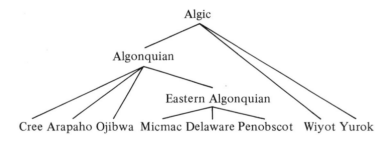

IROQUOIAN AND MUSKOGEAN

Splitting up the Algonquian family in the area of the St. Lawrence River and Lakes Erie and Ontario were the Iroquoian languages, of which the Mohawk, Oneida, and Seneca languages may be taken as representative. Southern outposts of Iroquoian are found in the Cherokee and Tuscarora languages spoken in the Carolinas and Tennessee. The predominant family in the southeastern part of the United States is Muskogean, which includes Alabama, Creek-Seminole, Choctaw, and Mikasuki.

SIOUAN AND UTO-AZTECAN

A large part of the Great Plains region of the United States was occupied by speakers of the Siouan languages; the most important of these are Dakota, Ioway-Oto, Hidatsa, and Crow. The predominant language family in the Great Basin and the Southwest was Uto-Aztecan, which includes Shoshone, Paiute, and Hopi. Another member of this family is Nahuatl, which is still spoken in Mexico and was the language of the pre-Columbian Aztec Empire. To complete our United States survey, note should be made of four other language families found along the west coast of North America: the Salishan, Wakashan, Penutian, and Hokan. Needless to say, there are other language families which we have not mentioned as well as a number of language isolates found in the United States. Among the more well known of the latter are Zuñi, spoken in a single pueblo in New Mexico, Yuchi, the language of one small tribe in the Southeast, and Kutenai, whose speakers are found in northern Idaho.

MAYAN

In the preceding paragraph, we mentioned Nahuatl, a Uto-Aztecan language, as one of the languages of Mexico. The other important family in the same area and extending further south into Central America is Mayan. Mayan includes a number of languages such as Mam, Quiche, Tzeltal, and Tzotzil. Yucatec, which is still spoken on the Yucatan Peninsula, was probably the language of the pre-Columbian Mayan Empire.

SOUTH AMERICAN INDIAN

The languages of South America are notoriously underinvestigated. The latest edition of *Les langues du mondes* lists some ninety-six separate families and language isolates. It is probably to be expected that better descriptions and more extensive research will reveal previously unnoticed relationships. The four most important of the established language families in South America are Arawak, Carib, Quechua, and Tupi-Guarani. Arawak appears to have once been quite widespread, since Arawak languages were spoken from the Antilles down to Paraguay. Carib languages were found all along the north coast of South America to the mouth of the Amazon; a few isolated members of this family are located further south. Quechua is the language family which is indigenous to Peru, and includes Inca (the language of the famous empire conquered by Pizarro). Tupi-Guarani is the name of the language family whose speakers occupy large portions of Brazil and most of Paraguay.

FOR FURTHER STUDY

In 1786, the empress Catherine the Great of Russia ordered C. S. Pallas to collect data on the languages of the world. The second edition of this work, entitled *The Comparative Vocabularies of the Languages of the Whole World,* was published in 1791, and contained data from languages of Africa and America. Ever since, as we have remarked in the text, linguists simply cannot resist the temptation to put languages together into families. The nonspecialist also finds this a fascinating topic, and often confronts a linguist with questions like "What is the origin of language X?" or "Where did language Y arise?" While these questions may not be scientifically phrased, the answer usually being sought is that of genetic relationships.

As a result of this interest, elementary linguistic texts usually carry a chapter such as the one we have just presented; for examples see Bloomfield, Chapter 4, or Gleason, Chapter 28. Such cursory surveys are not and cannot be complete, nor can they go into the complicated reasoning involved in setting up and subdividing each language family. They are intended to give "the names and numbers of all the players"; they locate in time and space, and in that sense *identify,* languages with which the student may be familiar or from which the author will draw his examples throughout the text.

To really understand the problems of similarities and differences among languages and genetic classifications, it is probably necessary to consult more detailed works. The most famous and best survey of the world's languages is that published by Meillet and his successors, *Les langues du monde.* In this two-volume work, we find not only lists and accepted genetic classifications, but also brief sketches pointing out peculiarities and interesting features of various languages and language families, as well as good bibliographies and indices. It should be the first work consulted for information concerning a language you know nothing about. A brief but nonetheless useful collection of facts and figures about the languages of the world today is Siegfried H. Muller's *The World's Living Languages.*

If you have an interest in a particular language family, very often you can find at least one book-length monograph which will give the details of the relationships and the development of the attested languages from the hypothesized parent. Among those dealing with unusual languages, we have Poppe's *Vergleichende Grammatik der altaischen Sprachen* (*Comparative Grammar of the Altaic Languages*), Greenberg's *Languages of Africa,* and Powell's *Indian Linguistic Families of America North of Mexico.*

5

Sound Change

Traditionally and for good reason, historical linguistic studies begin with sound change, and comparative studies begin with phonological reconstruction. In dealing with the phonemes of any given language, we are faced with a limited number of items whose interactions and shifts can be carefully plotted. No other area of linguistic research has yielded such fruitful results in terms of rigorous formulation and significant generalization as has the study of phonological history. In many senses then, we study sound change not only for its own intrinsic interest and importance, but also because it is where we see historical studies developed to their highest degree of formalization. Thus, it is the area in which it is easiest to see exactly what are the methods and aims of the historical linguist, and in some senses it provides the theoretical models toward which other areas of historical linguistics strive.

Let us begin with some simple observations about our own speech. In daily conversation there are certain words which we pronounce in different ways. Sometimes the difference is due to physical factors; when we are tired or rushed, words tend to be slurred. Sometimes the causes are social; for example, we may use some forms when speaking with dignitaries and others when speaking with friends. Sometimes, even after reflection, we cannot find any reason why we select one pronunciation over another. In this last-mentioned case the two (or more) pronunciations of the same word are said to be in *free variation*.

For example, there are the forms of *interesting* in the author's speech. In ordinary conversation, he uses in free variation the forms [ɪntrɛstɪŋ] and [ɪnərɛstɪŋ] whereas in a more formal situation he might use a pronunciation which more closely reflects the spelling of the word, namely [ɪntərɛstiŋ]. What is important to note is that any of the above three pronunciations may be used in any situation without impairing communication. All three are what we call *nondistinctive variants,* since using one for the other does not result in any differences of meaning. Nondistinctive variation is thus a broader term than free variation. Any free variation is nondistinctive, but some nondistinctive variants can be predicted by extra-linguistic, social situations. Therefore we reserve the term *free variants* to include only those alternations where criteria for choosing one or another defies explanation. It must be emphasized that variation in speech forms, either predictable or nonpredictable is an inherent fact of language and not some occasional occurrence.

If we take [intərɛstiŋ], the form which most closely reflects the spelling, as the original or oldest of the three pronunciations, we can say that the other two have developed from it in some way. Diagrammatically, we might look on [intərɛstiŋ] as being an ancestor of the other two forms:

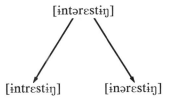

We explain this development by saying that they have undergone a sound change. In [intrɛstiŋ] the vowel which occurs between *t* and *r* in the second syllable has been dropped. In [inərɛstiŋ] the consonant cluster -*nt*- has been changed to -*n*-.

Over a period of time people tend to pick up variations such as these in their speech. But in what we normally consider sound change, there is a second step, and this requires additional time. The speech community as a whole must adopt one or another of these variants at the expense of the others. The newly accepted variant then becomes the normal or standard form, and may eventually find its way into the writing system.

The direction of sound change is difficult to observe in the short run, since it is impossible to tell which of the wide variety of alternate pronunciations in the speech of individuals and communities will survive and which will simply disappear and have no future or permanent effect on the language. However, given a sufficiently long time span, we observe many changes in the spelling of words in written records, and the new spellings indicate that the words involved have undergone a change in pronunciation.

REGULARITY OF CHANGE

In Old English there is a word spelled *hus* [hu:s]. In contemporary English the same word appears as *house* [haws]. Upon inspection of the older and newer forms of this word, it can be assumed that what is involved in their relationship is a shift of Old English [u:] to New English [aw]. But [u:] did not become [aw] in only this word; on the contrary, wherever [u:] appeared in Old English, we find [aw] in New English (when a word has survived). To express the same fact in other terms, we say that [u:] *regularly* becomes [aw] in the history of English. To verify this statement, we can cite many other examples:

Old English	New English
mūs [mu:s]	mouse [maws]
ūt [u:t]	out [awt]
sūð [su:ð]	south [sawθ]

In formal linguistics, we express phonological changes such as these by means of rules. The minimal form of a rule contains the earlier and later sounds linked by means of an arrow which shows the direction of change:

$$X \rightarrow Y$$

To account for the change of the vowel in the examples given above, we would write the rule:

$$[u:] \rightarrow [aw]$$

A rule such as this is a formalization in generally accepted symbols of a historical statement. It is intended to reflect the fact that, at some point in the history of English, a sound change occurred which replaced the sound [u:] by the sound [aw]. The rule can be read "Old English [u:] is replaced by (or changes into or develops into) New English [aw]." This means that those words which contained [u:] in Old English now have [aw] in New English.

PHONETIC ENVIRONMENTS

The development of Old English ū is what is known as an *unconditioned change:* every [u:] becomes [aw] no matter where it occurs in a word or what sounds are nearby. More often it is the case that sound changes are influenced or conditioned by neighboring phonemes. This we call *conditioned change.* Consider the vowels in the following words:

Old English	New English
cynn [kün]	kin [kɨn]
hyll [hül]	hill [hɨl]
synn [sün]	sin [sɨn]
pytt [püt]	pit [pɨt]

Given this data, the following rule can be written:

$$[ü] \rightarrow [ɨ]$$

Now, consider the development of some other words with Old English [ü]:

Old English	New English
wyrst [würst]	worst [wərst]
wyrcan [würkan]	work [wərk]
gyrdel [gürdɛl]	girdle [gərdl̩]
byrþen [bürθɛn]	burden [bərdn̩]

To account for the vowel change in this set, we would derive a different rule:

$$[ü] \rightarrow [ə]$$

If we write such statements which are obviously contradictory, our rules are of doubtful scientific validity. When faced with such a situation, our first step is to reexamine the data to determine under what circumstances the second change (which may be considered as an exception to the first) takes place. On examining these and similar words, we note that [ü:] develops into [ə] where it is followed by *r* plus some other consonant. This *r* + *C* (where C = any consonant) is called a *conditioning environment*.

In formal linguistics, we write a rule which specifies a conditioning environment in the following way:

$$X \rightarrow Y \,/\, \underline{\quad} Z$$

The slash is read "under the condition" or "in the environment." The low dash (__) indicates the position of the changing phoneme vis-à-vis its conditioning environment. The Z in the above example is the conditioning environment itself. A formal rule designed to express the change of [ü] to [ə] in the second group of words given above would be written as follows:

$$[ü] \rightarrow [ə] \,/\, \underline{\quad} rC$$

To translate it into words, the rule would read "[ü] becomes [ə] when it appears in the environment before [r] plus some other consonant."

ORDERING

The difference between Old English *hnecca* [hnɛka] and New English *neck* [nɛk] involves two sound changes: the loss of the initial consonant *h* and the loss of the final vowel *a*. Given just these two forms we would have no way of knowing which change took place first or whether there were any intermediate stages in the development of this word. Fortunately, in Middle English texts we find the same word spelled *nekke* [nɛkə]. We can therefore see that between Old and Middle English, two sound changes had taken place:[1]

1. h → ø / # __ n
2. a → ə / __ #

And then for the development from the Middle to the New English period, we can posit a third rule which drops the last syllable:

3. ə → ø / __ #

The phonological shape of the Middle English form is concrete evidence that the initial consonant was dropped before the final vowel. It also gives a bonus bit of information by telling us that there was an intermediate stage in the loss of the final vowel, i.e., there was not a simple a → ø, but rather a process such as a → ə → ø.

However, we do not always have texts adequately spaced in time to establish the order in which specific changes occurred or all the intermediate steps between two stages of a language. We might be dealing with a situation in which we have two widely separated stages attested and wish to describe the development from one to the other. An even more obvious case is when our starting point is a reconstructed language and we are faced with tracing its history to one of its daughter languages. In many instances, there will be no way to tell us in what order the given changes have occurred. The observed shifts are then listed in some convenient or logical order, grouped together as consonants, vowels, glides, etc. This would probably always be the case if all of the

---

[1] # is the sign used to indicate a word boundary. Thus, the notation # __ indicates an environment at the beginning of a word, and __ # denotes a final position.

changes involved were unconditioned. However, if often happens that after a conditioned change has taken place, the conditioning environment itself changes. On the other hand, we may find that a particular change must have taken place in an environment produced by another rule. By determining what sounds constitute the environments necessary for specific sound changes, we can often tell which changes occurred before others and so list our rules in relative chronological order.

For example, take the following pre-Sanskrit forms and their descendants in the attested langauge:[2]

Pre-Sanskrit	Sanskrit	
*kot-i	kat-i	'how much, how many?'
*ke	ča	'and'

We can note the following changes in these words:

1. The vowels *o and *e both become a.
2. *k becomes č before *e, but not before *o.

In our second statement above we see that we need the vowel e as opposed to a in order to describe the conditioning environment of the consonant sound change. Therefore, we must assume that this change took place before the vowel *e lost its distinction from *o. Our rules must consequently be ordered to reflect this relative timing. Thus, our two rules are in the order:

1. $k \rightarrow č / \underline{\quad} e$
2. $\left.\begin{array}{l} e \\ o \end{array}\right\} \rightarrow a$

According to our formal system, a sound change rule must be viewed as coming equipped with some kind of scanning device which notes every occurrence of a particular sound

---

[2] The asterisk is placed before a reconstructed form.

(with the specified environment, if necessary) and changes that sound in accordance with the instructions of the rule. We can view the application of each rule as giving us a separate stage of the language. In our examples above, the necessary stages would be:

Stage I   kot-i   ke

Stage II   kot-i   če   In between stages I and II, rule #1 has taken effect.

Stage III kat-i   ča   In between stages II and III, rule #2 has taken effect.

The easiest way to see whether or not two rules must be ordered with respect to one another is to reverse them and see whether or not they produce the desired results. For the above example, if we apply rule 2 first, we get the following stage II:

kat   ka

Rule 1 then has no effect since we have done away with *e* (the environment necessary for its operation), and as a result we do not get the Sanskrit forms which are actually attested.

CLASS CHANGES

We should note also that sounds tend to change in groups which form natural classes. By this we mean that sounds which share some feature, say, in point or manner of articulation will very often change in the same direction. Consider the following words in Ancient and in Modern Greek:

Ancient	Modern	
barus	varus	'heavy'
doksa	ðoksa	'glory'
lego	leɣo	'I say'

From these three words we can extract three separate sound laws:

1. b → v
2. d → ð
3. g → γ

Since ð and γ have the same relationship to *d* and *g* respectively, that *v* has to *b* (they are fricatives with the same point of articulation and voicing as the corresponding stop), we know that these three changes have something in common. They are reflections of the same process, namely, a voiced stop's becoming a voiced fricative. We want to express this generalization in our rules; so we combine the three rules into a single rule which more adequately describes what happened. We do this by naming the class to which the individual phonemes belong and the class to which they change. Thus, our rule summarizing the above three sound changes is:

[voiced stop] → [fricative]

By writing a rule of this type, we have achieved a measure of simplicity and generality in our description of changes since we have reduced three rules to one. In the history of languages it is most often true that similar situations prevail. Thus, when we discover one particular sound change in a language, it is likely that similar sounds will change in the same manner.

A further remark on our understanding and formal expression of *classes of sounds* is in order here. Basically, we look upon the sounds of language as consisting of various features, which we can define as particular articulatory actions. Some of these are voicing, the various points of articulation, being a stop consonant as opposed to a continuant, and being nasal or nonnasal. (For a complete list see the appendix on basic phonetics.) All of the sounds which have a particular feature can be designated as belonging to that class. Thus, instead of listing all the voiceless consonants in a language in its sound laws, one can simply write $\dfrac{C}{[-\text{ voice}]}$, and by this shorthand notation indicate the class of consonants (here designated by the letter C) which share the feature of voicelessness.

In our next chapter, we will give various examples of sound changes and the formal way of expressing them in rules. Before proceeding, the reader should go through the appendix on phonetics and refer to it later when necessary.

PHONETIC AND PHONEMIC CHANGE

In terms of classical American phonemic theory, when we speak of sound change, we should make a distinction between a phonetic and a phonemic change. A *phonetic change* presumably is one which merely affects the pronunciation of a given phoneme without altering the phonemic system of the language. Most of the time a simple phonetic change will merely add or delete an allophone with regard to a specific phoneme.

In New English, for example, we aspirate voiceless stops when they occur at the beginnings of words. Thus, we have a phonetic contrast between the *k* in *kit* [kʰɪt] and the *k* in *skit* [skɪt]. This was not always so. In Middle English an initial voiceless stop was unaspirated as it is in most European languages. Then English underwent a sound change which can be expressed by the rule:

$$[\text{voiceless stop}] \rightarrow [+ \text{ aspirated}] \, / \, \#\underline{\quad}$$

This rule, in terms of classical phonemics, merely adds another allophone to those of the voiceless stops. It does not change the status of those stops as independent phonemes, nor does it alter their position relative to the other phonemes of the language (see footnote on p. 75).

Consider now another example from the history of English: Old English forms *mōdor* 'mother' and *fæder* 'father'. The sound change we are interested in here involved a shift of the stop /d/ to the fricative /ð/ in between vowels, which can be expressed in the rule:

$$d \rightarrow ð \; / \; V\_\_V$$

While on some level we might count this as giving another allophone to /d/ in a certain position (between vowels), in fact it does more than that: it replaces the phoneme /d/ with the phoneme /ð/ in this context, for we already have in the Old English system an independent phoneme /ð/ in intervocalic position as in *æðele* 'noble'. Thus, we are forced to say that what we have here is a *phonemic change*. While the phonemic pattern of the language may reman unchanged, the words involved in this shift have undergone a phonemic change insofar as one phoneme has replaced another.

Let us go back to the Sanskrit example presented earlier in this chapter to see how a new phoneme can be created. Our data were:

*kot-i → kat-i   'how much, how many?'
*ke   → ča   'and'

and our first rule was:

$$k \rightarrow č \; / \; \_\_ \; e$$

At this point, in terms of phonemic theory, all we can say is that /k/ has acquired a new allophone [č] when it occurred before [e]. However, then we have our second rule:

$$e \rightarrow a$$

But [č] can no longer be considered an allophone of /k/ occurring in a particular environment since there is no longer a specific environment (i.e., the phoneme /e/ to predict its appearance), and with the two forms *kat-i* and *ča* we have

something approaching the necessary minimal pair.³ As prac-
titioners of classical phonemics, we are now forced to say that
/č/ is a new phoneme, independent of /k/ and of all other
phonemes in the language. This, then, is another case of phonemic change, a case where the phonemic system of the language is altered by the introduction of a *new* phoneme into
the system.

FOR FURTHER STUDY

The principles underlying the mechanisms of sound change
and their interpretation can be found, with only slight variations, in chapters from a number of elementary books; for
example, Chapter 8 of Sapir's *Language,* "Language as a
Historical Product: Phonetic Law," or Chapter 10 of Lehmann's *Introduction,* "Change in Phonological Systems." For
the more rigid explication of the neogrammarian position
one can consult their leading theoretician, Hermann Paul, by
reading Chapter 3 of *Principles,* "Sound Change." With less
psychological discussion, essentially the same position is presented in Bloomfield's *Language,* Chapter 20, "Phonetic
Change," and in more modern dress in Hockett's "Sound
Change."

For a more structured approach to sound change, there is
an article by Jakobson, "Principes de phonologie historique,"

---

3 "Minimal pair" is the term used by American phonemicists to describe a
set of linguistic forms (words or morphemes) which are different in meaning, but are identical in sound except for one item. Such pairs were felt to
prove that two sounds were indeed different phonemes. Thus, suppose we
were doing an analysis of English, and from the words we had already collected we were not sure whether [c] and [k] were different phonemes or
mere variations (allophones) of the same phoneme occurring in different
positions, say, [k] before back vowels and [č] before front vowels. When
we confront the words *cheese* [či:z] and *keys* [ki:z], we would find such a
position untenable since we have [k] and [č] occurring in exactly the same
phonetic environment. Therefore, we would be forced to say that /k/ and
/c/ are separate phonemes. This is proved by pointing to *cheese* and *keys,*
which form a minimal pair.

and the first part of Martinet's book, *Économie de change-ments phonétiques,* "Théorie générale." The idea of sound change was integrated with classical American phonemics in an article by Archibald Hill, "Phonetic and Phonemic Change." Finally, for a proper appreciation of sound laws and their rightful position within the phenomena of linguistic change, there is the excellent, very short paper of Jakobson, "The Concept of Sound Law and the Teleological Criterion."

6

Types of Sound Change

Anyone who has had experience with the phonological histories of different languages knows that, given a long enough time span, almost any sound can change into any other sound. Perhaps the current research on abstract models of phonology will shed some light on possible limitations of sound change between two *adjoining* stages of a language, but these studies are still in their infancy. However, it remains true that the most divergent languages show examples of phonetic change which are remarkably similar; these changes have been classified into types and named by linguists. When one investigates the history of a previously unstudied language, knowledge of the types of sound change provides a handy guide as to what one might expect to find. While these types show what changes might be likely or what *can* happen, in no sense should they be interpreted as covering all cases or as expressing limitations on the possible sound shifts a particular language may undergo.

When dealing with a previously unstudied language, one of the most powerful ways of identifying and making a case for the acceptance of a particular change is by pointing to a typological parallel, i.e., by showing that the same thing happened in the history of another, perhaps unrelated, language. Thus, when one finds in the history of a newly discovered language a situation whereby voiceless stops become voiced when located between two vowels, one can immediately point to the same phenomenon in the development of Spanish from Latin (p. 84) as a typological parallel.

In general, we should beware of explanations which state that a change proceeds in a particular direction because one sound or group of sounds is *easier* to make than another.

The problem with such an approach lies in defining, in any significant sense, what is an *easy* or a *difficult* sound or group of sounds. For example, continental Europeans have no trouble enunciating the pure vowels of their languages, whereas the diphthongized vowels of English are difficult for them. The reverse is true for speakers of English. In addition, we have no idea as to the relative complexity of the neurological processes involved in the production of any given sound.

LOSS AND ADDITION OF PHONEMES

Perhaps the most obvious type of sound change involves the simple loss of phonemes. Again this may be conditioned or unconditioned. For example, in the shift of Indo-European to the Celtic languages, the phoneme *p was lost in all environments. In formal terms:

$$p \rightarrow \text{ø}$$

Indo-European	Old Irish	
*pətēr	athair	'father'
*nepot-	nie	'nephew'
*tepent-s	tëe	'warm'

Of course a loss of phonemes may also be conditioned by a phonological enviroment. We have already seen the case in which initial Old English *h-* followed by the nasal *-n-* disappeared (pp. 68–69). In Northern Chinese all final stops were dropped between the Ancient and Modern periods:

Ancient Chinese	Mandarin	
fap	fa	'law'
pat	pa	'eight'
liuk	liu	'six'

This could be accounted for by a simple rule:

$$[\text{stop}] \rightarrow \text{ø} \: / \: \underline{\quad}\#$$

Much less common is the addition of a phoneme to a word. In New English we have the isolated examples of *nope* as an emphatic form of *no* and *yep* as an emphatic form of, perhaps, *yeah* (from *yes*). What happened was that in an emphatic *no* or *yeah* the flow of air was sharply cut off after the articulation of the vowel, first giving the impression of a glottal stop [noᵖ], [yəᵖ]. Later on, this glottal stop developed into the labial consonant -*p*.

A more usual occurrence of these "consonants from nowhere," or *excrescent* consonants, is a stop introduced to break up clusters of continuants. Most often the excrescent stop is homorganic (has the same point of articulation) as the preceding continuant. Thus in the history of the Greek word *ambrotos* 'immortal' we have the following situation: the word is formed from two elements of Indo-European origin, the negative prefix **a-* and the stem **mr̥t-*[1] 'death' in its alternate form **mrot*. Then a *b* was introduced into the cluster -*mr*-, giving us the attested Greek word:

$$*a\text{-}mrot\text{-}os \rightarrow ambrotos$$

In New English there are certain excrescent consonants which have not yet found their way into the writing system. For example, the cluster -*ns*- has been invaded by a -*t*-, yielding the three-member group [nts]. Thus, in most English dialects, there is no difference between the pronunciation of the words *dense* and *dents;* both are spoken [dɛnts]. Likewise, both *mince* and *mints* are generally pronounced [mɪnts].

There are, however, older cases of excrescent consonants which have found their way into the English writing system, as can be seen in the following words in Old and New English:

Old English	New English
æmtig	empty
ganra	gander
þunor	thunder
spinel	spindle

---

[1] Vocalic *r* is signified by *r̥*.

Loss of vowels (and therefore syllables) is especially common in languages with strong stress on one syllable of a word. As a result of the emphasis on the stressed syllable, other syllables in the word tend to become reduced (or "slurred") and may be eventually lost. When the lost vowel is at the end of the word, we refer to this loss as *apocope;* when a medial vowel drops, the process is called *syncope.*

English provides numerous examples of apocope. On p. 69, we saw one example in the reduction of [a] to [ə] to zero in the Old English *hnecca* (New English *neck*). This word was stressed on the first syllable [hnéka], and by the Middle English period, people had begun to slur the ending, and the final vowel eventually disappeared. There are numerous examples of the same process throughout the history of English. For instance:

Old English	New English
stícca	stick
náma	name
sónu	son
móna	moon

Syncope is more rare in English. We can see it reflected even in the spelling of a few words, such as the nautical term *focs'l* for *forecastle*. It was very common in the development of the Celtic languages. The following terms borrowed from Latin show the Old Irish form of syncope:

Latin	Old Irish	
apostolus	apstal	'apostle'
epīscopus	epscop	'bishop'
prædicat	predchid	'preaches'
nātālīcia	notlaic	'birth' or 'Christmas'

(The other changes in the words are due to processes in the history of Old Irish which will not be discussed here.) These would be accounted for by a rule of this sort:[2]

$$V_1CV_2C(C)V_3 \rightarrow V_1CC(C)V_3 \text{ or } V \rightarrow \emptyset \ / \ VC_1\_\_C_2(C)VC_3$$

ASSIMILATION

Perhaps the most common type of conditioned sound change is *assimilation,* whereby one sound becomes more like a neighboring one. Obviously, this can be considered a simplification of the muscular movements needed to pronounce a given word. Assimilation is a very frequent phenomenon in just about all the languages of the world. In terms of articulatory phonetics, assimilation of consonants usually involves one consonant becoming more like another in one or more of the following three ways:

1. point of articulation
2. manner of articulation
3. voicing

Assimilations are also divided into two broad groups depending on the linear direction of the change from the dominant to the changing phoneme. *Regressive assimilation* means that a consonant becomes more like one that follows; in other words, the force of the change proceeds backwards, from a phoneme to the one which precedes it. Presumably, this shift is explained as an anticipation of the muscular movements which go to make up the second phoneme. *Progressive assimilation* takes place when the first phoneme is dominant and in some way makes the second more like itself.

By far, the more common of the above two types is the regressive. An example of regressive assimilation in point of articulation is the New English word *comfort,* which ultimately derives from the Old French *conforter.* In this case,

2 Parentheses are used in writing rules to indicate optional elements. Thus an environment which is stated __(C)C means 'in the environment before one or two consonants'.

the dental nasal *n* has become *m,* more like the following labial fricative *f*; it has shifted its point of articulation from dental to labial.

Another very clear example of this type of assimilation is seen in the development of the consonant clusters *-ct-* and *-pt-* from Latin to Italian:

Latin	Italian	
noctem	notte	'night'
factum	fatto	'done'
septem	sette	'seven'
aptum	atto	'apt, fit for'

We see that immediately before *t*, the other voiceless stops, *p* and *k,* shift their point of articulation to match that of *t*. In formal notation, the rule might be written:

$$\begin{bmatrix} + \text{ stop} \\ - \text{ voice} \end{bmatrix} \rightarrow t \ / \underline{\quad} t$$

Much less common than regressive assimilation is progressive assimilation, in which a consonant assumes some of the qualities of the one that precedes it. For example, we have the following developments from Latin to French (with the loss of a medial vowel):

hominem → homme   'man'
nomināre → nommer   'to name'

The history of English presents us with examples of the Old English cluster *-ln-* becoming Middle English *-ll-*:

Old English	Early Middle English	Middle English	
eln	elne	elle	'ell' (a unit of measure)
myln	milne	mille	'mill'

Another type of assimilation involves the changes undergone by consonants when they appear between vowels. These changes have traditionally been subsumed under the general heading of *weakening* or *lenition* ("making lax"). Two principal processes are involved here: stops become continuants and voiceless consonants become voiced. We consider this to be a type of assimilation because vowels are both continuant and voiced, and so the processes of lenition can be looked upon as the assimilation of consonants to vowels with regard to these features.

The classic case of lenition with regard to stops becoming fricatives is the development of the Celtic languages. From the earliest attested stages of Irish (fourth century) to the Classical Old Irish period (beginning in the seventh century) all consonants which followed vowels were lenited (became continuants), as can be seen from the following examples:[3]

Fourth Century	Seventh Century	
*(p)ater	athair [aθar^y]	'father'
*dub-us	dubh [duv]	'black'
*aka(p)era-	a chorp [axorp]	'his body'

A similar but more limited type of lenition can be found in the development of noninitial Old English -d-; in certain cases it has become -th- [ð] in New English, as the following examples show:

Old English	New English
mōdor	mother
fæder	father
weder	weather
hider	hither

---

[3] Traditional Irish spelling indicates fricatives by placing an *h* immediately after the corresponding stop; thus *th* = [θ], *bh* = [v], and *ch* = [x] (*c* = [k]).

The conditioning environment for this change is that the *d* in question must be preceded by a vowel and be followed by either an ŗ (vocalic *r*) or by the syllable [ər], usually written *-er* or *-or*. In formal terms:[4]

$$d \rightarrow \eth \ / \ V \underline{\hspace{1em}} \left\{ \begin{matrix} ŗ \\ ər \end{matrix} \right\}$$

This rule explains the fact that certain other Old English words with intervocalic *-d-* maintain this sound in the modern language. For example:

Old English	New English
bodig	body
slīdan	slide
sadol	saddle

An example of the voicing of consonants between vowels can be seen in the development of Spanish from Latin:[5]

Latin	Spanish	
rīpa	riba	'shore'
mūtāre	mudar	'to change'
fāta	fada	'fate'
amīca	amiga	'female friend'

This change is accounted for in a single rule:

$$[\text{stop}] \rightarrow [+\text{voice}] \ / \ V \underline{\hspace{1em}} V$$

---

4 Braces { } are used in writing rules to indicate an either-or situation. Thus an environment written __ $\left\{ \begin{matrix} x \\ y \end{matrix} \right\}$ means 'in the environment before *either* x *or* y'.

5 The change of voiceless stops to voiced between vowels is very old and widespread in the Romance languages. In Modern Spanish the "weakening" of these consonants has gone even further, and they have become fricatives. The Spanish writing system preserves a stage where they were merely voiced stops, and this is what we are illustrating here.

Somewhat less frequent than consonant assimilations, but still widespread, are vowel assimilations, which are generally known by the name of *umlaut* or *vowel harmony*. They have been observed to proceed both regressively and progressively.

The most noted example of the regressive assimilation of vowels is probably that of the Germanic languages, which is clearly attested in texts from different stages of German. Observe the following words:

Old High German	Middle High German	
scōni	schöne[6]	'beautiful'
dunni	dünne	'thin'
mahti	mähte	'might'

In general terms, the shift can be described as one in which back vowels became front ones, and the motivation or assimilating element is provided by the final high front vowels -*i* in these words in Old High German. To express it more clearly, a final *i* (a high front vowel) in Old High German assimilated to itself in terms of frontness a preceding vowel. Later this -*i* changed to -*e*, phonetically [ə]. A rule to account for the first change would be as follows:[7]

$$V \rightarrow [+\text{front}] \; / \; \_\_C_0i$$

An example of progressive vowel assimilation can be seen in the history of the Turkic languages. Observe the difference between the following forms of Old Anatolian Turkish (fourteenth century) and Modern Standard Turkish:

Old Anatolian	Modern Turkish	
benüm	benim	'mine, of me'
bilür	bilir	'knows'
gelüp	gelip	'going'

[6] The vowels with the double dots (umlaut) are front variants of the undotted vowels.

[7] The notational convention C_0 means that zero or more consonants may be present in the environment.

The second vowel in each of the above words was rounded in Old Anatolian. By the time of Modern Turkish, the first vowel had assimilated the second with regard to the feature of rounding, and thus the second vowel also became unrounded. In formal notation, the rule for such a change is written:

$$V \rightarrow [- \text{round}] \ / \ \begin{array}{c} V \\ [- \text{round}] \end{array} C_o \text{---}$$

As we mentioned above, when consonants enter into any kind of assimilatory process, the conditioning environment (the phoneme they become more like) is usually one that is immediately adjacent. Vowels, on the other hand, are ordinarily separated by consonants, and the assimilatory feature leaps over the intervening consonants. But there is rarer situation in which one consonant is assimilated to another that is not directly adjacent.

Perhaps the most famous case of this is the Indo-European word for *five,* which can be reconstructed with some certainty as *penk^{w}e. In both Latin and the Germanic languages, the two stop consonants have become identical, though the assimilation proceeded in opposite directions:

> *penk^{w}e → Latin quīnque [k^{w}i:nk^{w}e]
> (k^w = *qu* in Latin orthography)
> *penk^{w}e → pre-Germanic *penpe → German fünf

(Indo-European *p regularly becomes Germanic *f* by a sound change known as Grimm's law, which we shall discuss in Chapter 8). So, for the Latin, our assimilation rule will read:

$$p \ldots k^w \rightarrow k^w \ldots k^w$$

In the shift from Indo-European to the Germanic languages, the rule is:

> p . . . k^w → p . . . p
> (with the later shift p → f mentioned above)

DISSIMILATION

Much less common than assimilation, though frequent enough to be worthy of mention is the opposite process of *dissimilation,* whereby one of two similar sounds will change so as to become even more differentiated from the other. The history of the development of French from Latin provides us with examples of dissimilation both in vowels and consonants:

Latin	French	
frāgrāre	flairer	L = 'to emit a smell'
		F = 'to smell out, scent, sniff'
frīgorōsum	frileux	L = 'cold' F = 'chilly'

We note that the Latin words have *r*'s in both of the above, and French has changed one of these *r*'s to *l* (the *g*'s are lost in another sound change). The history of French also includes situations in which vowels dissimilate before identical vowels in a following syllable, as the following examples show:

Latin	French	
dīvīnum	devin	'divine'
succussan	secousse[8]	'a jolt, shake'

In the Latin words we see two successive identical vowels. French has undergone a change which dissimilated the first; in one case *i* became *e,* and in the second *u* became *e.*

OTHER TYPES OF SOUND CHANGE

Besides assimilation, one of the most common types of sound change is the process of *palatalization,* which is found in many different languages of the world. Articulatorily, it involves the shift of a consonant to a palatal point of articulation. Usually this shift is triggered by a following front vowel

---

[8] *Ou* is the normal French method of writing [u].

(especially the high front vowel -*i*) or the glide -*y*-. Some examples from Old to New English should make clear what the process is:

Old English	New English
ceaf	chaff
cēse	cheese
cēap	cheap
cīld	child
cirice	church

In Old English the letter *c* generally represents [k]. In New English *ch* is the usual way to write the palatal [č]. The change involved in the above list of words is that from [k] to [č] under the influence of the front vowels *e* or *i*. This process of palatalization of the Old English *c* [k] before front vowels probably began even during the Old English period. We see that the change does not take place when a back vowel follows the *c*, as in the following examples:

Old English	New English
cuman	come
candel	candle

A particular type of change related to both vowels and consonants is the process known as *compensatory lengthening*. This situation involves a vowel which is followed by two consonants; when one of the consonants is dropped, the vowel is lengthened in compensation for the lost phoneme. In formal terms, compensatory lengthening is usually expressed as follows:

$$VC_1C_2 \rightarrow \bar{V}C_2$$

Compensatory lengthening is common in many Indo-European languages. Some examples from Old Irish are:

Common Celtic	Old Irish	
*magl	māl	'prince'
*kenetl	cenēl	'kindred, gender'
*etn	ēn	'bird'
*datl	dāl	'assembly'

A relatively infrequent type of sound change involves the reversing of position of two adjoining sounds, which is called *metathesis*. More often than not, it involves a liquid and a vowel. Thus, we have the following forms in Old and Middle English:

Old English	Middle English	
brid	bird	'bird'
hros	hors	'horse'
þridda	þirde	'third'

FOR FURTHER STUDY

The list of what sound changes are likely to take place is surprisingly short, and again probably the best way to know what to expect is not to memorize lists, but to become familiar with the histories of several languages. For a list similar to the one present in this chapter one can consult Chapter 21 of Bloomfield's *Language*, "Types of Phonetic Change." For more selective, but minutely described, examples of the types of sound change, there is the second part of Martinet's *Économie*, "Illustrations."

The third part of Cowan's *Workbook in Comparative Reconstruction* contains problems on sound changes to which solutions and explanations are appended. It might be worthwhile to look at them for further examples of what happens in a variety of languages.

7

Reconstruction

Historical investigation of particular languages ordinarily does not stop at the earliest written texts. Some of the most interesting work is investigating the prehistoric, unattested period and discovering facts about the development of languages in the period before they were written down. The most common method of investigation is the comparison of languages which are genetically related.

In Chapter 3 we discussed what is meant by genetically related languages: they are languages which are later developments of a single earlier tongue. Our goal in reconstruction is to get at that previous language, describe it as well as possible, and show what changes it underwent in evolving to its attested descendants. We do this by applying a technique which was developed in the nineteenth century and is known as the *comparative method*.

Basically, the comparative method is very simple. It involves taking corresponding elements in two or more related languages and projecting them backward in time by positing an ancestor whose development can be shown to have resulted in what is actually attested. In many senses the actual reconstruction of a parent language and the explanation of its developments to the daughter languages is the conclusive proof that two or more languages are genetically related.

PHONOLOGICAL RECONSTRUCTION

Usually the first reconstruction work that is done with any language family is an attempt to reconstruct the sound system and a collection of morphemes of the parent language. This is called *phonological reconstruction,* though its implications for other parts of the grammar are obvious. The initial step in this process is to group together words from languages which we suspect or know to have the same origin (i.e., genetically related languages). Quite often, these will be words which have the same (or approximately the same) meaning in the attested languages. But we must also be aware of possible semantic shifts which may result in somewhat different meanings. These sets of words are called *cognates;* a word in one language is called cognate to a word in another language if both have the same ancestor and neither is the result of any borrowing. Thus, English *father* and Latin *pater* are cognates, both having descended directly from Indo-European **pəter.* The details of this will be discussed in Chapter 8 in the section on Grimm's Law. The English adjective *paternal* is not a cognate of the Latin adjective *paternus,* but is simply a borrowing from Latin.

In the initial search for cognate sets, it is wise to start with words that have been in a language continuously for a long period of time and are not likely to be borrowings from other languages. Names for relatively new items, such as *airplane* or *telephone* or names of items of higher levels of culture, such as *piano* or *habeas corpus* are not of great value in proving genetic relationships and generally travel from one language to another in a relatively undisturbed phonological shape.

Experience has shown that the words least likely to be subject to outside influence and therefore most useful for reconstruction are those words which represent very common, universal items, such as the lower numerals, the parts of the body, familial terms, certain natural objects like *sun* or *day,* and so on.

As an example of reconstruction, we will examine words from four Polynesian languages and see how, using this data, we can reconstruct individual items and the phonemic system of the parent language. We start by arranging the presumed cognate sets in columns:

	Maori	Hawaiian	Samoan	Fijian[1]	
1.	pou	pou	pou	bou	'post'
2.	tapu	kapu	tapu	tabu	'forbidden'
3.	taŋi	kani	taŋi	taŋi	'cry'
4.	takere	kaʔele	taʔele	takele	'keel'

The next step is to break down the cognates into correspondence sets of individual phonemes. The equal sign (=) is used to indicate *corresponds to*. Thus, from the above cognates, we can extract the following vowel correspondences:

Maori		Hawaiian		Samoan		Fijian	Example Number
o	=	o	=	o	=	o	(1)
u	=	u	=	u	=	u	(1 & 2)
a	=	a	=	a	=	a	(2 & 3)
i	=	i	=	i	=	i	(3)
e	=	e	=	e	=	e	(4)

Once the correspondence sets have been put in proper order and observed, the first step is to hypothesize a phoneme in the parent language from which each of the descendants could have developed. In the case of the vowels given above, there is no question. Since the same vowels appear in all the different languages, we have no reason to assume that anything different existed in the common language from which they are all descended. Therefore, we reconstruct the following vowel phonemes:

$$*o \quad *u \quad *a \quad *i \quad *e$$

---

[1] Some scholars feel that Fijian, strictly speaking, is not a Polynesian, but a Melanesian language. Even in this system of classification, Polynesian and Melanesian are closely related branches of the Malayo-Polynesian family. This opinion is noted in passing and has no bearing on our use of the language for purposes of illustrating the principles of reconstruction.

More normally, one arranges them in a phonetic chart indicating relative features:

	Front	Mid	Back
high	*i		*u
mid	*e		*o
low		*a	

This, we say is the vowel system of Common Polynesian.

The consonant correspondences which can be extracted from the same data are:

	Maori		Hawaiian		Samoan		Fijian	
A.	p	=	p	=	p	=	b	(1 & 2)
B.	t	=	k	=	t	=	t	(2 & 3 & 4)
C.	ŋ	=	n	=	ŋ	=	ŋ	(3)
D.	k	=	ʔ	=	ʔ	=	k	(4)
E.	r	=	l	=	l	=	l	(4)

The consonant correspondences present a bit more difficulty because they do not agree in all cases. Remember that many more examples could be added to substantiate the patterns in each of the sets given. This regularity of correspondence can be explained in no other way than to assume that for each correspondence set there existed a single phoneme in the parent language, which may have undergone some change in one or more of the daughters. These attested descendants are referred to as *reflexes* of the parent phoneme.

Where the daughter languages show different reflexes, the choice of which pheneme to reconstruct will depend on several factors. The most important of these are:

1. Likelihood of a change in one direction as opposed to another, as shown by experience with a wide number of languages.

2. Considerations of what the whole phonological pattern of the parent language will look like.

The first factor might also be called *historical likelihood* or *probability*. Thus, suppose we have a situation where in one language we find the phoneme k, and in a related language we find a $\check{c}$ corresponding to it before front vowels. We know already, from many attested cases, that k often becomes $\check{c}$ before front vowels (pp. 87–88); the reverse process is unknown. Therefore we would have no hesitation in reconstructing a phoneme $*k$ in the parent language and assuming a change $k \rightarrow \check{c}$.

As an illustration of the second factor, suppose we have already reconstructed for a parent language the following consonants:

$$\begin{array}{ccc} *p & *t & *k \\ & *d & *g \\ & *s & \end{array}$$

Further data reveals the correspondence set $b = v$. We would immediately assume that the ancestor phoneme of this set is $*b$, thus yielding a system:

$$\begin{array}{ccc} *p & *t & *k \\ *b & *d & *g \\ & *s & \end{array}$$

Such a result is much more likely or natural than the system we would end up with if we reconstructed $*v$:[2]

$$\begin{array}{ccc} *p & *t & *k \\ & *d & *g \\ & *s & \\ *v & & \end{array}$$

Suppose then, that for our first correspondence set (A), we assume a protophoneme $*p$. This involves positing a sound rule, which says that proto-Polynesian $*p \rightarrow b$ in Fijian.

---

[2] A phonological system such as this, with an irregular pattern or gaps, is known as a *skewed system*. While a language may have such a collection of sounds, a normal or well-patterned collection is more common.

Likewise for the second set (B), we propose *t, which becomes k in Hawaiian. For the fourth set (D), we set up a *k, which becomes ? in Hawaiian and Samoan. For the last (E), we posit an *l, which becomes r in Maori.

We have now a very symmetrical and "normal" pattern for the stop consonants, namely:

$$*p \qquad *t \qquad *k$$

(which are all voiceless) and also a single liquid *l. Note that if we had set up a *b (voiced) for set A, at this point our stop system would be the rather unlikely:

$$\qquad\qquad *t \qquad *k$$
$$*b$$

Furthermore, the choice of *k for set B, would have necessitated the selection of some other phoneme, probably *? for set D, and also would have produced a skewed, much less likely, phonemic pattern:

$$*p \qquad\qquad *k \qquad *?$$

We might also note that the change $k \rightarrow$? is much more common than the reverse.

Before deciding what to reconstruct for set C:

$$C. \quad ŋ = n = ŋ = ŋ$$

let us consider another set of cognates:

5.	hono	hono	fono	vono	'stay, sit'

From this, we can extract two or more consonant correspondence sets:

$$F. \quad h = h = f = v$$
$$G. \quad n = n = n = n$$

For the set G, where *n* occurs in all the daughter languages, we will obviously want to reconstruct the phoneme **n.*[3] Therefore for our set C, we reconstruct **ŋ*, with the accompanying rule that **ŋ* becomes (or merges with) *n* in Hawaiian. Another group of cognates will fill out our inventory of nasals:

---

6.   marama malama malama malama 'light, moon, dawn'

These cognates yield the new correspondence set:

H.   m = m = m = m

for which we obviously reconstruct **m,* thus yielding the nicely patterned set of nasals:

*m   *n   *ŋ

Let us return now to the correspondence set F given above, where our reasoning will have to be a bit more sophisticated:

F.   h = h = f = v

In terms of mere numbers we might be tempted to reconstruct an **h*; however, several other factors should be considered. First of all, sound change very seldom, if at all, proceeds in the direction $h \rightarrow x$ (where $x =$ any other phoneme); most often sounds become *h*. Second, the sound change $f \rightarrow h$ is very common in the world's languages, e.g., Latin *factum* → Spanish *hecho* 'done'. Third, and most important here, we already have posited a sound change which says that $*p \rightarrow b$ in Fijian. Thus, a change from $*f \rightarrow v$ can be looked upon as part of the same process, and we revise our rule to become more general and so read [voiceless labials] → [voiced labials].

---

[3] As we pointed out when we reconstructed the vowels at the beginning of this chapter, where all reflexes are identical there is simply no reason to suspect that the common language had any other sound.

By this single rule we capture both sound changes ($*p \rightarrow b$ and $*f \rightarrow v$). The evidence thus favors $*f$ as the source of this set.

Finally, let us examine one more set of cognates:

| 7. | kaho | ʔaho | ʔaso | kaso | 'thatch' |

From this we extract the new correspondence set:

I. h = h = s = s

Here again, starting from the principle that $x \rightarrow h$ is more likely than $h \rightarrow x$, we propose to reconstruct $*s$, which becomes h (and therefore merges with the h reflex of f) in Maori and Hawaiian.

While we have not handled all the difficulties involved in reconstructing a parent language, we have some idea as to how it is done. Basically, a short explanation such as we have presented is no substitute for experience in knowing what to expect. From our Polynesian examples we now have reconstructed the sound system of proto-Polynesian as follows:

Consonants: Vowels:

$*p$ $*t$ $*k$ $*i$ $*u$
$*f$ $*s$ $*e$ $*o$
$*m$ $*n$ $*\eta$ $*a$
       $*l$

The list of words we used are transcribed in their proto-form as follows:

1. $*pou$
2. $*tapu$
3. $*ta\eta i$
4. $*takele$
5. $*fono$
6. $*malama$
7. $*kaso$

The rules necessary to account for the reflexes of these words in the daughter languages are as follows (no rules are written for sounds whose reflexes are the same as the proto-phonemes):

Hawaiian	Maori
1. $k \rightarrow ?$	1. $l \rightarrow r$
2. $t \rightarrow k$	2. $\begin{Bmatrix} f \\ s \end{Bmatrix} \rightarrow h$
3. $\eta \rightarrow n$	
4. $\begin{Bmatrix} f \\ s \end{Bmatrix} \rightarrow h$	Samoan
	$k \rightarrow ?$

Fijian

[voiceless labials] $\rightarrow$ [voiced labials]

INTERNAL RECONSTRUCTION

In traditional historical linguistics a technique known as *internal reconstruction* complemented the comparative method. Basically, internal reconstruction involves comparing forms *within a single language* to determine if these give any indication regarding an earlier state of that language. In present-day linguistics, much of what has previously been subsumed under internal reconstruction is taken over by descriptive linguistics, specifically under the heading of morphophonemic analysis. Nonetheless, from the historical point of view internal reconstruction remains a valid device for getting at earlier stages of a language.

Internal reconstruction was "discovered" and its classical examples produced by Hermann Grassman, a noted Indo-Europeanist of the nineteenth century. Certain Indo-European correspondence sets were causing difficulty in that they seemed not to fit in with previously established patterns. Grassman examined the data in Greek and Sanskrit and was able to show that developments peculiar to these languages resulted in the apparent irregularities. Consider the Greek forms:

1. a. trekh-ō 'I walk'   b. threk-s-ō 'I will walk'
2. a. thrik-s 'hair'   b. trikh-os 'of the hair'

First we note that in each of the above forms only *one* aspirated consonant occurs, but this varies in each of the two sets: in 1a and 2b we have a *kh* and in 1b and 2a we have a *th*. In other words, in these paradigms we find aspirated consonants (*th, kh*) alternating with nonaspirated (*t, k*), and this gives us different forms of the stem (*trekh-, threk-*; *thrik-, trikh-*).

Internal reconstruction is based on a principle that alternations such as these in a language were at some previous stage not present, and the current situation is due to specific sound changes. From the above forms Grassman was able to deduce that in pre-Greek the original stems were:

*threkh-
*thrikh-

Greek then underwent two sound changes. The first of these removed the aspiration from the consonant when it was followed by *s*; the second deaspirated a consonant when it was followed by another aspirated consonant in the same stem. In formal terms:

1. Ch → C/ __s
2. Ch → C/ __ . . .Ch

By applying these two rules in order to the pre-Greek forms we can account for what appears in the attested words.

As it turned out, the pre-Greek forms thus reached by Grassman were precisely those needed to deal with the Indo-European problem at hand. The second rule above, that two aspirated consonants may not occur in the same stem, also applied in Sanskrit and came to be known as *Grassman's Law*.

One final word of caution should be made about the use of internal reconstruction. When we reconstruct forms and posit sound laws to account for alternations in a single language we have no guarantee that these forms actually existed at a previous stage of the language. The alternations might have been present for an indefinitely long time or other irrecoverable sound changes might have taken place. Grassman's internal reconstruction was accepted because the earlier forms which he posited could be verified by comparison with other languages.

In this chapter we have concentrated on phonological reconstruction because determining the phonology, at least in its broad outlines, must be the first step towards establishing the rest of the grammar. In addition, most of the principles used in reconstruction can be easily seen in phonological examples. Ideally, of course, the comparative linguist does not stop with the reconstruction of the sound system of the parent language and a few more-or-less isolated roots. The goal of reconstruction is to reconstruct the entire grammar of the parent language insofar as this can be done with the evidence provided by the attestations. Thus, in more advanced studies we will find attempts to reconstruct the morphological systems and even the syntax.

Basically, reconstruction on these other levels of language is similar to reconstruction in the phonological system. We begin with the attested morphological and syntactic systems, compare them, and hypothesize corresponding systems in the parent language; then we show how this system underwent changes to become the various daughter languages. On these levels, also, we will be guided by our knowledge of possible or likely changes in the development of well-attested languages. In later chapters we will study examples of this kind of reconstruction.

FOR FURTHER STUDY

The technique of reconstruction is perhaps the most elusive of all linguistic practices for the beginner; he generally cannot see exactly how choices among possible reconstructions are made. Yet it remains true that even after a moderate amount of experience, linguists intuitively know what to expect and there is remarkable agreement on proposed reconstructions. If you want to read more about the principles underlying reconstruction, there are the following three items: Chapter 18 of Bloomfield's *Language,* "The Comparative Method"; Paul Thieme's excellent article, "The Comparative Method for Reconstruction in Linguistics"; finally, there is Mary Haas's paper, "Historical Linguistics and the Genetic Relationship of Languages." With certain revisions and additions, the Haas paper was republished as a separate book entitled *The Prehistory of Languages.*

That the principles of reconstruction could be extended to languages with no written tradition was shown by Bloomfield in his historical sketch "Algonquian." A sympathetic and extremely important statement of the ramifications and importance of Bloomfield's work is Hockett's "Implications of Bloomfield's Algonquian Studies."

Two exercise books offering examples and explanations of reconstructives are available. Pike's *Axioms and Procedures* provides detailed analyses of why particular reconstructions of real languages were made and also gives exercises made up of artificial data which are manageable for the beginner. Cowan's *Workbook* contains seventeen problems on comparative reconstruction and seven on internal reconstruction.

8

Indo-European

As an example of what has been done and what can be done in writing the prehistory of related languages, we will examine the Indo-European family. No other language family has been studied so intensively, and the reconstruction of the parent language is generally acknowledged to be one of the real achievements of nineteenth-century science. The very methods of historical linguistics were developed while exploring Indo-European, and still today, prospective historical linguists, even those who definitely intend to investigate other language groups such as Algonquian or Bantu or Tai, are trained by learning about the results of Indo-European studies. Indo-European is also a very interesting family because many written records of its branches have been preserved from various points in time. Within the family itself there is also a wide range of divergence or difference among the various member languages, so that modern Indo-European languages may look very little like one another. This makes the study interesting (all solutions are not obvious), and it shows the very different parallel paths along which daughter languages might develop within one family.

Furthermore, Indo-European is a very well-defined family. Linguists are in agreement as to which languages are and which languages are not Indo-European. As we saw in Chapter 4, the same cannot be said of most other putative language families. For example, many scholars are uncertain about the position of Japanese vis-à-vis Korean, which most assume to be a member of the Altaic family. Likewise there is some question whether the Tai languages belong to the Sino-Tibetan family or are themselves a separate group. And when we consider the little-known groups, such as the languages of Africa, there are almost as many opinions regarding genetic groupings as there are linguists who write about them.

The Indo-European phonology we will be giving in this chapter is that known as "classical" Indo-European; it is basically the system presented by Karl Brugmann in his famous *Comparative Grammar of the Indo-Germanic Languages*.[1] Essentially the same system is reflected in Antoine Meillet's *Introduction to the Comparative Study of the Indo-European Languages*. This is not to imply that there has been no progress in Indo-European studies since the time of Brugmann and Meillet in the early twentieth century. Yet it remains true that in its basic points the Brugmann system is still valid and should be known to all historical linguists. At the end of this chapter we will examine one rather exciting advance over Brugmann and Meillet when we discuss the history of the so-called laryngeal theory.

THE INDO-EUROPEAN LANGUAGES

Brugmann reconstructed Indo-European by using data from the following eight branches or subfamilies:

1. Indo-Iranian (Aryan)
2. Armenian

[1] The term "Indo-Germanic" is equivalent to "Indo-European," but it is not often used nowadays except by German scholars. In naming language families, one practice is to call the family by the names of the areas which lie at the extremes of the family's geographic spread. Thus, Indo-European was so called because its members stretched from India in the east to Europe in the west. On the same principle, some scholars refer to Hamito-Semitic as Afro-Asiatic since languages of this family are found in a belt through Africa and Asia. Likewise, Sino-Tibetan is sometimes known as the Indo-Chinese family because members of this family are found in northern India at one end and in China at the other.

The term Indo-Germanic derives from a slightly different practice of calling a language family after the two of its own branches which are farthest apart geographically. Thus Indo-Germanic simply points out the fact that the Indic languages are the easternmost branch of the family and a Germanic language (Icelandic) is its westernmost member.

3. Greek
4. Albanian
5. Italic
6. Celtic
7. Germanic
8. Balto-Slavic

Besides these branches, which were well known by the end of the nineteenth century, Meillet used data from two additional Indo-European subfamilies, whose written records were discovered in the early part of the twentieth century.

9. Anatolian
10. Tocharian

The Anatolian group, especially important because of its great antiquity, consists of three principal languages: Hittite, Luvian, and Lydian. Of these the most important is Hittite since there are a large number of Hittite documents, some dating back as far as 1300 B.C. This makes them even older than the Vedas, and therefore of great interest in reconstructing the parent tongue. Luvian and Lydian are attested in only a few inscriptions. We will return to one very important contribution of Hittite when we discuss laryngeals at the end of this chapter. The Tocharian languages, which are found in texts unearthed in Central Asia, are attested in the seventh century A.D.

The Indo-Iranian branch consists of languages (ancient and modern) of present-day India, Iran and certain neighboring areas. The most important and oldest of these is Sanskrit, the sacred language of Hinduism and, in a later form, of Buddhism. Our oldest Sanskrit texts are the Vedas, parts of which date back to approximately 1200 B.C. Most of the modern languages of India, such as Bengali, Hindi, and Marathi are descendants of varieties of Sanskrit. On the Iranian side, we have two important ancient languages: Old Persian and Avestan. In Old Persian there are the inscriptions of the kings of ancient Persia from the sixth and fifth centuries

B.C., and in Avestan we have the sacred books of the Zoroastrian religion. Modern Iranian languages include Persian, Kurdish, Pashto, and Ossetic.

Three branches of Indo-European which consist of a single language each are Armenian, Greek, and Albanian. Early Indo-Europeanists considered Armenian to be a member of the Iranian branch, but in 1875 Hübschmann showed that the Iranian elements in Armenian were due to borrowing and that Armenian was an independent branch of Indo-European. Our oldest Armenian texts date from the fifth century A.D. Greek is attested in inscriptions from the seventh century B.C., though some parts of the Homeric epics the *Iliad* and the *Odyssey* may date back to 1000 B.C. Tablets containing an older dialect of Greek, known as Mycenean, were discovered and deciphered in the twentieth century; these were written in script called Linear B. Another script appearing on the same tablets, Linear A, has so far resisted decipherment. Our earliest written records of Albanian date back to the fifteenth century A.D.; the language is still spoken in Albania and adjoining regions as well as in scattered pockets in southern Italy.

Among the Italic languages, the most important is, of course, Latin, the language of ancient Rome and the ancestor of the modern Romance languages, including French, Italian, Spanish, Portuguese, and Rumanian. Contemporaneous with early Latin are the lesser-known, but often helpful, dialects of Oscan and Umbrian, of which we have several inscriptions.

Some scholars had previously grouped the Celtic languages together with Italic in a supposed Italo-Celtic branch of Indo-European. Recent scholarship has cast doubt on the existence of this intermediate common language, and currently Italic and Celtic are generally considered to be two independent developments of the parent language.

The Celtic languages themselves divide into two groups: Continental and Insular. The Continental branch is known through a single language, Gaulish, which was spoken in an area centering around present-day France. Gaulish is meagerly attested in a few inscriptions and proper names from the first

Major Language Groups of Europe

Key to map of Europe

Germanic
Romance
Balto-Slavic
Greek
Albanian
Celtic
Armenian
Finno-Ugric
Altaic
Caucasian

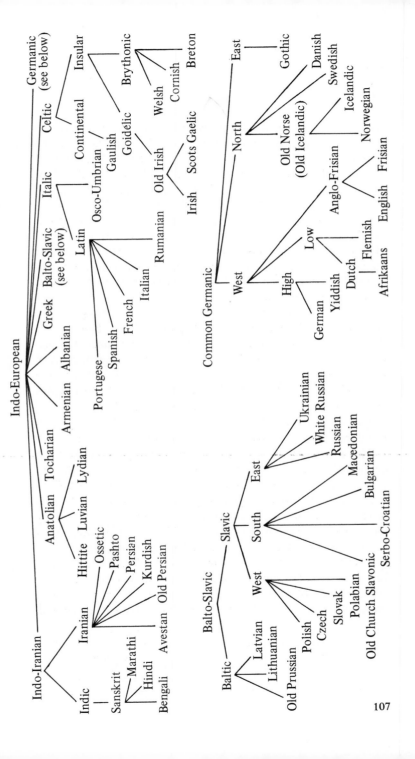

107

millennium B.C. Insular Celtic is further subdivided into two branches: Brythonic and Goidelic. Welsh, attested since the eleventh century, is a Brythonic language; also Brythonic is Breton, spoken in northern France, and the Cornish language, which became extinct in the eighteenth century. The first attested Goidelic language is Old Irish, which is recorded in inscriptions of the fourth century and extensive texts from the sixth century. Old Irish has two present-day descendants: Modern Irish, still spoken in the western part of Eire and taught in Irish schools, and Scots Gaelic, which continues to be used in the highlands and islands of Scotland and on Cape Breton Island in Nova Scotia.

The Germanic branch of Indo-European is generally broken down into three main divisions: East, North, and West. East Germanic is known from a single language, Gothic, which was attested in a Bible translation of the fourth century A.D. Our first records of North Germanic, the so-called Runic Inscriptions, date from the third century A.D. Modern North Germanic languages are Danish, Norwegian, and Swedish, as well as Icelandic. Texts in Old Norse (also known as Old Icelandic) date from the end of the twelfth century A.D.

There are several schemes for subdividing the West Germanic languages, and here we will present that of Meillet, who separates them into three major subgroups: High Germanic, Low Germanic,[2] and Anglo-Frisian. Various dialects of High German have been attested since the seventh century A.D.: Modern Standard German is a High German dialect, as is Yiddish. Low German is attested in the ninth century A.D. and is represented by modern languages such as Dutch, Flemish, and Afrikaans, an offshoot of Dutch spoken by the Boers (descendants of Dutch farmers) in South Africa. The most important member of the Anglo-Frisian branch is, of course,

[2] The terms "High Germanic" and "Low Germanic" are in no sense to be interpreted as social or class judgements; they are merely terms descriptive of the geographical areas in which the speakers of these languages lived. Thus, "High Germanic" refers to the language of people who lived in mountanous regions, such as the Bavarian Alps. "Low Germanic" means simply the speech of those who settled in the lowlands along the North Sea coast.

English. Old English (formerly called Anglo-Saxon) is attested as early as the seventh and eighth centuries A.D.; the Middle English period extends from the twelfth to the fifteenth centuries; New English continues the same language down to the present. The other member of this group, Frisian, is still spoken in various northern regions of the Netherlands.

The Balto-Slavic group splits up into two large subgroups: Baltic and Slavic. Three principle languages make up the Baltic group: Old Prussian, Lithuanian, and Latvian. Old Prussian, which is attested in lists and texts of the fifteenth and sixteenth centuries, is extinct today. Lithuanian and Latvian, whose written records extend back only as far as the sixteenth century, are still spoken along the southern coast of the Baltic Sea in the Lithuanian and Latvian republics of the Soviet Union.

Speakers of Slavic languages are quite numerous and are found throughout Eastern Europe, from north to south. The Slavic languages are grouped into three main branches: Eastern, Western, and Southern. The most important Slavic language is Russian, which together with Ukrainian and White Russian (Byelorussian) forms the Eastern group. The Western group is represented by such languages as Polish, Czech, Slovak, and Polabian.

Among the languages of the Southern branch we find the most anciently attested Slavic language: Old Church Slavonic, whose texts date from the tenth century A.D. and which is in fact remarkably similar to the common Slavic language reconstructed by linguists. It remains today the liturgical language of numerous Eastern churches. Some modern South Slavic languages are Serbo-Croatian, Bulgarian, and Macedonian.

CONSONANTS

The phonemes of Indo-European are divided into three main groups: consonants, vowels, and resonants. The last named are phonemes (e.g., *r* and *l*) which can function as either consonants or vowels and are involved in the system of alternations known as apophony, which we shall examine later. First we will give the consonant phonemes of Indo-European together with the principal sets of correspondences from Latin, Greek, Sanskrit, and Germanic which define them. By *principal correspondence sets,* we mean those correspondences which hold in most cases. Needless to say, there are specific environments where a reflex will appear which is different from that shown in the charts.

Indo-European had the following consonants:

Stops	Labial	Dental	Velar	Labio-velar
voiceless	p	t	k	k^w
voiced	b	d	g	g^w
voiced aspirates	bh	dh	gh	g^wh
Fricative		s		

The principal correspondence sets together with an example for each are in the table on pp. 112–113.

GRIMM'S LAW AND VERNER'S LAW

When we examine the Indo-European consonant phonemes given above together with their reflexes in Germanic languages, we find an interesting situation. Indo-European has the following system of stops:

p	t	k	k^w
b	d	g	g^w
b^h	d^h	g^h	g^wh

The Germanic consonant system looks like this:

f	þ	h	hw
p	t	k	kw
b	d	g	

Putting the two together, with arrows showing the direction of the developments, we obtain the following scheme, which is really noteworthy for its beautiful patterned movement:

f	þ	h	hw[3]
p	t	k	k^w
b	d	g	g^w
bh	dh	gh ←	g^wh

With the minor exception of the g^wh, we can summarize the Germanic consonant shift in three simple rules:

voiceless stops →	voiceless fricatives	(e.g., p → f)
voiced stops →	voiceless stops	(e.g., b → p)
voiced aspirated stops →	voiced unaspirated stops	(e.g., bh → b)

It was the identification of precisely these sound changes from Indo-European to Germanic which set in motion much of the nineteenth-century research on historical linguistics. First noted by the Danish scholar Rasmus Rask in his *Prize Essay* of 1818, they were later codified and given further supporting examples from Sanskrit by the German linguist Jacob Grimm in the second edition of his *German Grammar* (1822).

Neither Rask nor Grimm, of course, were dealing with reconstructed Indo-European. The actual attempt to reconstruct the parent language did not come until August Schleicher (who also gave us the family tree model) did so in 1861. Grimm started with Latin, Greek, and Sanskrit as

---

[3] In the older Germanic languages, the letter *h* is presumed to represent the voiceless velar fricative [x]; likewise *hw* was phonetically [xʷ].

Indo-European Consonant Correspondences

INDO-EUROPEAN	SANSKRIT	GREEK
*p	p	p
*sųep- 'to sleep'	svap-ati 'he sleeps'	hup-nos 'sleep'
*t	t	t
*trei- 'three'	trayas	treis
*k	ś	k
*kųon 'dog'	śun-	kuōn
*kʷ	k/č⁴	p/t⁵
*kʷis 'who?'	kas	tis
*b	b	b
*bel- 'to be strong'	bal-am 'strong'	bel-tiōn 'better'
*d	d	d
*ped- 'foot'	pad-	pod-
*g	ǰ	g
*gen- 'knee'	ǰānu-	gonu-
*gʷ	g/ǰ	b
*gʷiu- 'to live'	ǰīv-ātus 'life'	bi-os 'life'
*bh	bh	ph
*bher- 'to carry, to bear'	bhar-	pher-
*dh	dh	th
*dhē- 'to place'	dhā- 'to set'	e-thē-ka 'I placed'
*gh	h	kh
*ųegh- 'to pull'	vah- 'to pull'	okh-os 'chariot'
*gʷh	gh	ph/th⁶
*gʷher- 'warm'	ghar-ma- 'heat'	ther-mos 'hot'
*s	s	h
*septm̥ 'seven'	sapta	hepta

⁴ In Sanskrit the Indo-European *kw appears as k, and gw appears as g when they precede a back vowel. When a front vowel follows, kw and gw become the palatals č and ǰ, respectively.
⁵ In Greek, kw becomes t before front vowels and p before back vowels.
⁶ In Greek, gwh becomes th before front vowels and ph before back vowels.

LATIN		GERMANIC[7]	
p		**f**	
	sop-or 'sleep'		swef-an (OE) 'to sleep'
t		**þ**	
	tres		þrēo (OE)
k		**h**	
	can-is		hund (OE)
qu		**hw**	
	quis		hwas (Goth.)
b		**p**	
	dē-bil-is 'without strength, weak'		pal (Dutch) 'firm'
d		**t**	
	ped-		fōt (OE)
g		**k**	
	genū-		cnēo (OE)
v		**kw**	
	viv-us 'alive'		cwi-cu (OE) 'alive'
f		**b**	
	fer-		ber- (OE)
f		**d**	
	fē-ci 'I did'		dō-n (OE) 'to do, to put'
h		**g**	
	veh-o 'I pull'		ga-vig-an (Goth.) 'to pull'
f		**g**	
	for-mus 'warm'		gyr-we-fenn (OE) 'marsh'
s		**s**	
	septem		sibun (Goth.)

[7] In providing the Germanic words, we have selected those forms from the ancient Germanic languages which illustrate the particular correspondence most clearly. Which language provides the form is noted in parentheses by the following abbreviations: OE = Old English; Goth. = Gothic; ON = Old Norse; OHG = Old High German. In one case, our best example was from a modern Germanic language, Dutch.

bases and looked upon the differences between these languages and Germanic as some kind of change. To use Grimm's term, they were called a *Lautverschiebung* or "sound shift." In later times this sound shift of the consonant system from Indo-European to Germanic came to be known as *Grimm's Law*.

After Grimm's Law had been accepted, various scholars began to take up the seeming exceptions and attempted to explain them by pointing out conditioning phonetic environments. One of the first of these found and explained was the case of the voiceless stops after *s*. For example, where one finds *p, t,* and *k,* after *s* in Latin, one finds the same sounds in Germanic; in other words, the environment *s-,* so to speak, prevents the operation of Grimm's Law as regards the voiceless stops. For example:

Latin	Germanic	
spu-ō	spit (English)	
stāre	stand (English)	
scab-ō	skab-an (Goth.)	'to shave, scrape'

In the early and mid nineteenth century, certain other exceptions were also accounted for. Grassman's Law which we have already seen (p. 98) handled certain "irregular" correspondences. However, one particularly large group of exceptions seemed to defy explanation. In some Germanic words *b, d,* and *g* were found corresponding to Latin *p, t,* and *k.* From Grimm's Law, the expected Germanic correspondences should have been *f,* þ, and *h.* In the ancient Germanic languages, there were also certain alternations between the expected and the unexplained correspondences. Note the medial consonants in the following examples:

Old High German:	sla*h*an 'to strike'	gi-sla*g*an 'struck'
Old English:	sniþan 'to cut'	sni*d*en 'cut'
		(past participle)

Here we see *h* (← IE*k) alternating with *g* (← IE*?), and þ
(← IE*t) alternating with *d* (← IE*?).

In order to show how Karl Verner solved this problem,
let us consider the following kinship terms:

Old English	Latin	Sanskrit	
fǽder	páter	pitár-	'father'
brṓþor	frā́ter	bhrā́tar-	'brother'
mṓdor	mā́ter	mātár-	'mother'

From the Latin and the Sanskrit, for the moment we will
reconstruct the following Indo-European ancestors:

$$*\text{pətér}$$
$$*\text{bhrā́ter}$$
$$*\text{mātér}$$

Note that what we have done is to assume the Sanskrit
accent pattern as being present in the reconstructed forms.
By so doing, Verner was able to explain seeming exceptions
to Grimm's Law, and he was then blessed by having a law
named after him. *Verner's Law,* which operates after Grimm's
Law, says that when *f, þ,* and *h* are preceded by an unac-
cented vowel, they become the corresponding voiced stops.
Thus in formal notation, the following sequence of events
occurred between Indo-European and Germanic:

1.   Grimm's Law

    p   f
    t   →   þ
    k   h

2.   Verner's Law

    f   b
    þ   →   d   /   V
    h   g   [− accent] __

3. Accent shift
    In Germanic the accent shifts
    to the first syllable.

It has been said that Grimm's Law proved that sound laws
existed, and that Verner's Law proved that they worked. In
addition to its importance for understanding the Indo-European–Germanic phonetic relationship, Verner's Law also had
a crucial impact on the history of linguistics. The publication
of Verner's paper led to a tremendous amount of intellectual
optimism on the part of linguists. Now that the last large
group of exceptions to Grimm's Law had been accounted for,
there seemed to be no reason why all language change could
not be analyzed. Linguists now felt that their subject matter
was as receptive to scientific analysis and understanding as
was the physical world.

The most vocal proponents of the power of sound laws
were centered in the German University of Leipzig and came
to be known as the Neogrammarians. Flourishing for more
than half a century, they ranked among their numbers the
leading linguists of the day, including Karl Brugmann, Hermann Paul, and August Leskien. As basic principles, the Neogrammarians held that *sound laws operate without exception*
and *no exception operates without a rule.*[8] What this meant
was that whenever something appeared to be an exception to
a sound law, it should be possible to define the phonetic conditions under which the "exception" appeared and so write
another rule. Nowadays, we do not regard sound laws as such
powerful devices, but it remains true that, had it not been for

[8] As is often the case, complex ideas can be summed up in a single German
word. For the Neogrammarians, the word was *Ausnahmslosigkeit,* which
can be analyzed into *Ausnahm-* 'exception', plus *-los-* 'without, -less', and
-keit '-ness', a suffix used to form abstract nouns from adjectives. The complete word summing up the Neogrammarian belief can thus be translated
'exceptionlessness'.

Interestingly enough, the term Neogrammarian (German *Junggram-
matiker*) was originally just a local university term used in Leipzig to describe those students of linguistics who had "rebelled" against their teachers.

Verner's Law and the faith of the Neogrammarians, modern linguistics would probably not have progressed as far as it has.

VOWELS

In the beginning of the nineteenth century, the early Indo-Europeanists posited for the parent language the same vowel system as is found in Sanskrit, namely, a system with only three vowels (which may be either long or short):

i   u

a

Yet, in the classical languages of Europe (Latin and Greek) they found a five-vowel system:

i   u

e   o

a

The development from a three-vowel system to one consisting of five vowels was explained by some vague and unscientific sort of reasoning about a breakdown or corruption of the original system.

With the advance of research in the field, the original slavish devotion to Sanskrit, together with the accompanying assumption that Sanskrit always reflected the parent language, began to wear thin. By the 1870s, it was generally accepted that the five-vowel system of the classical languages was indeed a closer reflection of the parent tongue. We now place the vowels *i* and *u* in with the resonants, and one additional vowel, ə, is added to produce the Indo-European system of four pure vowels, which is:

e   ə   o

a

Indo-European Vowel Correspondences

INDO-EUROPEAN	SANSKRIT		GREEK		LATIN	
*e	a	e		e		
*ed-	ad-mi		ed-omai		ed-ō	
'to eat'	'I eat'		'I will eat'		'I eat'	
*ē	ā	ē			ē	
*plē-	prā-ta		plē-res		plē-nus	
'to fill'	'filled'		'full'		'full'	
*o	a	o		o		
*oktō 'eight'	aṣṭā		oktō		octō	
*ō	ā	ō			ō	
*gnō- 'to know'	jñā-		gnō-		gnō-	
*a	a	a		a		
*ag-	aj̆-		ag-		ag-	
'to drive'						
*ā	ā	ā			ā	
*māter	mātar-		mātēr (Doric)[9]		māter	
*ə	i	a		a		
*pəter	pitar-		patēr		pater	

With the exception of ə, the vowels may be either long or short. Because of the particular developments of the vowels in the Germanic languages, we have limited our correspondence sets to Latin, Greek, and Sanskrit, as shown above.

RESONANTS

The Indo-European phonemes which are called resonants can function as either vowels or consonants. The group consists of the following sounds:

[9] In citing the Greek correspondence for long *ā, we give the form in the Doric dialect, which preserved the original sound. In standard classical Greek (Attic), the Indo-European *ā became ē. Thus, the Attic word for 'mother' is mētēr.

As vowels	As consonants
i	i̯ (y)
u	u̯ (w)
m̥	m
n̥	n
r̥	r
l̥	l

Some examples of the principal correspondence sets which define resonants can be found in the table on pp. 120–121.

APOPHONY

Very often in trying to set up correspondence sets among the Indo-European vowels and resonants, difficulties are encountered of a seemingly insurmountable nature. There is, for instance, the case of Latin *ped-* 'foot' and Greek *pod-* 'foot'. The words are obviously cognate, yet why should the vowel not show a regular correspondence (e = e or o = o)? Problems such as these could lead the budding comparativist to cynically remark that only the consonants count, because people are careless about vowels, anyway. Not so. We have every right to expect that vowels should fall into correspondence sets with reconstructable ancestors, just as consonants do. We have already given the normal correspondence sets which define the Indo-European vowels. How, then, do we account for facts such as the *ped-* = *pod-* equation?

The solution to this and any number of vowel problems lay in the discovery that Indo-European possessed a flourishing system of *apophony*. Apophony, also called *ablaut* or *vowel gradation,* is a collection of processes whereby meanings and functions of roots are indicated by altering the quality of the root vowel (= changing the vowel).

Apophony is very productive in any number of the world's languages. Let us take an example from Semitic. In Arabic, there is a root *slm,* which means 'to be peaceful, safe, sub-

Indo-European Resonants Functioning as Consonants

INDO-EUROPEAN	SANSKRIT	GREEK	LATIN	GERMANIC
*i̯	y	z	j[10]	y
*i̯ugo- 'yoke'	yuga-	zugo-n	jugu-m	yuk (Goth.)
*u̯	v	w[11]	v[12]	w
*u̯ik- 'house, dwelling'	viś- 'home'	woik-os 'home'	vīc-us 'village'	weih-s (Goth.) 'village'
*r	r	r	r	r
*reg- straight, to set straight'	rāj̆- 'king'	o-reg-ō 'I stretch'	reg-ō 'rule'	reik-s (Goth.) 'ruler'
*l	r	l	l	l
*legʷh- 'light' (in weight)	raghu- 'light'	e-lakh-us 'small'	lev-is 'light'	lēoht (OE) 'light'
*m	m	m	m	m
*meg- 'great'	mah-ā-	meg-as	mag-nus	mic-el (OE)
*n	n	n	n	n
*gʷhen- 'to strike'	ghn-anti 'they strike'	phon-eus 'murder'	de-fen-dō 'defend'	gan-dr (ON) 'stick'

10 In Latin the letter j is phonetically [y].
11 The sound [w] had disappeared from Greek by the time of the classical period. That it existed earlier in particular places can be inferred from the metric patterns of the Homeric poems. In very early Greek inscriptions it is represented by the letter F (digamma).   12 In Latin, the letter v is phonetically [w].

Indo-European Resonants Functioning as Vowels

INDO-EUROPEAN	SANSKRIT	GREEK	LATIN	GERMANIC
*i̯ *u̯id- 'to see, to know'	i vid-ma 'we know'	i wid-men 'we know'	i vid-eō 'I see'	i wite (OE) 'knowledge'
*u *mūs 'mouse'	u mūṣ-	u mūs	u mūs	u mūs (OE)
*r̥ *mr̥-tó- 'death'	r̥ mr̥tá- 'death'	ro a-mbrot-os[13] 'immortal'	or mort- 'death'	or mord (OHG) 'murder'
*l̥ *u̯l̥kʷos 'wolf'	r̥ vr̥kas	lu lukos	lu lupus	ul wulfs (Goth.)
*m̥ *dekm̥ 'ten'	a daśa	a deka	em dekem	um tiun-d (ON)[14]
*n̥ mn̥to-s 'mind'	a mat-ís 'mind'	a auto-mat-os 'self-acting'	en ment- 'mind'	un munda (Goth.) 'mind'

[13] The intrusive b in the Greek form was explained on p. 79.
[14] The n which occurs instead of m in Germanic is the result of an assimilation (in point of articulation) to a following dental suffix.

missive'. By inserting a short *a* after each of the letters, one gets the form *salama* 'he was peaceful'; if one inserts a short *a* after the *s* and a long *ā* after the *l*, the noun *salām* 'peace' is obtained; a short *i* before the *s* and a long *ā* after the *l* yields yet another noun, *islām* 'submission, reconciliation'; finally, if one prefixes the participial marker *mu-* and adds a long *ī* after the *l*, the participle (or verbal noun) *muslīm* 'one who submits' is the result.

It has been shown that in the common Indo-European language there also was a system of apophony, though by no means was it either identical or genetically related to that found in the Semitic family. Remnants of this apophony are found in all the Indo-European languages. One obvious case is the alternations found in the English words

sing   sang   sung

in which we can say that the pattern of the (written) vowels (i ~ a ~ u)[15] indicates the tense of the verb. By giving still another vowel quality, *o*, we are even able to form a noun from the verb, namely *song*.

The basic pattern of Indo-European apophony consisted of

e ~ o ~ ø

That is, a root was modified, different tenses of a verb were given, nouns were formed, etc, by the alternation of *e* with *o* and with zero. These are known as *vowel grades,* and so one speaks of the *e-grade, o-grade,* and *zero-grade* of a root. Prefixes and suffixes were also used, but these are not essential to our point here.

Not all grades are preserved in all roots or in all daughter languages, and it took a great deal of sophisticated reasoning to determine *some* of the functions of the different grades in

---

[15] The sign ~ is used to indicate alternation. The formula here reads "*i* alternating with *a* and *u*."

the parent language. Even now, not all uses are understood perfectly, but in broad outline the system is clear. One of the more patent reflexes of Indo-European apophony can be found in the Greek verbal system. Consider the following principle parts of the verbs *peith-* 'to believe' and *leip-* 'to leave':

Present	Perfect	Past
peith-omai	pe-poith-a	epe-pith-men
'I believe'	'I have believed'	'I believed'
leipō	le-loip-a	e-lip-on
'I leave'	'I have left'	'I left'

We note that in the present, we have e + resonant (i), in the perfect o + resonant, and in the past only the resonant. From this we can extract the formula (where R stands for any resonant):

$$eR \quad \sim \quad oR \quad \sim \quad \underset{\circ}{R}$$

Or omitting the notation for the resonant:

$$e \quad \sim \quad o \quad \sim \quad \emptyset$$

A clear case in which the apophonic alternation of e/o is used to form nouns from verbs is found in both Latin and Greek, where we have the following pairs:

Greek	Latin
leg-ō 'I read'	teg-ō 'I cover'
log-os 'word'	toga- 'Roman garment' (← 'covering)

Apophony helps us to explain the seeming exceptions to vowel correspondences by showing that it is possible for one vocalic grade of a root to survive in one language and a different grade to appear in another. Thus, to explain the problem found in the correspondence set of Latin *ped-* and Greek *pod-*, we say that Latin preserved the *e*-grade of the root and Greek retained the *o*-grade, though we may not be sure what functions the *e*- and *o*-grades bore in this particular root. To draw a somewhat simplistic analogy, let us assume that in a few thousand years English evolves into several different languages. In a few twentieth-century English words we still have vocalic alternations to indicate functions; take for example *foot ~ feet*. Now suppose one descendant language inherits only the form *foot* (and probably would form a plural *foots*) and another language preserves the form *feet* (pl. *feets?*). Whatever correspondence sets are proposed to reconstruct the vowels of twentieth-century English, these two words would present a problem. The solution would be found when our future historical linguists discovered that English had some words with vocalic alternations, indicating different forms or functions of one word.

LARYNGEAL THEORY

In addition to the alternations of apophony given above, there is another type of apophony in Indo-European, which is generally referred to as *lengthened grade apophony*. As its name implies, it involves alternations of long vowels. The basic pattern for lengthened grade apophony is:

$$\bar{e} ~\sim~ \bar{o} ~\sim~ \partial$$

(Long *ē* alternates with long *ō* and with schwa, the reduced grade.) Some examples of this are:

Greek	ē-grade	ō-grade	Reduced grade
	ti-thē-mi	thō-mos	ti-thĕ-men (ĕ ← IE*ə)
	'I place'	'heap'	'we place'
Latin	fē-ci		făc-io (ă ← IE*ə)
	'I did'		'I do'

In the 1870s, Ferdinand de Saussure studied this pattern bearing in mind the alternations we have seen with the short vowels, namely:

$$eR \sim oR \sim R$$

Why not, asked Saussure, assume that this lengthened grade apophony is of basically the same pattern as the normal grade (at least at some earlier stage of Indo-European)? That is, assume that ə was originally a resonant of some type, which functioned as did the other resonants in short-vowel apophony. A second assumption then would be that later this resonant merged with e and o to produce the long ē and ō which we can safely reconstruct for late Indo-European. The pattern then would be:

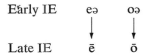

Early IE   eə   oə

Late IE   ē   ō

Through a complicated system of reasoning, which we shall not go into here, Saussure made a further intuitive leap in trying to describe even earlier changes in Indo-European vowels than those that had been reconstructed. Suppose, he said, there were different resonants, now lost, which combined with one single vowel to produce the vowels which reconstruction had yielded? The single vowel would, of course, be e, the basic form of the root. Saussure then posited two more resonants (O̯ and A), which he called *sonantic coefficients,* and which, he claimed, could explain the origin of many of the a and o vowels in late Indo-European. Saussure's formulae ran as follows:

$$eO̯ \rightarrow ō$$
$$O̯ \rightarrow o$$
$$eA \rightarrow ā$$
$$Ae \rightarrow a$$

In general, Saussure's theories about sonantic coefficients were ignored by Indo-Europeanists, who doubtless felt that they were too algebraic and too abstract, were not sufficiently proved, and besides really did not seem to explain any extant problems. The only group of people who took Saussure's theory seriously were those scholars who were trying to connect the Indo-European family with the Semitic languages.

In proto-Semitic there were large numbers of consonants, called *laryngeals* (primary point of articulation somewhere in the region of the larynx) such as h, ʾ(alef), and ʿ(ain). In some of the Semitic languages, one or more of these laryngeals were lost, but often the loss did not take place until the laryngeal had changed or lengthened an adjoining vowel. Consider the following examples in the development of Akkadian from Common Semitic:

	Proto-Semitic		Akkadian	
*ḫaqlu-	(cf. Arabic ḫaql)	→	eqlu-	'field'
*ziʾbu-	(cf. Hebrew zəʾeb)	→	zību-	'wolf'
*baʿlu-	(cf. Hebrew baʿal)	→	bēlu-	'lord'

Obviously, the prospect that such a similar process occurred in Indo-European was extremely attractive. Herman Möller in his book *Semitic and Indo-Germanic* (1906) used Saussure's sonantic coefficients in an attempt to establish a genetic relationship between Semitic and Indo-European. In terms of proving any such relationship, this study was a failure, especially from the Indo-European point of view; for the work was simply not a competent piece of scholarship. However, one important thing was left with Saussure's sonantic coefficients (which were previously undefined phonetically), and this was the name *laryngeals*. Even so, as far as Indo-Europeanists were concerned, the existence of the laryngeals or sonantic coefficients was a dead issue.

Then, in the early twentieth century, the first Hittite tablets were discovered and were deciphered during the First World War by the Czech linguist Hrozny. In an article published in

1927, Jerzy Kuryłowicz examined the Hittite words of definite Indo-European etymology in light of the work of Saussure, and the results were amazing. Where Saussure had predicted the sonantic coefficient (laryngeal) *A*, Kuryłowicz found an *ḫ* in Hittite. Consider:

Greek	anti	= Hittite ḫanti	'in front'
Greek	arges	= Hittite ḫarkis	'white'
Latin	pāsco	= Hittite paḫsanzi	'protect'

We note the similarity down to the point where Saussure has said that when *A* precedes, the vowel becomes *a*; when A follows, the vowel becomes long *ā*. The existence of laryngeals at some stage in Indo-European could no longer be doubted, and linguists began to restudy old problems to determine if the newly accepted laryngeals could shed new light on them.

By assuming the existence of laryngeals, the French scholar Émile Benveniste was able to show that every root in Indo-European (with a few exceptions such as numerals and pronouns) was of the form CeC-.[16] This enormously simplified explanations of the different types of suffix addition.

Nowadays, Indo-Europeanists generally accept the existence of three laryngeals, which are usually written ə with proper subscript numerals. Starting with the single vowel *e* and assuming interaction with laryngeals, the vowels *a* and *o* develop.

Early Indo-European		Late Indo-European	
dheə$_1$-	→	dhē-	'to place'
steə$_2$-	→	stā-	'to stand'
deə$_3$-	→	dō-	'to give'
ə$_1$es-	→	es-	'to be'
ə$_2$eg-	→	ag-	'to lead'
ə$_3$ed	→	od-	'to smell'

---

[16] Benveniste posited the CeC (consonant-vowel-consonant) by assuming a lost laryngeal at the beginning of roots which had been previously reconstructed with an initial vowel. Similarly, a final laryngeal was assumed for roots that had been reconstructed with a vocalic ending.

In some works, the symbol H is used instead of ə to indicate the laryngeal, and the same subscript numbers are used (H_1, H_2, H_3).

Today, Indo-Europeanists who use laryngeals in their work on reconstruction can be divided roughly into two groups. The first group employ the laryngeals merely as algebraic symbols and make no attempt to define their phonetic characteristics; this camp includes such scholars as Benveniste, Kuryłowicz, Watkins, and Boling. The second group, which counts Sapir, Lehmann, and Martinet among its members, have attempted to determine the phonetic value of laryngeals. Among the assigned values are ʔ (glottal stop), the glottal fricative h, and the voiceless velar continuant x.

FOR FURTHER STUDY

The amount of work already done and presently being done on the origins and development of the Indo-European languages is voluminous. The standard complete reference work remains Brugmann's *Elements of the Comparative Grammar of the Indo-Germanic Languages,* which contains all kinds of data from the various languages together with reconstructions and remarks on development. Meillet's *Introduction à l'étude comparative des langues indo-européenes* is still the best short survey of what is known about the family. At the present time, an international team of distinguished scholars under the editorship of Jerzy Kuryłowicz, is producing a complete new comparative grammar. So far, two volumes have appeared: Kuryłowicz's *Akzent und Ablaut* and Watkins's *Geschichte der Indogermanischen Verbalflexion.*

An exhaustive list of the reconstructed Indo-European roots, together with their principal reflexes, is found in Julius Pokorny's *Indogermanisches Etymologisches Wörterbuch.* A less complete, but nonetheless useful list is Buck's *A Dictionary of Selected Synonyms in the Principal Indo-European Languages.* Mention should also be made of the *American Heritage Dictionary,* which has an appendix containing all

Indo-European roots which have reflexes in contemporary English.

The exciting history of Indo-European studies can be read about in two books: Holger Pedersen's *The Discovery of Language: Linguistic Science in the Nineteenth Century* and W. P. Lehmann's *A Reader in Nineteenth Century Historical Indo-European Studies.* The Lehmann reader contains excerpts (in English translation) of the original epoch-making works of Rask, Grimm, Grassmann, Verner, and others.

There are also numerous comparative grammars of the branches of Indo-European. Some of these which might be of interest are Buck's *Comparative Grammar of Greek and Latin* and Prokosch's *Comparative Germanic Grammar.* For the comparative study of the Romance languages, a standard reference work is Bourciez's *Éléments de linguistique romane.*

9

Analogy

Many changes in language cannot be explained by rigidly operating sound laws, that is, laws which operate only with regard to phonetic factors. Certain other important types of change have been grouped under the heading of analogy. To give analogy a purposedly vague and general definition, we might say it is a process whereby one form of a language becomes more like another with which it is somehow associated. Our definition is intended to be vague because as we shall see there are many different degrees to which forms can become more alike, and there are various types of associations which might motivate the changes involved. But one generalization which can be made about analogical operation is that its effect is the disappearance of irregular or anomalous forms. There is one very important restriction on analogy that should be stated quite clearly at the outset of our discussion: the workings of analogy do *not* create any new forms or categories in a language. Analogy only causes the spread or extension of *already existing* items.

ANALOGY IN STEMS

Perhaps the clearest examples of analogy occur in the disappearance of stem alternations within a given paradigm. A *paradigm* is a list of the different forms which a word may assume to indicate different functions or meanings within a particular sentence. Thus, we refer to the declensions of nouns or the conjugations of verbs as paradigms.

When we speak of simple analogy in stems, we mean that one phoneme will replace another in a given form in order to make it more like other forms in the same paradigm. For example, the following partial paradigm of the noun *honor* 'honor' appears in Classical Latin as follows:[1]

Nom.	honor
Gen.	honor-is
Dat.	honor-i

As it stands, this paradigm appears perfectly regular, with the stem *honor-* having the same phonological shape in each of the given cases. If we look at the oldest Latin records, however, we find not *honor* for the nominative, but *honos*. Furthermore, by comparison with other languages we can posit the following paradigm in the pre-Latin period:

Nom.	*honos
Gen.	*honosis
Dat.	*honosi

It is known that pre-Latin underwent a general sound shift called *rhotacism,* which changed every *s* to *r* when it occurred between vowels. In formal terms:

$$s \rightarrow r \: / \: V\_\_V$$

After this change took place, we have the oldest Latin forms:

Nom.	honos
Gen.	honor-is
Dat.	honor-i

But this rule has produced what is generally termed an irregular paradigm because the nominative now has a stem different from that found in the other cases. Presumably, the learner of Latin at this time had to learn two alternate stems (*honos* and *honor-*) in order to decline the word properly.

[1] In the forms cited here, the length of the Latin vowels are not indicated since they have no bearing on the point we are making.

Then the process of analogy proceeds to make the paradigm regular by leveling out the irregular element of the different form. In the case at hand, it does this by replacing the phoneme -s, which makes the nominative different, with the -r- that is found in the other forms of the same word. We say, then, that the -s has become -r, not by any general sound change (since there are many Latin -s's in the same phonetic position which do not change), but by analogy with the other members of this particular declension.

ANALOGY IN AFFIXES

Analogy is much more common in the spread of grammatical morphemes: one morpheme expressing a particular function extends its domain of application to other forms which previously had different morphemes expressing the same function. Consider the following singular nouns in Old and New English:

Old English	New English
hand	hand
gear	year
ēage	eye
stān	stone

The changes between these Old and New English forms can be accounted for by general sound laws which operate on strictly phonetic conditions.

In Old English, every noun belonged to a particular class, and each class had a particular suffix (or vowel change) for forming the plural. Let us compare the Old and New English plurals of the above nouns:

Old English	New English
handa	hands
gear	years
ēagan	eyes
stānas	stones

As we can see from the Old English forms, *hand* belonged to the class of words that formed plurals by *-a;* words of the *gear* class added nothing to make a plural; nouns like *ēage* changed the final *-e* to *-a* and added the letter *-n;* and finally, the *stān* class simply added the suffix *-as* to the singular form.

In terms of the phonological changes of English, only the last case *stānas → stones* can be considered regular. In other words, there are no sound laws which account for the development of the plurals of the first three words. We simply cannot justify writing individual rules of the type:

1. a → s
2. ø → s
3. an → s

What has happened is that the usage of the *-s* suffix to indicate plurality spread to these words at the expense of their original plural endings. These other endings have, in fact, just about disappeared from the language. We say that by analogy with the plurals in *-s* (← *-as*) (which was the most widespread plural suffix even in Old English times) the plurals of the other words were replaced.[2]

In traditional terms, we express the operation of this type of analogy by means of a proportion; in the case of the word *hand*, the proportion would be expressed as follows:

stone:stones::hand:X

(Read: *stone is to stones as hand is to X; solve for X.*) The solution of the proportion is intended to simulate the thinking of a speaker who knows the plural of the first word, but does not know the plural of the second. He makes the assumption that if he forms the plural of one noun in such and such a way, then he should form the plural of noun X in the same way.

[2] The variability of the plurals in Old English is of course, an inheritance from Common Germanic. It is interesting to note that most other Germanic language underwent a similar leveling, but with other suffixes emerging as predominant (e.g., *en* in Dutch). Only German appears to have maintained the original variability.

In this case we can also add that -*s* has acquired a plural "feel" for the individual speakers of English. Bréal terms this phenomenon *specialization,* in that the expression of the meaning "plural" has come to be concentrated or specialized on the single form -*s*, instead of being scattered among various other possibilities as was the prior situation.

It had been objected that a device such as the analogical proportion is simply too sophisticated to assume its operation in the minds of countless native speakers of a language. But the Danish linguist Otto Jespersen pointed out that he once heard a small child create his own proportion to justify an incorrect form. To substitute English words for Jespersen's Danish example, consider that a child said the word *brang* as the past tense of *bring*. His elders, of course, immediately corrected him, and told him that he should say *brought* instead of *brang*. To this the child replied: "ring, rang, bring, brang." By analogy with *ring:rang*, the child had formed the past tense of *bring* as *brang*. But it happens to be false analogy, in the sense that the form *brang* is not considered standard English. (Nor, for that matter, is *bringed*.)

It is probably best to regard analogy as operating slowly through the lexicon of a language, absorbing one word at a time, perhaps originally operating only in substandard speech. Gradually, the new analogical formations may become accepted and used by the whole speech community.

In the case of the English plurals, we can see that the triumph of the -*s* suffix is just about complete. There are, however, still a few words which have resisted its advance. Among these are nouns which still add nothing, such as *sheep,* or still preserve an -*en,* as in *ox-en* or *childr-en*. (Among educated speakers, certain borrowed words retain the plural of their original languages, e.g., from Latin, the plural of *alumnus* is *alumni;* from Greek the plural of *octopus* is *octopodes;* from Hebrew, the plural of *cherub* is *cherubim*.)

The upshot of all this is that we can use analogy to explain a large number of language changes in the past; its operation is basically simple and straightforward. We are, however, seriously restricted in using analogy as any kind of a predictive

ANALOGY   135

device. In other words, we simply do not know when it will
operate or how widespread its effect will be.

KURYŁOWICZ'S LAWS

There have been various attempts to predict the direction that
analogy might take, and perhaps the most successful of these
(or at least the most widely known) is that of Jerzy Kuryłowicz. Kuryłowicz first formulated his ideas in an article entitled "The Nature of the So-called Analogical Processes."
The notions therein presented later proved a powerful tool for
Kuryłowicz in his further refinements of the reconstruction
of Indo-European, and culminated in his large work on Indo-
European apophony.

In the article, Kuryłowicz presented six "laws" of analogy.
They are still the subject of great controversy among linguists, both as regards their actual performance, and even as
regards the possibility of formulating such laws. One can find
examples from various languages which seem to go in directions opposite from those which Kuryłowicz's law would predict. Nonetheless, Kuryłowicz's laws are valuable and should
be known because they represent a serious attempt to put
some order and restraint on analogical processes. Further
research which seeks tendencies or general directions of
morphological change is needed in order to prevent the operation of analogical processes from becoming a convenient rug
under which all problems can be swept and subsequently
ignored.

Perhaps the first of Kuryłowicz's laws that we should mention is the one that he presents last. (In its actual statement,
it is very difficult to understand, but Kuryłowicz's subsequent
discussion clarifies it somewhat.) Basically, law six is a kind
of disclaimer. It states that *we are never sure when analogy
will operate, but when it does it will follow the direction indicated by one of the previous "laws."* In a comparison with
drainage systems, Kuryłowicz claims that analogy is like rain.
Nobody can tell when it's going to rain, but when it does,

anyone who knows the plan of the local drainpipes and gut-
ters can tell the way the water is going to flow.

Kuryłowicz's first law is based upon a specific example. In
Old High German there were, among others, two suffixes for
forming plurals: -i and -a, depending on which class a noun
belonged to.

	i-class	a-class
Sing.	Gast 'guest'	Topf 'pot, container'
Pl.	Gast-i	Topf-a

Somewhat later in time, the language underwent a sound
change, whereby back vowels became front when they appeared in front of a syllable which contained -i. In formal
terms:

$$\begin{matrix} V \\ [+ \text{ back}] \end{matrix} \rightarrow \begin{matrix} V \\ [- \text{ back}] \end{matrix} \Big/ \underline{\quad} C_o i$$

This process is known as umlaut (see Chapter 5, p. 85).
As a result of this sound change, plural nouns in the i-class,
which had an original back vowel in the root, now had a front
vowel. (In accordance with traditional German orthography,
we will indicate the front version of a as ä.) After this change,
the plurals of the two words given above were:

Gäst-i   Topf-a

At the end of the Old High German period, the vowels -i and
-a (in unstressed syllables) at the ends of words merged into
[ə], written -e. Our original plurals had then developed into:

Gäst-e   Topf-e

Note the formal difference between the two plurals in this
stage. The plural of Topf, Topf-e, is marked by a single item,
the suffix -e; the plural of Gast, Gäst-e, is, however, marked
by two items: the suffix -e and the umlauted form of the root
vowel (ä in place of a). The indication of the plural in words

such as *Gäst-e* is called *a bipartite* or *doubly marked morpheme;* whereas that in *Topf-e* is called a *unitary* or *singly marked morpheme.*

Now analogical leveling begins to take place, and we ask in which direction it will go. Will *Gäst-e* lose its umlaut and become more like *Topf-e,* or will the reverse take place, and words like *Topf-e* gain an umlauted vowel? For anyone who knows German, the answer is already known: the modern plural of *Topf* is *Töpf-e.* The *o* in the root did not become *ö* by any general sound shift, but by analogy with the plurals that already had an umlauted vowel.

From an example such as this, the first law can be derived: *A bipartite morpheme tends to replace a unitary one;* that is, a language "prefers" to add a second, corroborating marker of meaning or function wherever it is possible. This also involves the principle of polarity, which states that two linguistic forms of the same root which have different meanings or functions will tend to polarize or become maximally distinct. In the example under question, the singular and plural of *Topf* have become more distinct than they previously were.

In contemporary English we can see the operation of this law in the double marking of adjectives. For example, there is a perfectly normal English adjective *syntactic* (from *syntax* + *ic,* with phonological adjustments). Some speakers add on to this word the additional adjectival suffix *-al,* yielding the form *syntactical.* This is done by analogy with the other doubly marked adjectives ending in *-ical,* such as *phonological* or *morphological.*

Kuryłowicz's second law is stated as follows: *Analogy proceeds from a base to a derived form.* In terms of the usual form of a proportion as we have presented it in this chapter, the law means that the first term of the proportion must be a base form and the second must be somehow derived from it, and not vice versa. Thus the following proportions are acceptable by this law:

$$\text{stone:stones::word:X}$$
$$\text{ring:rang::bring:X}$$

In these cases, the singular of the noun and the present tense of the verb are looked on as being *basic,* and the plural and past tense are derived from them by the addition of marks which add more information.

An immediate difficulty with the second law is seen in the case of *back-formations.* These involve starting off with a form which the speakers of a language come to interpret as being derived from a basic form; then that basic form is created. Thus, at one point of time, English had the noun *orator* with no accompanying verb. Because of similar formations speakers of English interpreted the *-or* suffix as signifying the agent, and created the verb *to orate.* They did this on the pattern of many other English words such as *sing:singer; read: reader,* etc. (Note that there is no difference in pronunciation between the *-or* or the *-er* suffixes.) In order to express the formation of *orate,* we need a proportion of the following type:

$$singer:sing::orator:X$$

Unfortunately, Kuryłowicz's second law would not allow such a proportion since *sing* is clearly the base form from which *singer* is derived. The second law is designed to place a restriction on the items which can serve as a model for new analogical formations. We see that Kuryłowicz's original formulation is too restrictive, and that it must be revised to include back-formations. In order to preserve the important point in the law, and yet allow for back- formations, law two might be revised to read as follows: *The two terms which make up the first half of a proportion must be related by a productive morphological process.*

Here we should introduce the concept of *productivity* versus *nonproductivity* of grammatical forms and processes. These refer to a language as existing at a particular point in time. Some of the affixes of the language are productive in the sense that they may be added to *any* word of the proper grammatical class in order to form new words or new inflections; other affixes are not productive and exist in relatively few forms and are not understood if extended to other forms. Take, for example, the English plural -s (as in table-s) versus the plural -en (as in ox-en). Clearly, the -s is productive and is understood if added to any English noun, including new words, such as hippie (plural hippies). If a noun is borrowed from a foreign language, such as sputnik, its plural is formed by the addition of the productive suffix -s, and we get sputniks. Surely, if we added the unproductive suffix -en and came up with the form sputnik-en, it would seem strange, and most likely would not be understood as the plural of sputnik.

Productivity of any given form will, of course, change in the course of time. Some years ago the suffix -wise, which is used to form adverbs from nouns, was rare indeed and occurred in only a few forms such as clockwise. Now, thanks to Madison Avenue, it is an extremely productive suffix and may be added to almost any noun, as in:

> Moneywise, I'm in bad shape.
> She has terrible taste clotheswise.

Thus we see a productive relationship in what is necessary for analogy to operate. In the following three sets of English verbs in their present and past tenses, only the last represents a productive process of past tense formation. Note the phonological similarity of the present tenses (bases) all of which end in [ik].

Present	Past
speak	spoke
seek	sought
reek	reeked

We can understand a child or a foreigner who says "I speaked" or "I seeked," but if he says "I spought" or "I rought" on the pattern of seek or if he says "I soke" or "I roke" on the pattern of speak, we would scarcely understand these as the past tenses of given verbs. By accepting the revised verson of the second law, we can rule out the possibility of such formations.

On the other hand, the case of the "false" analogical form *brang* indicates that a productive morphological process is involved here, because *brang,* though incorrect, can be understood by speakers of English. What we would have to say, then, is that the apophonic variation *i-a-u* is productive in contemporary English, but only for monosyllabic verbs whose stems end in *-ing.*

Kuryłowicz's third law is obscurely written, and there is much controversy as to its exact meaning and import. The examples he gives are apparently connected with details of more or less minor importance, and we can safely ignore the third law here.

The fourth law deals with the results of the operation of analogy. This law states that *when a new analogical formation is accepted in the language, it takes on the primary function of the word.* If the older, irregular form remains in use, it is restricted to secondary functions.

Thus, when the new analogical formation *brothers* replaced the older form *brethren, brethren* was limited to religious usages and *brothers* became the normal plural of the word *brother.* Another example is the development of *older* and *elder.* In a previous stage of English, the comparative of the adjective *old* was *elder.* When by analogy (with pairs such as *bold:bolder*) the new form *older* appeared, it assumed the primary function of expressing the comparative of *old. Elder,* in turn, was relegated to limited usage in expressions such as *elder brother* or *elder statesman.*

The analogical formation of *old:elder* on the pattern *bold: bolder* may seem to be violation of the first law, and indeed it is, since the unitary morpheme (suffix *-er*) has replaced the bipartite morpheme (vowel change $o \rightarrow e$ plus suffix *-er*). This should not be too surprising if we bear in mind the restrictions imposed by the second law: that only productive processes are involved in analogical formations. By the time of the creation of the form *older,* the vowel change (umlaut) was no longer a productive process for comparatives in English; therefore, the forms without umlaut had to serve as the model for the analogical change.

Kuryłowicz's fifth law is intended to explain why certain analogical operations take place, and is stated as follows: *in order to reestablish a central grammatical distinction, a language will abandon one that is more marginal.* Needless to say, the concept of marginality versus centrality of grammatical distinctions may face a good deal of debate in any given situation.

However, in some cases they are clear, as in the development of the Latin nouns (of the third declension) into Spanish. Given the Latin forms for the word *key* in the left column, the forms on the right are what would be expected in Spanish, considering only the operation of the sound laws by which Spanish developed:

		Latin	Expected Spanish
Sing.	nominative	clāvis	llaves
	accusative	clāvem	llave
Pl.	nominative	clāves	llaves
	accusative	clāves	llaves

As can be seen in the above chart, the nominative and accusative of the plural have merged, while the singular and plural of the accusative have been kept distinct. But more important is that the nominative singular has become identical with both plural forms, and thus the distinction between singular and plural has been erased. So the two grammatical distinctions we are concerned with here are: (1) singular versus plural; and (2) nominative versus accusative. Which distinction is more important to the language?

Given the state of the development of Spanish and the other Romance languages, it is not at all difficult to see that the singular-plural distinction is central, while the nominative-accusative distinction is marginal. It is marginal because word order was replacing case endings as the indicator of grammatical relationships (cf. Chapter 10). Therefore, according to this fifth law, what we would expect is that Spanish would give up the case distinction in order to preserve the number distinction. And this is precisely what we find has happened. The "expected Spanish" form given above for the nominative singular does not occur. Instead, we have the form *llave,* which is identical with the accusative singular. The proportion which provides the mechanism for this change could be stated as follows:

Acc. Pl.   :   Nom. Pl.   ::   Acc. Sing.   :   Nom. Sing.

llaves   :   llaves   ::   llave   :   X

Interestingly enough, this is an example given by Kuryłowicz himself, yet it seems to violate his own second law in that the direction of change moves from the accusative to the nominative singular. In no grammatical theory is an accusative considered as a base from which a nominative is derived; in fact, the reverse is true, Of course, this presents no difficulty for our revised version of the second law.

IMPLICATIONS OF ANALOGY FOR RECONSTRUCTION

It should be fairly obvious by now that the operation of analogy can seriously block attempts to reconstruct particular morphemes, since it is quite possible that original forms which were in some way irregular have been lost because of the operation of analogical processes. If leveling has taken place in all the attested daughter languages, an original form will be hopelessly lost and frequently there is nothing that can be done about this.[3]

However, it is often true that one daughter language will preserve the original form as an irregularity or *anomaly* in an attested stage of that language. In comparing daughter languages for the purposes of reconstructon, we must contually bear in mind the fact that analogy is constantly at work leveling out paradigms and causing the disappearance of ir-

[3] This statement does not, of course, refer to cases where the ancestor form does not have to be reconstructed, but is itself attested, as in the case of Latin and the Romance languages.

regular forms. Therefore, in seeking the oldest stages we pay special attention to those forms that appear anomalous and could not possibly be the result of analogy.[4]

The following cognate infinitive and participial forms from Middle English and German are an example:

	Infinitive		Past Participle	
ME	fres-an	'to freeze'	fros-en	'frozen'
German	frier-en		ge-fror-en	

In Middle English we have the consonant -s- as the last consonant in both the infinite and the past participle stems, in German there is an -r- in the same places. But $s = r$ is not the usual English-German correspondence, even considering phonetic environments. Given this fact, we would suspect that originally (i.e., in Common Germanic), there was an -s- in one tense and an -r- in the other. Further, by analogy in English, the -s- (later replaced by -z-) took over as the only stem-final consonant. The German analogy must have worked in the opposite direction with -r- replacing -s-. With just the German and English data above, we would be unable to decide which form originally contained the -s- and which had the -r-.

By looking at a third, cognate langauge, the solution becomes evident, for the Dutch cognates for the same words are:

vries-en   ge-vror-en

Given this additional evidence we conclude that in the original paradigm, the infinitive had an -s- and the past participle had an -r-. English has leveled out the paradigm in favor of the present form, and German in favor of the past participle. Our hypothesis receives final confirmation when we look at the Old English forms:

frēos-an   ge-fror-en

4 Meillet was very fond of pointing out the fact that corresponding irregular or anomalous forms found in two languages is perhaps the surest proof of genetic relationships.

Meillet has a very interesting example of the problems of reconstruction in which two related languages show similar forms which wrongly point back to a common ancestor extant in the parent tongue. This concerns the past participle of the Indo-European root *bher- 'bear, carry', which we have seen several times before. Taking a sample of the Indo-European languages we find the following stems in the present tense:

Sanskrit	Greek	Latin	Old Irish
bhar-	pher-	fer-	ber-

There is no difficulty in reconstructing an Indo-European present stem *bher- from this data. However, when we look at the passive past participles, we find a bewildering situation:

Sanskrit	Greek	Latin	Old Irish	
br̥-tá-s	ois-tó-s	lā-tu-s	bre-th-	'borne, carried'

The Irish and the Sanskrit forms make a cognate set with perfect correspondences and seem to point to an original Indo-European participle *br̥-tó-. Ordinarily, when Irish and Sanskrit, which are far apart geographically, agree on a given form, we are quite safe in ascribing that form to the parent language.

It should be noted at this point that in Common Indo-European and in many Indo-European languages (including Irish and Sanskrit) the normal way of forming past participles was to use the zero-grade of the root followed by the accented suffix *-tó-. Thus, there are serious reasons why we should reject these Irish and Sanskrit forms as being representative of Indo-European. If we accept the *br̥-tó-, we will have accounted for Irish and Sanskrit, but will be totally unable to deal with or explain Latin or Greek. On the other hand, if we reject *br̥-tó- as existing in Common Indo-European, we can explain the Irish and Sanskrit participles by saying that they were formed by analogy with other passive past participles in those languages. What we mean is that at any time in the history of either Irish or Sanskrit, some irregularity might have been leveled out and replaced by a "normal" form. In other words, their origin need not be in the parent language. But the question remains as to how to decide whether either the Latin or the Greek past participles are reflections of what existed in Common Indo-European.

First, we look for an origin in some verb other than *bher-. It appears that the Latin participle, *lātus,* belongs to another verb, namely, *tollō* 'to take away' and is a normal past participle of that verb. (*Latus* comes from an earlier **tlǝ-tó-s,* the normal Indo-European formation with zero grade of the root and the **-tó-* suffix; the **tl-* cluster in Latin has been simplified to *l-.*)

This leaves us with the Greek form. If we remove the *-tos* suffix, we are left with the root *ois-,* and in Greek this *ois-* is only found in the future of the same verb *pher-* in the form *ois-omai* 'I will carry'. The conclusion is now clear. The Irish and Sanskrit forms are indeed later developments; we have shown that the Latin form was borrowed from another verb. Only the anomalous Greek cannot possibly be derived from a source other than the word for 'to carry'. The only possible explanation for the presence of the stem *ois-* in the Greek paradigm of the verb *pher-* is that it was part of the Indo-European paradigm for 'to carry,' and was preserved in Greek, but lost in the other languages through the process of analogy or the process of suppletion.[5]

ANALOGY IN WORD ORDER

In much the same way as we look upon the operation of analogy in the spread of morphemes, we can observe the spread of particular syntactic constructions. For our present purposes, *syntactic construction* refers only to the order of

---

[5] Suppletion is the occurrence of two or more unrelated stems in a paradigm. Thus in English the paradigm of the verb *go* is *go, went, gone.* The words *go* and *gone* are obviously related, but the past tense *went* comes from a completely different stem *wend.* We say that *went* is a suppletive form in the paradigm of *go,* since it has replaced whatever the "normal" form of *go* would be with an unrelated word. In the same vein the Latin past participle *latus* is suppletive in the paradigm of *ferō.*

words in a particular utterance. An example is the adjective-plus-noun constructions in modern English. With the exception of a few borrowed expressions, adjectives are always placed before nouns, with or without the word *and* to link the adjectives together. We can express the construction in the following formula:

Adj. + Adj. + Adj. . . . . + Adj.   Noun
(e.g., good, decent, friendly . . . cheerful   men)

This was not always the case. In Old English, if there was more than one adjective, only the first preceded the noun, and all the others followed it. Thus, we have:

gōd	man	and	clǣne	and	swiðe	ǣðele
good	man	and	clean	and	very	noble

In New English translation, the above phrase would read:

(a) good and clean and very noble man

By analogy with the pattern for positioning the first adjective, the second, third, fourth, etc., adjectives have come to be placed before the noun. The language has become more regular or simpler in the obvious sense that previously speakers of English had to learn two positions for adjectives, depending on their location in a given sequence, whereas now, only one position (before the noun) is required.

Let us consider another example from the history of English. In New English, the order of words in a clause is:

Subject   Verb   Object

Again, this was not always the case. In Old English the above pattern held only for most main clauses; in subordinate clauses the order was:

Subject   Object   Verb

as in:

SVO: man   ferode   hine
        they   carried   him

SOV: (paet   synd   þā)   ðe   þaet   word   gehȳrað
        (they   are   those)   who   that   word   heard

'(They are those) who heard that word.'

In the development from Old to New English, we again have a simplification in that now we only have one pattern for the elements in a clause, and this is followed in both subordinate and main clauses.

There might be some question of whether the two cases given above are actually types of analogy or should be treated as some kind of grammatical or syntactic change. On closer study of the question, it appears that there is no change in grammar or syntax in any significant sense. What has happened is merely that one pattern of word order, already existing in the language, has replaced another, which has the same meaning, much in the same way that an already existing morpheme replaces another one of the same function. No new patterns are introduced into the language, nor are any meanings changed. Thus, these cases are not treated as matters of syntactic change; that they are a type of analogy is obvious.

The problem of *new* morphological and syntactic structures is the problem of grammatical change, and we turn to that in the next chapter.

FOR FURTHER STUDY

The basic problems and processes involved with analogical change are quite straightforward and there is not much point in belaboring the obvious. Chapter 23 of Bloomfield's *Language*, "Analogic Change," might prove a useful supplement, with further examples, to what we have presented here. For quasi-psychological theories regarding analogy, one should also consult the master Neogrammarian Hermann Paul, *Prin-*

ciples, Chapters V–VIII. The article by Kuryłowicz, to which reference was made in this chapter, has not been translated into English; its full title is *La nature des procès dits analogiques.* An article proposing somewhat different "laws of analogy" is Mańczak's "Tendences générales des changements analogiques." The Meillet tale of **bher-* can be found in the article entitled "A propos de οἰστός." Finally, as an example of how one attempts to reconstruct word order, there is Watkins's "Preliminaries to a Historical and Comparative Analysis of the Syntax of the Old Irish Verb."

10

Change in Grammar

As was pointed out in the previous chapter, the operation of simple analogical processes does not result in any change of the grammatical system of a language.[1] Analogy simply extends the domain of applicability of some forms and reduces that of others (perhaps to zero), but it does *not* affect the phonological shape, the meaning, or the function of the forms so involved. For example, -*s* remains /s/ or /z/ and signifies "plural" no matter what word it is added to. We now turn our attention to consider what is involved when there is change in the actual grammatical system of a language, that is, when new grammatical elements are created, old ones are lost, or there are new means of expressing grammatical categories and relationships. To use (slightly modified) the terminology of Benveniste, we can divide all grammatical change into two groups: conservative and innovative. A *conservative change* is one in which a grammatical notion or category continues to exist, but the means of expressing it (its *marker*) has changed. When a new grammatical category is created or an existing one is lost we are dealing with an *innovative change*.

There is undoubtedly some overlap between what we will consider in this chapter and what appears in the next ("Semantic Change") since both are concerned with shifts of meaning of one sort or another. For practical purposes, we will consider now those changes which affect grammatical systems, and in our next chapter we will deal with changes that affect lexical items whose shifts of meaning have no bearing on the morphology or syntax.

[1] We are using the terms *grammar* and *grammatical system* in a more traditional sense to refer to the morphology and syntax of a language.

GRAMMATICAL RELATIONSHIPS

By grammatical relationships, we mean the meaningful connections which hold between the individual items of a phrase, clause, or sentence. For example, consider the following string of English words:

The friendly aardvark eagerly chewed the tasty zucchini.

The noun *aardvark* bears a grammatical relationship of *subject* to the verb *chewed;* to the same verb, *zucchini* has a relationship of *object*. The relationship between *friendly* and *aardvark, tasty* and *zucchini, eagerly* and *chewed* is a relaship of *modification*. In the former two cases, it is a question of adjectives modifying nouns, and in the latter, we have an adverb modifying a verb. The grammatical relationships in the normal English sentence are indicated by the word order: the subject appears before the verb, the object after, and adjectives and adverbs generally stand next to the words they modify.

If we rearrange the words, we may get either a new sentence (i.e., a collection of words with a different meaning), or we may get something that is simply not an English sentence and has no meaning or content. The following variations are understandable and grammatical, if somewhat bizarre semantically:

The tasty aardvark eagerly chewed the friendly zucchini.
The tasty zucchini eagerly chewed the friendly aardvark.

Certain other arrangements will not be English sentences and will produce strings of words that make no sense at all simply because we cannot understand the grammatical relationships between the words:

Zucchini the chewed tasty the eagerly aardvark friendly.

It should be pointed out that various languages have different ways of expressing (or marking) the grammatical relationships between the elements of a sentence. At the present time, it appears that a large number of the commonly known grammatical relationships are in some sense universal. What this means is that every language has a means of expressing the subject of a verb, the object of a verb, a modifier for noun or verb, definiteness in a noun, etc. From time to time a statement is made that some language does not have these relationships, but usually closer inspection reveals this claim to be erroneous.

If then, these grammatical relationships are universal and found in every language, we do not expect the relations themselves to be subject to change. What can change, however, is the marker or the means used to express these relationships. In Benveniste's terms, we will be dealing with a conservative change.

A most obvious example of this sort of change is a loss of inflection and a consequent requirement that word order become rigid in order to express the grammatical relations among the words of a sentence. This development is found in the histories of a number of the world's languages including the development of English and the evolution of the modern Romance languages from Latin. To take a simple example, consider the following sentence in Latin:

Marcell -us	Sophi -am	ama -t
Marcello -nom.	Sophia -acc.	love -3rd pers. sing. present

'Marcello loves Sophia'

The nominative ending, -us, on the stem Marcell- tells us that Marcello is the subject of the verb, and the accusative ending (-am) on Sophi- indicates that Sophia is the object of the verb. As a result of the presence of these endings, a Latin speaker was able to put these words in any order he liked and still preserve the same meaning (with, perhaps, varying degrees of emphasis). Thus, all of the following are acceptable Latin sentences with the same meaning, "Marcello loves Sophia":

Marcell-us ama-t Sophi-am.
Sophi-am ama-t Marcell-us.
Ama-t Marcell-us Sophi-am.
Sophi-am Marcell-us ama-t.

In modern Italian (as well as in the other Romance languages) case endings have been lost; as a result, the only way to express the relationships of subject and object of the verb is by the order of the words. Thus if we want to say "Marcello loves Sophia," we must say:

Marcello ama Sophia.

If we reverse the order (a perfectly acceptable practice in Latin), we have:

Sophia ama Marcello.

This sentence, however, has a rather different meaning, namely, "Sophia loves Marcello."

Thus, in this case, we can say that the grammatical system has undergone a shift. The grammatical relationships of subject and object to the verb have not changed, but the relationships are now expressed by the position of the words rather than by the endings. Of course, in Latin, the words had to be in some order, but the order was not crucial for determining grammatical relationships. The grammatical change in Italian involves word order being used in a *new way,* and this cannot be explained as an operation of simple analogy. In other words, word order has replaced case endings as the marker of the grammatical relationships of subject and object.

Let us take another example from the history of the Romance languages. In Modern French a relationship of modification between an adjective and a noun is indicated by putting the adjective next to the noun. Most adjectives occur after the noun but a few special ones occur before it. In Latin the primary indicator that a particular adjective modified a particular noun was the fact that the adjective *agreed* with the noun; that is, the adjective was equipped with an ending which indicated the same number, gender, and case as the noun it was modifying. Thus, it was often possible to separate adjective and noun, and still the meaning would be clear. For example, the poet Virgil was able to write 'because of the remembering hatred of cruel Juno' as follows:

saev -ae   memor   -em
cruel -fem. gen. sing.   remembering -fem. acc. sing.

Jūnon -is   ob   īr   -am
Juno -fem. gen. sing. because of   hatred -fem. acc. sing.

The relationships indicated by the endings of the words give an interlocking grouping of adjectives plus nouns, with a preposition thrown in for good measure. The connections can be expressed by the following diagram:

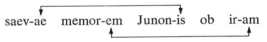

saev-ae   memor-em   Junon-is   ob   ir-am

A modern French translation of the above might read:

à cause de   l'implacable   haine   de la cruelle   Junon
because of   the remembering   hatred   of the cruel   Juno

Of course, in French an adjective agrees in gender and number with the noun it modifies. However, this is unnecessary information since the rules of French grammar do not allow an adjective to be placed next to any noun other than the one it modifies. Thus, even though this remnant of agreement is present in the language, the way of expressing modification is by putting the adjective next to the noun. The grammatical change is that word order has replaced agreement as marking the fact that a particular adjective modifies a particular noun.

PARADIGM RESTRUCTURING

Another type of conservative change involves the replacement of one overt mark for another in the continuation of a single grammatical category. Principles regarding how certain formal changes are likely to take place within a verbal paradigm without disturbing a particular function or meaning were clearly elucidated in Watkins's investigation of the development of some verbal categories from Indo-European to the Celtic languages. The forms of the preterite (past tense) of the verb 'to carry' in Old Irish can, with the comparative evidence from other Celtic languages, be traced back to reconstructed Common Celtic forms:

Common Celtic		Old Irish	
*ber-t-ū	→	-biurt	'I carried'
*ber-t-ī	→	-birt	'you carried'
*ber-t	→	-bert	'he carried'

The Common Celtic forms appear quite straightforward morphologically. There is the known root *ber- (from Indo-European *bher-), followed by a marker of the past tense -t-, followed by the personal endings: -ū for the first person, -ī for the second, and zero for the third. In most languages of the world (English is a notorious exception), the third person does not bear any mark.

The problem that Celticists and Indo-Europeanists faced with these forms was that there was no obvious Indo-European ancestor of this particular past tense formed with -t-. Some scholars tried to attribute it to the influence of some unknown language that was spoken on Celtic territory before the arrival of Indo-European Celts. In other words, it was argued that the presence of this tense in Celtic was due to a linguistic *substratum*. (A substratum of language X is the language originally spoken by a speech community who later adopt language X; presumably some elements of the old lan-

guage will remain and be incorporated in the new one).[2] One
problem with the substratum explanation here is that we have
absolutely no idea what this previous language might have
been. Thus, to say that the unknown origin of something is
due to the influence of an unknown language does nothing
more than substitute one unknown for another, and hardly
offers any advance in knowledge.

Leaving aside the specific problems of the Celtic *t*-tense
for a moment, let us seek a typological parallel by turning our
attention to developments of verbal paradigms that were already understood. For example, consider developments in
Iranian (from Avestan to Modern Persian), and in Slavic
(from Common Slavic to Polish) in the present tense of the
verb 'to be':

Avestan	Modern Persian	
ah-mi	hast-am[3]	'I am'
ah-ti	hast-i	'you are'
as-ti	hast	'he is'
Common Slavic	Polish	
*es-mi	jest-em	'I am'
*es-i	jest-eś	'you are'
*es-ti	jest	'he is'

Ignoring minor sound changes, the development of these
paradigms is parallel, and should appear quite clear. What
has happened is that not every member of the paradigm has

2 An oft cited example of a language with a substratum is French. We
assume that before the armies of Rome moved into ancient Gaul (modern
France) in the first century B.C., the inhabitants of that country spoke a
Celtic language known as Gaulish. The Roman occupation lasted several
centuries, and the people of Gaul adopted the language of their conquerors.
It has been claimed that certain features of the Gaulish language "seeped
through" to the new tongue. Thus French is sometimes spoken of as a
descendant of Latin with a Gaulish substratum.

3 The origin of the initial *h-* in Persian and the *j-* in Polish are phonological
developments which are of no concern to us here. Likewise of no import to
our current discussion is the fact that Polish has replaced the Common
Slavic *-i* of the second person singular with the ending *-eś*.

left a *direct* phonological descendant in the later languages; rather, only one form survived and this one became, as it were, a new stem, upon which the paradigm was rebuilt.

In more detail, we see that only the third person singular in each of the above paradigms has survived; what was previously the ending of the third person has been incorporated into the stem and so a new stem is formed; the endings of the other persons are added to this new stem. Formulaically, we look upon the transformation of the third singular in the following manner:

old stem + 3rd person ending		new stem + 3rd person ending
Iranian	as + ti	ast + ø
Slavic	*es + ti	est + ø

The final -*i*'s of the 3rd person ending drop out by a phonological rule. The fact is that the third person singular marker has been interpreted as part of the stem, and subsequently, the third person singular marker was considered to be zero. As we remarked before (p. 154), most of the world's languages have a zero marker for the third person singular. This appears to be the result of identification of the third person as the (semantically) most indefinite member of the paradigm. First and second persons are always people, since they, by definition, are participating in the speech act; but the third person, which is only the party spoken about, could be anything—an animal or a quality as well as a person. Since third person does not have to be identified, except as "not-first or second," it does not have to have a special mark; the absence of the marks for first or second person serve to identify it.

This then gives us a principle (Watkins's Law) that *the third person occupies the pivotal position in the historical development of a verbal paradigm.* If the paradigm is to undergo change by incorporation of a personal marker into the stem, the personal marker so incorporated will be the third. Witness also the substandard English "So I says to him."

Let us now return to our Celtic example. Drawing from our typological parallel, suppose we hypothesize that something similar happened in the development of Celtic from Indo-European. Our first task then will be to locate the functional equivalent (i.e., the form with the same meaning) of the Celtic -*t*- tense in Indo-European. This is easily found since there is already reconstructed on solid evidence a preterite marked by an *-*s*-, which is preserved in Greek and other languages. The preterite of the verb *bher- in Indo-European is:

*bher-s-m̥	'I carried'
*bher-s-s	'you carried'
*bher-s-t	'he carried'

By normal phonological development coupled with certain analogical reformulations, we can postulate the following pre-Celtic forms:

$$\text{*ber-s-ū}$$
$$\text{*ber-s-ī}$$
$$\text{*ber-t}$$

In pre-Celtic we see that the -*s*- tense marker is still present in the first and second persons. However, in the third person, it has dropped out due to a phonological rule which reduces the cluster -*rst*- to -*rt*-. There is evidence for this change in other cases; for example, the Old Irish word *tart* 'drought, thirst' corresponds to the English *thirst,* where both are reflexes of an Indo-European **tr̥sto*-.

Given the above pre-Celtic forms, the rest of the development to Common Celtic will parallel the development we have presented in Avestan → Persian and Common Slavic → Polish. Starting with the third person singular of the pre-Celtic **ber-t,* we have the following reinterpretation:

stem + tense + person	→	stem + tense + person
ber- + ø + t		ber- + t + ø

This form, *bert, was understood as having a zero marker for the third person singular; it is the only member of the paradigm which really survives into Common Celtic. The rest of the Common Celtic paradigm is built on this new base, thus yielding the forms of the structure given above:[4]

$$
\begin{array}{lll}
\text{stem} + & \text{tense} + & \text{person} \\
\text{ber} - & t - & \bar{u} \\
\text{ber} - & t - & \bar{\imath} \\
\text{ber} - & t -
\end{array}
$$

Working with methods like this involve a process which Watkins has dubbed *reconstructing forward*. It consists of accepting the starting and ending points of particular developments (here they were chosen on the basis of function or meaning, e.g., past tense), bringing to bear all the relevant evidence from phonological history of the language involved and typological parallels from other languages while moving forward from the starting to the ending point, and showing how the former developed into the latter. The principal point that must be made is that the -t- past tense in the Celtic languages is the functional descendant of the -s- past tense in the Indo-European. The same grammatical category has continued to exist, its means of expression has changed by the restructuring of the paradigm. While the spread of the -t- as past-tense marker from the third to the other persons may be attributed to some sort of analogy or leveling, the same cannot be said for the original misinterpretation of the -t- as a tense marker, which is a clear case of conservative grammatical change.

INNOVATIVE CHANGES

Besides changes in the way of expressing grammatical relationships and categories it is also possible to have changes in

---

[4] It might be noted that the Celtic example differs slightly from those taken from Slavic and Iranian. In the latter two cases we saw the third-person marker incorporated into the verbal root, since the present tense has a zero marker. Nonetheless, the principle is the same: the mark of the third person is interpreted as being zero, and the previous overt mark is incorporated (or reinterpreted) as part of the preceding morpheme.

the grammatical categories themselves. These categories are the sets of forms which express particular grammatical meanings. For example, in English we have a category of plural for nouns, of present and past tenses for verbs, etc. Grammatical categories may vary widely from language to language. Thus, Ancient Greek has a verbal category of mood called the optative, which expresses a wish; and modern Turkish has a "hearsay" past tense which the speaker must use when he narrates a past action which he himself did not witness. Just as there are varying grammatical categories in the languages of the world, there is no reason to suspect that all the grammatical categories of any given language are inherently stable and not susceptible to change. We will be dealing here with innovative changes, whereby grammatical elements are created and lost.

Perhaps the most significant way of introducing new grammatical elements into the morphological system of a language is by the process Meillet calls *grammaticalization,* which is the shift of an element from being a full root word with an independent meaning to being a mere grammatical marker of some kind, usually modifying or marking the meaning of some other word or phrase in the sentence.[5] If a new category is to be created, the linguistic material out of which its expression comes is often already existent in the language, but with a different meaning or function. This is a crucial difference between grammaticalization and analogy. In analogy, the morpheme which spreads does so with no change in its seman-

---

[5] Meillet finds the motivation for grammaticalization in what he calls the "expressive function of language." In his brilliant study on the history of conjunctions, he shows that words (such as conjunctions) which are sprinkled throughout a conversation tend to become clichés, and in essence, they lose their punch and become meaningless connectives. In order to restore some element of meaning or expressiveness, speakers may create new conjunctions by compounding. Meillet noted that in the spoken French of his own day, many were replacing the simple conjunction *et* 'and' by *et puis* or *et alors,* or even by *et puis alors.*

Besides compounding, the other obvious way of restoring expressiveness to conjunctions was by the grammaticalization of full words. Thus, the French *mais* 'but' finds its origin in the Latin word *magis* 'more'. Apparently, this word was originally grammaticalized for use as an *expressive* conjunction in the sense of 'moreover', 'furthermore', etc., in place of conjunctions which no longer had any expressive content.

tic content; in the earlier stage of the language the analogical form already existed in the same function as it does in the later. In grammaticalization we have a full word taking over a new, purely grammatical function.

In Old English, for example, there was really no form of the verb comparable to our future tense, which is formed with the auxiliaries *shall* and *will*. Instead, Old English speakers usually employed the present tense and let the context infer that the given action was to take place at some time in the future. Here is an example from the parable of the Prodigal Son:

ic arīse and ic fare tō mīnum fæder, and ic secge him
I arise and I go to my   father and I say   to him

'I will arise and I will go to my father and I will say to him'

By the twelfth century, however, two verbs which were formerly modals had moved into the position of becoming simple auxiliaries indicating a future tense. They were *sculan* (→ New English *shall*), which originally meant 'to have to' and *willan* (→ New English *will*), originally 'to wish to'. At that time, we find them in their familiar function as indicating a simple future tense:

ich schulle vor þe luve of þe nimen þis figt upon me
I   shall   for the love of you take this fight upon me

While the tenses of English have undergone this broadening and expansion, it appears that the moods of the English verb are being continually reduced. Old English had a flourishing subjunctive mood expressing wishes, desires, and contrary-to-fact conditions. But there are few remnants of this in New English. One such is contained in expressions such as "If I were rich, I would. . . ." Doubtless, this remaining trace of an English subjunctive owes its survival to the insistence of school teachers who consider "If I was king . . ." to be incorrect English.

We can see that this loss of moods and gaining of tenses created a great difference between the grammatical systems of Old and New English. In Old English, what had to be expressed in the sentence was the speaker's attitude toward whatever he was talking about, since the subjunctive always carries with it a degree of doubt or uncertainty. New English, with its elaborate system of tenses, requires instead detailed expression of time as opposed to mood.

A contemporary case of a grammatical change is the appearance of what seems to be a question particle in conversational French. Interrogative particles exist in many langauges of the world; they are simply markers whose presence in a sentence turns a statement into a question. Thus, in Chinese, there is the interrogative particle *ma,* the usage of which can be seen in the following examples:

Statement: ta   shr   Junggwo   ren
             he   is   China   man   'He is Chinese.'

Question: ta shr Junggwo ren ma   'Is he Chinese?'

In Standard French many questions are formed by reversing the pronoun subject *il* (phonetically [i]) 'he, it' and the verb; often, this results in the phonetic appearance of a -*t*- between the end of the verb and the pronoun. Thus,

Statement: il vient [iviɛ̃] 'He is coming'

Question: vient il [viɛ̃ti] 'Is he coming?'

Von Wartburg points out that in the minds of many French speakers, the sequence [-ti-] is being interpreted not as a pronoun, but as a reflection of the questioning nature of the utterance. Therefore, in some varieties of French, a particle *ti* is now in use which simply indicates that a question is being asked; as the following examples show:

je   savais   ti
I   knew   (question particle)   'Did I know?'

vous	passerez	ti	par	là?
you	will pass	(question particle)	by	there

'Will you pass by there?'

We have here the creation of a totally new grammatical category, namely, the question particle. Its immediate ancestor is a -t ending on certain verbs and [i], which is a reduced form of the masculine pronoun il, 'he'.[6] The further impact of this new particle on the whole French syntactic system remains to be seen. Perhaps it will completely take over the marking of a sentence as a question, and so remove the necessity of reversing pronoun and verb to do so. The example given above (je savais ti?) might seem to indicate this.

LOSS OF GRAMMATICAL CATEGORIES

Just as new grammatical categories or means of expression can be created, so can they be lost. We have already mentioned the fact that in the shift from Old to New English the category of verbal mood has been greatly reduced.

Another example of the reduction or loss of categories is the history of the three grammatical genders (inherited from Indo-European) in Germanic: masculine, feminine and neuter. Various forms of articles and adjectives would have to "agree" with the gender of noun they modified. There would be but few cases where natural gender or sex would be involved since all nouns, including inanimates, would have to fall into one of the three classes. Thus, in Common Germanic, we have:

Masculine	Feminine	Neuter
*sáe gódaé dagaz	*so gódón bótó	*þata gódón wórd
'the good day'	'the good booty'	'the good word'

[6] The -t ending is historically a descendant of the Latin -t, marker of the third person singular. Cf. the form ama-t, cited in the text above (p. 151). Considering starting and ending points we have a question particle eventually arising from a personal suffix combined with a personal pronoun.

Modern German still preserves the three original genders, and each is still indicated by the forms of articles and (in some cases) adjectives:

Masculine	Feminine	Neuter
der gute Tag	die gute Buss	das gute Wort

Modern Dutch however, had reduced the system somewhat by merging the masculine and feminine categories into one: the so-called common gender. Still opposed to this is the neuter.

Common	Neuter
de goede dag	het goede woord
de goede boete	

Still further along the same line of development, New English has completely abolished the category of grammatical gender. We have a natural gender which is reflected in the pronouns *he, she* and *it,* but with nouns there is no trace of a gender system requiring alternative forms of modifying articles and adjectives.

From this example we can learn that there is no *inherent* reason for the reduction of such grammatical categories. While other influences (which we will not go into here) may have been at work, we find that German preserves the original gender system, English abolishes it completely, and Dutch occupies a middle position with a partial reduction.

FOR FURTHER STUDY

Quite frequently changes in grammatical systems have been either mixed up with analogy or ignored. Thus, for example, Bloomfield has a chapter on analogy, but none on grammatical change. Lehmann apparently does not observe any difference and calls his Chapter 11: "Changes in Grammatical Systems; Analogical Change." In fact, he observes that "analogy may be viewed as the central process in modifications introduced in grammatical systems" (p. 190). This is essentially misleading since there is a definite distinction between the two. One of the clearest statements of certain types of grammatical change is Benveniste's "Mutations of Linguistic Categories." Also of importance is Meillet's "L'evolution des formes grammaticales," where he discusses at length his term 'grammaticalization' and its motivation. Another interesting article of his, "Le renouvellement des conjonctions," treats in detail the shift of forms from being "full" words to being mere grammatical markers (i.e., conjunctions). The investigations by Watkins into the pre-history of the Celtic past tense can be found in his *Indo-European Origins of the Celtic Verb*. Interest in syntactic change has increased enormously since the advancement of knowledge of general syntax which accompanied the progress of the various schools of transformational grammar; we will look at some of the results in Chapter 14.

11

Semantic Change

For various reasons, linguists generally divide their study of morphemes (minimal units of meaning) into two parts, one dealing with grammatical elements, the other treating root morphemes or full words. In our chapters on analogy and change in grammatical systems, we discussed the shifts in form, meaning, and range of application that grammatical morphemes might undergo, including the borderline case where full words have become grammatical markers. Now we turn our attention to root morphemes. Changes in the meanings of root morphemes are usually subsumed under the heading of *semantic change.*

More than any aspect of linguistic change so far discussed, semantic shifts are related to the life and culture of a speech community; they are somewhat free of the mechanisms that may be peculiar to language systems, but are by no means completely independent of linguistic explanation. Semantic change concerns the changes in *lexicon* or *vocabulary,* the most variable and shifting part of any language. Studies in semantic change so far have not resulted in the formulation of abstract models or even in the reasoned educated guesswork that pervades the study of phonological, morphological, and syntactic change. One reason for this is quite obvious: the semantic models of general or synchronic linguistics are themselves quite limited and not applicable to all cases. Nonetheless, some interesting observations have been made, and we shall discuss some of the mechanisms which cause or promote various shifts of meaning, as well as some attempts to classify the types of semantic change.

Much of the interesting work on semantic change has been produced by the school of so-called *sociological linguistics* centered in Paris among the students of Meillet. This school finds its headwaters in the work of Michel Bréal, a late nineteenth-century French linguist who opposed the neogrammarian belief in the blind operation of laws of language change and insisted on the importance of considering the social aspects of language.

For anyone seriously interested in semantic change, a caveat is in order: *every word has its own history*. While we have observed similar semantic changes in different languages, it nonetheless remains true that much painstaking philological work, involving the close study of texts, must be done before the true history of a word's meanings will emerge. The etymologies given in many dictionaries abound with fanciful and unproved speculations about how and why a word shifted meaning. Another linguistic fact that should constantly be kept in mind is that at any given point in time a particular word may have more than one meaning. To this phenomenon, Bréal gave the name *polysemia*. In most instances, a context or general topic of conversation will tell which of the many meanings is appropriate in the particular situation.

Thus, for example, we have the English word *root,* which has several related, though different, meanings, as can be seen in the sentences below:

> Victor trimmed the roots of the plant.
> Peter took the square root of sixty-four and multiplied it by the cube root of twenty-seven.
> Janice reconstructed the Indo-European root for "armpit."
> Penny keeps trying to get at the root of Steve's problem.

Perhaps we might say that all of these share a meaning something like "base" or "foundation," but nonetheless each carries a very specific semantic connotation in each of the above contexts. The root Victor is dealing with is a physical object; Peter's root is a number; Janice's consists of phonemes; and Penny is looking for a root that is probably an experience (of Steve). For our purposes, it is important to recognize this fact because a complete shift of meaning is often not abrupt and because a word may exist with several meanings for indefinite periods of time.

In order to illustrate exactly what happens in semantic change, let us return to the diagram of the linguistic sign presented by Saussure (p. 33):

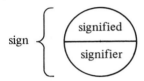

In terms of this diagram, when the speech community has an idea or object it wants to talk about (the signified), symbolizing it will be an accompanying collection of sounds (the signifier) in the vocabulary or lexicon of the language. Thus, when a new signified enters the culture, it will be accompanied by a signifier in the language; vice versa, when a signified is no longer in use, its signifier will tend to disappear. We refer to these two processes as *appearance* and *obsolescence* of lexical items. (The term *obsolescence* is employed instead of *disappearance* because a word may live on for sometime within small groups, and will probably survive indefinitely in the speech or writings of professional antiquarians.)

APPEARANCE

Let us first take up the question of appearance. When an object or institution is taken into a speech community from another culture, as often as not, the name of the object or institution will be borrowed from the lending culture. Thus, English has borrowed *pizza* and *pâté de foie gras* from Italian and French, respectively. Problems connected with linguistic borrowing will be discussed in the next chapter.

Suppose, however, that the item in question is discovered or invented within the given society; then its name often comes about by the simple creation of a new word. This process is known as *coining*. A word is coined according to the particular habits of the coining language. In English, when there are new objects to be named, the tendency is to create the word from Latin or Greek roots. Thus, we have *astronaut* from the Latin roots *astro-* 'star' plus *naut-* 'sailor'; from Greek roots we have the word *megalopolis* from *megalos* 'great' and *polis* 'city'. Of course, roots already existing in English can also be used, as in the words *spacecraft* and *townhouse.*

The process of coining is not, of course, limited to nouns, though they probably form the largest class of new words. Among quite recent English coinings, we have the adjective *psychedelic,* used to describe states of euphoria or expanded consciousness induced by hallucinogenic drugs or audio-visual stimulation. The word is formed from the Greek roots *psyche-* 'pertaining to the mind' and *delos* 'clear, visible'. A new verb in the language is *trash,* which refers to the actions of young people who for political or recreational reasons destroy property by smashing windows and looting. The new verb is an obvious derivation from the noun *trash,* and finds its semantic connection in the idea of turning into trash that which should be trash (at least in the minds of those doing the trashing).

Certain names, especially trade names, are not necessarily coined because they have any root or etymological meaning, but merely because they have a pleasant ring and are easy to remember. Thus, for the chemical substance polytetrafluoro-ethylene, which is supposed to create a slick surface on cooking utensils, the name *Teflon* was coined.

It is also possible that proper names will enter a language as ordinary words. Witness the rise of *McCarthyism* in the early fifties, or the practice of labeling a collaborator a *quisling.* For years people have been talking about *boycotts,* an action that takes its name from Charles C. Boycott (1832–

1897). He was a hapless Irish landlord who was evicted by his own tenants for refusing to lower rents. Mr. Boycott has been immortalized by having his name applied to any action that involves refusal to do business with someone as a means of protest.

OBSOLESCENCE

The opposite process, namely obsolescence, takes place when the speech community ceases to use the item in question and as a result the word falls out of everyday usage. Thus, we might consider the fact that nowadays the vocabulary of falconry or alchemy is used only infrequently. For all practical purposes, these words have left the language, and their current usage is essentially restricted to antiquarians or historians of science. Obviously, it is the process of obsolescence which requires that current editions of Shakespeare and similar writers be provided with notes or glossaries. Shakespeare expected his audiences to know what a *placket* or a *foin* was, or what is meant by *to rash*. (A placket is an opening in a woman's petticoat; a foin is the trust of a sword; and to rash is to slash, as by a boar's tusks.) These are items or actions simply no longer represented in our culture.

Besides the obsolescence of a word merely because it has ceased to be of use to the society (as an object is no longer present in the culture, or an action is no longer performed), certain words tend to become obsolete simply because of their unfavorable connotations. For example, in the history of recent American English, we have witnessed the obsolescence of two ethnonyms: *Jew* and *Negro*. In the former case, we have tended to replace the noun with the already-existing adjective *Jewish,* probably because of the existence of derogatory phrases employing the form *Jew* as a noun or as a verb. It now sounds more "polite" to say that someone is *Jewish,* rather than a *Jew.* Likewise, in emphasizing their pride in the color of their skin, many Negroes have preferred to be called *Blacks,* and in order not to be offensive, an increasing number of the present-day white community have adopted this appellation.

SHIFTS

Besides the obvious cases in which items are introduced into the culture and consequently vocabulary into the lexicon, there is also the situation of an already existing word which gains a new meaning. In Ullmann's formulation, "a semantic change will occur whenever a new name becomes attached to a sense and/or a new sense to a name." In terms of our Saussurean diagram, there will be a shift in the relationship between signified and signifier.

It should also be fairly obvious that a semantic shift cannot take place abruptly throughout a speech community, but must take place gradually through various associations of meanings and the phenomenon of polysemia. This statement, of course, ignores the possible, if unlikely, situation where some absolute ruler might simply decree: "Tomorrow, the leather thing worn on the feet shall be known as a *cabbage.*" In such a case, the semantic shift has been ordered for whatever reason, and all loyal subjects will be bound to follow it.

SEMANTIC CONTACT

As an extreme case of a shift of meaning let us take the well-known example of the English word *bead*. A recent dictionary defines this as "a small, ball-shaped piece of glass, metal, wood, or other material pierced for stringing or threading." A Saussurean diagram for this linguistic sign might look as follows:

If we trace the word back to Old English, we might find the form **gebet,* which surprisingly enough does not mean 'bead', but rather means 'prayer'. Again, a diagram:

The obvious question at this point is: "How did a word, which originally meant 'prayer' come to mean 'bead'?" Barring the existence of our aforementioned tyrant and his linguistic decrees, we would try to look for some connection between the two meanings.

Fortunately, the cultural history of this word is well attested. An old custom, still living today among some members of the Roman Catholic Church, is to count specific prayers on strings of beads called *rosaries*. So there arose the expressions "to count one's beads" or "to tell one's beads,"[1] which included both 'bead' and 'prayer'; and in Middle English the word *bede* ~ *bead* (both spellings are found) had the following glosses: 'prayer, prayer bead, bead'. This gives us, then, our semantic shift, which can be expressed in Saussurean diagrams as follows (ignoring the phonological changes in the signifiers):

We might well ask, though, what additional circumstances were necessary to allow this word to give up its old meaning

[1] In this context the word *tell* is used in its older meaning 'to count'.

completely and assume a totally new one. Our answer here lies in the fact that the signified acquired a new signifier *prayer,* which was borrowed from French. To some extent this freed the old signifier *bead* from its original primary duty of meaning 'prayer' and allowed it to be used more often for its original secondary duty of signifying . The case of the 'prayer' → 'bead' shift is one that we attribute to semantic contact. In other words, in the life of the people who spoke English there was a contact between prayers and beads, and this contact was reflected linguistically by the fact that at some point in time the word *bead* meant both 'prayer' and 'bead'.

ISOLATION OF FORMS

One factor which will definitely increase the possibility of a semantic change is the phonetic or morphological isolation of a particular form from other members of the same word family (i.e., words formed from the same semantic root). The association of a word with words similar in sound and meaning will tend to keep in the speakers' minds that connection, and so hinder semantic shift. When, for one reason or another, the link is broken, a word is more free to wander. The breaking of this link usually happens when a root word drops out of the language, or when the morphological process linking a base and a derived form either disappears or ceases to be productive.

As a very obvious example, take the history of the English word *quick,* which now means 'fast, speedy'. *Quick* is a descendant of the Old English word *cwicu,* which meant 'alive'; in this old meaning it is found only in a few archaic expressions such as the liturgical formula *the quick and the dead.* The figurative extension from 'alive' to 'fast' is not difficult to see (e.g., *lively* and *live*), but an additional factor is involved in the complete semantic shift. In Old English there was also a verb *cwician* 'to be alive, to live'; this was lost and replaced completely by *live* (← Old English *libban* 'to live'). Now that *cwicu* no longer had a direct phonetic/psychological connection with a verb meaning 'to live', it was free to assume exclusively the meaning 'fast'.

A similar case is that of the French adjective *chétif* 'miserable'. This word finds its origin in the Latin *captivus* 'taken captive', which is the past passive participle of the verb *capere* 'to take'. In French the verb *capere* was lost, and the notion of 'take' was expressed by descendants of the Latin verb *prehendere* 'to seize' (→ French *prendre* 'to take'). Therefore, the originally metaphorical meaning of 'miserable' (what captive is not miserable!) now became the only meaning because there was no longer a verb with which to associate the notion of 'taking'.

As we mentioned at the beginning of this section, it is also true that a word may very likely assume a specialized meaning when the morphological processes which relate it to its root are no longer productive. In our section on apophony, we gave the example of *teg-ere* 'to cover' and *tog-a* 'a toga, Roman robe' (p. 123). If the relationship were simply one of derivation, we might ask why does not *toga* mean simply 'covering'? The answer lies in the fact that the *e* (verb) ∼ *o* (noun) apophony was no longer productive in Latin, and so the relationship between *teg-ere* and *tog-a* is weakened. Consequently, *toga* was free to assume a specialized meaning.

Another example from the same root is the case of the Latin noun *tec-tum* 'roof'. This, too, was originally from *teg-* plus *-tum* (a suffix used to form nouns from verbs) with the devoicing of *g* to *c* [k] before *t*. By the time of Classical Latin, this *-tum* suffix was also no longer productive, and, as expected, the semantic links between *teg-ere* and *tec-tum* had been loosened. Thus *tectum* could assume its specialized meaning of 'roof' (and eventually become French *toit,* Spanish *techo* and Italian *tetto,* all meaning 'roof').

An almost identical case is found in the history of Irish. From the Indo-European root **teg-* (the source of Latin *teg-ere*), Old Irish had a verb *tuig-ithir* 'to cover'. In a pre-

Celtic stage, a verbal noun was formed from this with the normal Indo-European suffix *-ye; however, when this noun appeared in Old Irish as *tuig-e,* it did not mean simply 'covering', but more specifically it meant 'thatch'. For 'covering', the word was *tuig-iud.* The reason for this specialization was that after the formation of *tuig-e,* the suffix *-e* ceased to be productive, and its place was taken by the suffix *-iud.* This allowed *tuige* to assume the narrower meaning of 'thatch'.[2]

SUBGROUPS WITHIN A LINGUISTIC COMMUNITY

At the beginning of this chapter we mentioned the linguistic phenomenon of polysemia (p. 166), whereby one word might have several different meanings and a linguistic context is necessary to tell which of the meanings is intended. We now extend that idea to include social or professional contexts; that is, a single word will assume more or less different meanings within different interest groups of a single speech community. To go back to our original example, the word root has different meanings when spoken by

1. gardeners
2. mathematicians
3. linguists
4. psychiatrists

This brings up the fact that one very important mechanism for the actual working of polysemia in semantic change lies in the existence of the subgroups or subcultures within any human society. Linguistically, it follows that these subcultures will have a language which differs somewhat from that of the speech community at large. The primary difference between these languages and the general language will be in the

[2] The notion of the unproductive suffix also explains the *live* (verb) and *lively* (adj.) divergence of meaning which has been mentioned above (p. 172). The suffix *-ly* used to derive adjectives from verbs is simply not productive. The adjectives which were so formed were free to move along semantic paths different from their "base" verbs. Cf. also *seem* and *seemly*.

area of vocabulary. By subcultures we do not mean groups that are looked down upon or denigrated by the society as a whole, but merely groups that share certain interests or occupations. And these groups will have special vocabularies which unambiguously reflect the items, actions, and institutions of their subcultures. These specialized vocabularies are called *jargons*, or *cants* or *argots,* and obviously they are found in the various professions such as the medical, the military, or the theatrical. The reason why the small specialized social or professional group is a more likely vehicle for semantic change than society at large is not difficult to see. Using a particular word has been compared to using a particular type of money; its only value derives from the fact that the other person is willing to accept it with the same understanding as we have.

Thus, if on my own I decided to substitute *foot* for *head, head* for *file cabinet, file cabinet* for *roast beef,* etc., there is, theoretically, nothing to prevent me from so doing. However, it would be impossible to communicate with anyone else unless I had told him of my new meanings personally. Thus, within a small group, it is possible to create new meanings or to shift the meaning of a word, simply because continual contact (in speech or in writing) as well as closeness in thought and subject matter are already present.

The way semantic change in this sense would work is that a word with meaning X would enter the particular subculture where it would acquire the meaning Y. It would then re-emerge into the general speech community with this new meaning.

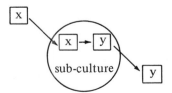

One very good example of this is the history of the verb *arrive* (borrowed from French), which is an emanation from sailors' jargon. Etymologically, we can trace the word back to a form **adrīpāre* 'to reach the shore' which, in turn, is composed of three Latin elements: *ad* 'to', + *rīp-* 'bank, shore' + *-āre,* a verbal ending. Presumably, in a sailor's jargon "reach the shore" could extend its meaning to "reach anyplace," because when a sailor got to the shore, he got to where he was going. The word then emerges into the general speech community with the new meaning of "reach the place you're going to" and is not limited to "reaching land" from the sea.

TYPES OF CHANGE

While it might be possible to give an indefinitely long list of the supposedly different types of semantic shifts that a word may undergo, such lists add little to our understanding of semantic change. We will therefore limit ourselves to listing four types, examples of which we have seen in our previous sections. These should certainly suffice for an elementary understanding of semantic change. They are:

1. Extension
2. Narrowing
3. Figurative use
4. Subreption

It should be remembered that these types form a quite different system of classification than what has appeared in our previous sections on semantic contact, morphological isolation, and social groups. The latter three form classes of mechanisms, or causes, or simply means of facilitating semantic change. Types 1–4 involve the direction in which semantic shifts may go.

EXTENSION

By extension of meaning, we mean simply that the number of things that a word refers to has increased. In other terms, the word widens its meaning, as did the English word *salary,* which means 'wages of any kind'. The Latin ancestor of our word, *salārium,* was of more limited usage, meaning 'the wages of a soldier'; even further back, usage of *salārium* was limited to the allotment that a soldier received for salt (*salārium ← sal* 'salt'). Using concentric circles we can see how the meaning of this word has been widened or extended:

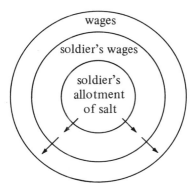

Its development is like the earlier example of *arrive ← *adrī-pāre,* where the word extended its meaning from 'reaching a shore' to 'reaching any place'.

From the history of English we have the case of the word *dog.* The ancestor of this word is Middle English *dogge* (late Old English *docga,* and no further etymology), which meant a particular breed of powerful canine. Between the Middle and New English periods, this word extended its meaning so that it now includes the whole species of domesticated canines.

NARROWING

The exact opposite of the expansion of meaning is its narrowing. What is involved is that the number of things a word refers to is reduced, or we might say that a word becomes more specialized. Meillet gives an example from the French word *saoul,* which in Modern French means 'drunk, intoxicated by means of liquor'. At a previous stage of French, the word meant simply 'seized, possessed' by anything. Perhaps because within the given culture, the primary agent for seizing one's soul or personality was liquor, the word *saoul* narrowed its field of reference and came to mean exclusively 'seized by the power of alcoholic beverages' or simply 'drunk'.[3] Again, a set of concentric circles can illustrate this shift, but this time it moves from the outside in.

3 Meillet's contention is that a narrowing such as this is due to a fact of language transmission. Adults for whom the word *saoul* had its original, wider, meaning of 'seized, possessed', might have uttered this word only in reference to individuals intoxicated by liquor. Since the children would not hear *saoul* in any other context, for them it would have only the narrower meaning of 'drunk'.

A possible similar case of semantic narrowing has recently been pointed out by Oswalt, though he makes no mention of Meillet's theories. In the Pomo languages of northern California, Oswalt found a set of obviously cognate words: Kashaya Pomo *putílka* 'broken glass fragments', Southern Pomo *pʰotilka* 'broken glass fragments' and Central Pomo *pʰtilka* 'glass in any form' but especially 'broken fragments'. This word is originally a borrowing from Russian *butílka* 'bottle'.

In American English of the past decade or so, we have an excellent example of a narrowing of meaning in the history of the word *pill.* Ten years ago, if a woman remarked that she had to take her pill, the curious listener might well inquire if the pill was intended to cure a headache, relieve arthritis pain, or perhaps settle an upset stomach. With the advent of oral contraceptives, and the consequent phrase *birth-control pill,* the word *pill* itself has been narrowed in meaning and has come to mean almost exclusively 'oral contraceptive'. Thus, writers of newspaper headlines have no fear of ambiguity with statements such as:

> The pill is safe says Dr. X.
> The pill is unsafe says Dr. Y.

Everyone knows precisely what pill Drs. X and Y are talking about. What, we might ask, has happened to the older, wider meaning of this word? As any watcher of television commercials can testify, we find that a totally different word, *tablet,* is taking over the function of *pill* as meaning any kind of compressed medication that is taken orally.

FIGURATIVE SPEECH

It is often the case that a word acquires new meaning by way of figurative usage. We are all familiar with the use of figurative language in poetic or expressive speech, such as referring to old age as the *evening of life,* thus drawing an analogy between the end of a day and the end of life. Almost any word can be used figuratively on a given occasion, but when the metaphor sticks and comes into general usage, the word

Oswalt comments: "The semantic development of this set is easy to understand when it is known that the informants (who are now mostly in their seventies) first learned the words as children admonished by their grandparents in a context (in the appropriate language) like 'Don't play there barefoot, putilka!' Here the earlier generation may have meant *bottle* but the child understood it as *broken bottle* or *any broken glass.*"

can be said to have acquired a new meaning. If the old meaning still remains primary, the new meaning may seem figurative; if not, the figurative meaning becomes the primary meaning of the word.

Some linguists might like to classify the effect of figurative usage on semantic change into various categories, usually based on the classification of figures of speech known from traditional poetic and rhetorical studies. Thus, they would distinguish *metonymy* from *synechdoche* from *metaphor*. In terms of the effect on semantic change such subclassification is really of no value and only adds a list of complicated technical terms which must be learned. Since it does not lead to any further insights into semantic change, we can, I believe, safely subsume all such changes under the heading of *figurative use of language.*

There is one significant difference between the two types of semantic change we have already mentioned (extension and narrowing) and figurative use of language. Extensions and narrowings may be relatively unconscious processes which very gradually expand or limit the referents of a word.[4] In Ullmann's terms, though, semantic change due to the figurative use of language in its early stages *involves a more conscious and deliberate transfer serving aesthetic purposes.* In other words, when one uses language figuratively, one is consciously aware of the resemblance between two items; and for the sake of novelty or expressiveness, one deliberately uses a figurative term. Of course, this reminds us again of Meillet's insistence on the importance of the expressive aspect of language in language change (p. 166).

Take, for example, the word *bottleneck*. Because the slowdown of traffic at narrow points in a road reminded people of the slow passage of liquids through the neck of a bottle, such points came to be known as *bottlenecks*. The metaphor remains obvious since both *bottle* and *neck* are still in current usage. However, in this compound form it has definite meanings, namely, a place where vehicular traffic is usually tied up

---

[4] Or, as we saw above, (p. 178, note 3), certain narrowings may be due to factors connected with the transmission of languages.

or by further extension, a place in a bureaucratic chain where business is held up.

The history of the Turkish word *yurt* is an example of figurative usage resulting in semantic change. In Old Turkic (and in many modern Turkic languages) *yurt* means simply a type of tent which Central Asian nomads use. In the modern language of Turkey, however, the primary meaning of the word is 'country, fatherland'. The figurative use involves seeing the home of the individual family, the tent, as symbolic or similar to the home of the whole nation. Undoubtedly, the originators of this semantic shift achieved a great deal of expressiveness in conjuring up the concrete image of the tent as the home of all the people.

SUBREPTION

Another type of semantic change which has been discussed by Meillet and others is that which Wellander calls subreption. Basically, subreption is the continued existence of a signifier, while the signified changes either in some real or some intellectual way (i.e., in terms of its understanding) without a disruption or sharp break in the history of the word. For example, consider the developments in military hardware from medieval to modern times; we still use the word *artillery* (← Middle English *artillerie*) to refer to the physical means of ground warfare. The word has continued on, but with new weapons of destruction replacing older ones, the reference for *artillery* has shifted slightly, at one point meaning catapults and cross bows, and at present meaning mortars, howitzers, and cannons.

Likewise we know that the New English word *house* is the direct descendant of the Old English *hūs,* yet since the dwellings we live in hardly resemble those of sixth-century England, we can say that the object referred to by *hūs* ~ *house* has changed. Similarly, the word *book* (← Old English *bōc*) or French *livre* (← Latin *liber*) are words that have remained in uninterrupted use, undergoing only normal phonological changes; but with the invention of printing, the objects they refer to have changed considerably.

One thing that remains constant in all the cases of subreption that we have seen is the function of the object in question: artillery is still used for ground warfare, houses are for living, and books are for reading. As Ullmann points out, though, psychologically it is probably not these similarities between objects at different stages in a word's history which cause people to go on using the same word. Much more likely, it is the fact that speakers ignore or do not notice the differences or the changes in the referent.

One of Meillet's favorite examples of subreption is the history of the Indo-European words *pəter 'father' and *māter 'mother'. Apparently, in Indo-European society, these words referred not to physical parentage, but to specific positions within the social order. This is most clearly reflected in Roman society, where the Latin words māter and pater refer to the heads of families and not strictly to physical parents. For the latter concept, the terms genitor 'physical father' and genitrix 'physical mother' were employed. For a Roman it would be unthinkable to refer to the māter or pater of an animal. A further proof of the original concept of māter is contained in the etymology of the Latin word mātrimōnium 'marriage', which is formed from māter plus the suffix -mōnium, a legal term found in other words such as testimōnium 'testimony, witness'. Therefore, mātrimōnium obviously does not mean 'becoming a mother' in the sense of bearing a child, rather it means 'becoming a māter', assuming the position of māter in the social structure.

As we all know, in the course of time, the referents of the original Indo-European *māter and *pəter have changed in the descendant languages. In English, we use the terms mother and father to refer to mere physical parenthood. If we wish to add the notions of correct devotion and care for children, we might reinforce the meaning by referring to a real mother, as in speaking of a childless woman who brought up someone else's child by saying "She was a real mother to to him." Meillet has recorded French dialects in which the

French descendants of these words (*mère* and *père*) have gone even further in shift of meaning and now mean merely 'female' and 'male', respectively, even with respect to animals. This last example of subreption shows that even where no function has remained stable, the word has continued in history with only a slight shift of referents at any one point in time. It does indeed substantiate the position of Ullmann that what is psychologically noteworthy in subreption is not that the speakers of a language bear in mind similarities as a word is applied to different things, but that they ignore the differences.

FOR FURTHER STUDY

Perhaps the best short study of semantic change is Meillet's "Comment les mots changent de sens"; like almost all other works of Meillet, this is a brilliant, concise, well-written piece of theory with copious examples. The work of Meillet's teacher, Michel Bréal, *Semantics: Studies in the Science of Meaning,* is also worthwhile in that it is the first serious attempt to classify and explain many different types of semantic change. For a more recent, and well-illustrated, theoretical work, one should consult Stephen Ullmann's *The Principles of Semantics: A Linguistic Approach to Meaning.* Especially valuable is Chapter IV, "Historical Semantics." Oswalt's study of the 'bottle' to 'broken fragments' shift is found in his article "The Case of the Broken Bottle." Finally, for detailed semantic histories of individual words resulting from precise philological work, one can read Benveniste's article "Problèmes sémantiques de la réconstruction."

12

Borrowing

The study of linguistic borrowing is inextricably bound up with the social and political history of a speech community. The historical point of interest here is the contact of one group with speech communities outside itself. Speaking generally, we define borrowing as the *process by which one language or dialect takes and incorporates some linguistic element from another*. The appropriateness of the term "borrowing" might be debated. Einar Haugen has pointed out that since the borrowing language incurs no obligation to return anything, "stealing" might be a better term, except for the fact that the lending language does not feel offended by having something taken from it and, in fact, has not lost anything.

LEXICAL BORROWING

For the moment, we will restrict ourselves to the question of lexical borrowing, or the borrowing of whole words, which is the most common type of interaction between languages. Words can be taken very freely from one language into another, with very little, if any, effect on the rest of the grammar or lexicon of the borrowing language. The vocabulary or lexicon is the most unstable part of any language, and words may be picked up or discarded as a given community feels the need. To take the most simple and obvious case, suppose a speech community borrows some foreign cultural item. At the same time, it might well take into its language the name of that item from the language of the culture supplying it. Some clear examples are the names of foods. Most of us are familiar with the words *bagel* (from Yiddish), *goulash* (from Hungarian), *enchilada* (from Mexican Spanish), or *moo goo gai pan* (from Cantonese). On a less concrete level, we may speak of someone's *savoir faire* (from French), an organization's *aggiornamento* (from Italian), or a social situation as being *gemütlich* (from German). These last-mentioned foreign words were borrowed because it was felt that they express an attitude or feeling not adequately expressed in any native words.

It is not, of course, necessary to absorb an item culturally before borrowing its name linguistically. For a word to travel from a lending to a borrowing language, all that is necessary is that the concept be within the borrowing speech community or at least within a subgroup that desires to speak about something "foreign." Thus, while neither a *lama* (Tibetan monk) nor a *llama* (Peruvian beast of burden) has become a part of the culture of any English-speaking group, both are acceptable English words, known to even moderately educated speakers. Likewise, when the first English speakers reached the New World, they borrowed into their language many words related to the native cultures whose referents they may never have dreamed of using in their own societies: *wigwam, wampum, pemmican.* And even today we can speak freely of a *junta,* without necessarily wanting one as our government.

Borrowing from one specialized subgroup by a similar one in a different speech community is something that takes place all the time. Such borrowed words may not make their way out of specific areas or specialized groups for a long time, if ever. Thus, English-speaking linguists are familiar with the German words *ablaut* and *umlaut,* and psychiatrists talk about *Weltschmerz* and *Angst* daily, though these words may not be known to the general public.

One very significant fact about borrowing is that the borrowed words are assimilated into the phonemic (or sound) system of the borrowing language. What this means is that after a word has been fully absorbed into a new language, it sounds like an ordinary word of that language and is subject

.

to all its rules. (Individuals who know the source language may still affect the original pronunciation, in which case the word is still felt as being foreign. No one would think of giving *theatre* its French pronunciation, for it is now completely assimilated; but many English speakers who know French will at least approximate a French pronunciation of such words as *savoir faire, déjà vu, nom de plume.*) Sounds which do not occur in the borrowing language are either dropped or replaced by familiar, native ones.[1]

An example of the complete loss of phonemes is the borrowing from tonal languages into nontonal ones. We completely ignore the tones of Chinese words, such as *chow mein* or *kowtow,* though in Chinese they must be pronounced with specific pitch contours or registers in order to convey the proper meaning. Ordinarily, though, foreign sounds in borrowed words are simply replaced by native sounds which are similar. Take the common expression *déjà vu;* the French [ü] sound does not occur in English, so an ordinary English speaker simply replaces [ü] with [u], a normal sound in his language. Or in the English pronunciation of the German name *Bach* we find the German -*ch* (the voiceless velar fricative [x]) replaced by the English voiceless velar stop [k]. In Spanish borrowings from Arabic we find that the Arabic pharyngealized consonants have been replaced by unpharyngeal-

---

[1] It is an interesting fact that in present-day English, people generally tend to say foreign proper names with a pronunciation at least approaching that of the source language. This has not always been the case, and in previous centuries English speakers tended to pronounce foreign names as they were spelled (from the English point of view). Thus, we now pronounce the name of the noted Austrian composer Mozart as [motsart], recognizing the fact that in German spelling *z* represents the sound [ts]; the accepted pronunciation in the nineteenth century would have been [mozart]. A clear example of these different habits can be found in the case of contemporary English pronunciation of the adjective *quixotic* [kwɪksatɪk] and the pronunciation of the source name *Quixote* [kihoti]. We see that at a previous stage of English, when people referred to Don Quixote, they pronounced his name according to the rules of English spelling, probably something like [kwɪksot]. From this pronunciation the adjective *quixotic* was formed with the normal adjective suffix -*ic*. As it became linguistically fashionable in the twentieth century to give names at least an approximation of their original pronunciation, the name [kwɪksot] was replaced by [kihoti], but the adjective was so completely integrated into English that it was untouched by this change of habit.

ized Spanish equivalents, e.g., *alcalde* 'mayor' from Arabic *(al-) qadi.*[2]

Another example of words conforming to the sound pattern of the borrowing language can be seen in Turkish. According to the rules of Turkish phonology a word may not begin with an *s*- followed by a stop consonant. When words from European languages which have an *s* + stop cluster at the beginning are borrowed into Turkish, often an initial *i*- is prefixed. For example:

Turkish	Source
ispirto	← spirito (Italian) 'spirit', 'alcohol'
istasyon	← station (French)
iskoč	← scotch (English)

Finally, we might note that morphological boundaries present in a lending language can be lost in transit. This usually happens when speakers of the borrowing language interpret two or more words in the lending language as being only one word. In Spanish borrowings from Arabic we find that the majority are adopted with the Arabic article *al-* 'the' whose force as an article is not felt at all in Spanish. That is, with *alcalde* 'mayor' from Arabic *qadi,* a Spanish speaker will use the regular Spanish definite article: *el alcalde* 'the mayor'. Other similar words include *almacen* 'store, grocery' from Arabic *mahzan* 'granary'; *alcoba* 'bedroom, anteroom', from Arabic *qubba* 'domed edifice' and *almaden* 'mine' from Arabic *ma'din* 'mine, lode'.

In terms of the traditional parts of speech, it is possible to show which ones are more likely to be borrowed. As might be expected, nouns are by far the most frequently borrowed class of words. Haugen's study of English borrowings into the Norwegian spoken by bilingual Norwegian-Americans revealed that the total of borrowed words consisted of the following percentages:

[2] A pharyngealized consonant is one which in addition to its primary point and manner of articulation, has a secondary articulation formed by narrowing the pharynx during production. They are common in the Semitic languages, where they are known as emphatic consonants. *q* is a pharyngealized velar, i.e., a *k* pronounced with a narrowed pharynx.

Nouns	75.5%
Verbs	18.4
Adjectives	3.4
Adverbs and Prepositionals	1.2
Interjections	1.4
	99.9

We might note the total absence of pronouns in this list. In point of fact it is very rare that pronouns are borrowed, which is one of the reasons that comparative linguists often look first to pronouns when seeking to establish genetic relationships. Borrowing pronouns is, however, possible, and one of the few examples of this occurrence is in the history of English. The third person pronouns in Old English were as follows:

	he	*she*	*it*	*they*
nom.	hē	hēo	hit	hīe
acc.	hine	hīe	hit	hīe
dat.	him	hiere	him	him
gen.	his	hiere	his	hiera

Perhaps because of possible confusion with the nominative and dative of the masculine singular and with the genitive of the feminine, the plural forms were gradually replaced with items from a related language, Old Norse. Before the end of the twelfth century, we have attested in forms spreading down from the north of England the following forms:

Old Norse

nom.	þei-r		þei
acc.	þeim	→	þeim
gen.	þeir-a		þeir

These forms, which were borrowed from Old Norse, became the standard English third person plural pronouns, and with small phonological changes are with us today.

LOAN TRANSLATIONS

English stands out as being almost unique with regard to the extent to which it indifferently borrows words from any language for whatever purpose. English speakers do not ordinarily worry about the notion that extensive borrowings cause their language to be corrupted or less "pure." In English a native word and a borrowed word may exist comfortably side by side with very similar or identical meanings. Such is the situation with words like *handbook* (native) and *manual* (borrowed from French, with further origin in Latin *manus* 'hand'). Or a borrowed word may completely oust the usage of a native word for no apparent reason. In our first Bible selection (p. 3), we saw the Old English verb *astigan,* which has been replaced by *ascend* (borrowed from Latin *ascendere*).

This is certainly not the case for a large number of other speech communities where there may be an official government policy or an unofficial feeling that the purity of the language must be preserved from the incursions of foreign words. As a result of this attitude, when the need arises to borrow a word, these languages tend to use a process known as *loan translation* or *calquing.* What is basically involved in loan translation is *translating* the component parts of a foreign word into roots native to the borrowing language. In English there are a few examples of this, one of the most famous being the expression *lightning war,* a loan translation of the German word *Blitzkrieg,* which is itself a product of compounding *Blitz* 'lightning' and *Krieg* 'war'. In the literature of Freudian psychoanalysis, we may find the word *unpleasure,* a loan translation of the German technical term *Unlust,* a concept which Freud kept distinct from *Schmerz* 'pain'.

In certain other languages, such as French and German, there has been a decided tendency to prefer loan translation to simple borrowing. Thus, while English simply borrowed the Latin word *compassion* (through French), the Germans broke the word down into its component parts (*com-* ← *con-* 'with' + *passio* 'feeling'), translated these elements individually in German *mit* 'with' and *Leitung* 'feeling', and produced the calque *Mitleitung* 'compassion'. The same process can be seen in the German equivalent of the English verb *to impress,* another word of Latin origin. Instead of borrowing the word, the Germans translated the parts: *im-* (← *in* 'in') translated as German *ein-* 'in'; *press-* translated as German *drucken* 'to press'; and the result was the calque *eindrucken.*

In the nineteenth century when Alexander Graham Bell invented a device for transmitting the human voice by electronic means, the name *telephone* was coined from the Greek roots *tēle* 'at a distance, far off' and *phōnē* 'sound, voice'. Many cultures which adopted the device (such as French and Russian) borrowed the English word with the usual phonetic modifications. The Germans, however, preferred loan translation and created the calque *Fernsprecher* from *fern* 'distant' + *sprecher* 'speaker'.[3] A recent example of a loan translation, is the slang English expression *out of sight* 'really terrific'. The French segment of the international youth culture chose to render this in French by the calque *loin de la vue* 'far from sight'.[4]

An interesting example in which the spread of American institutions involved calquing in one language and simple borrowing in another is the case of the words *boyfriend* and *girlfriend* in the Far East. With the spread of the previously unknown phenomena of casual dating in these cultures

[3] The spread of the name for "telephone" in the Far East is also interesting. The Chinese coined a word *dyanhwa* from *dyan* 'electric' and *hwa* 'speech.' This is not, strictly speaking, a loan translation because Chinese used the word for 'electric' instead of that for 'distant.' The Japanese simply borrowed the Chinese word, with appropriate adjustments to the Japanese phonological system, and emerged with *denwa.*

[4] In the author's recent experience, he has encountered a somewhat amusing calque in French which was created by a group of French-speaking Americans. In this group, it so happened that nobody knew the French word for "dumbwaiter." Instead of borrowing the English word, they chose to loan-translate it as *garçon stupide,* from *garçon* 'boy, waiter' and *stupide* 'dumb' (in the sense of stupid). A later, probably more correct from the etymological viewpoint, calque formed by the same group for 'dumbwaiter' was *garçon muet* with *muet* 'dumb' (in the sense of mute).

through American influence, the aforementioned words were adopted to express the new social relationships. The Japanese simply borrowed the English words, fitted them into the Japanese phonological pattern and emerged with *bōifurendo* and *gārufurendo*. The Chinese, on the other hand, chose to loan translate the terms and came up with *nan pengyu* (← *nan* 'male' + *pengyu* 'friend') and *nü pengyu* (← *nü* 'female' + *pengyu*).

PHONOLOGICAL BORROWING

As was clearly implied in our section on lexical borrowing, sounds, or groups of sounds, do not ordinarily travel from one language to another. A borrowed word, fully integrated into its new language, loses whatever phonetic properties it had originally that would make it sound foreign. The sounds (or sound pattern) of a language at any given point in time, we generally considered to be exclusively the product of internal history, of phonemes in some sense evolving from previous phonemes in the same language.[5]

However, phonological borrowing is not unknown. For example at some point in the history of English, there was a sound change which dropped *k* when it appeared at the beginning of a word and before *n*. Our writing system has not yet caught up with this, and we still write *knife, know, knee* where we say [nayf], [no:], [ni:]. In other words, we could say that the initial cluster *kn-* does not exist in contemporary English. In a recent dictionary, however, two such clusters were listed as the *only* pronunciation for the words *knish* 'potato pancake' (← Yiddish) and *Knesset* 'parliament' (← Hebrew). What has happened is that in borrowing these words, English has borrowed what amounts to a *new* consonant cluster and has somewhat altered its own phonological rules in permitting the full integration of these words into the

---

[5] We are, of course, ignoring here the previously mentioned case (p. 186) of people who speak the source language and may use the original pronunciation of a word.

language. It should be fairly obvious that the introduction of new groupings of already extant phonemes will be more common than the introduction of new phonemes themselves.

The borrowing of a new phoneme is not very common and takes place only when there are large numbers of bilinguals speaking both the source and the borrowing language. The borrowed sound comes into the language within particular words and is accepted into the sound pattern of the language. Thus, the New English phoneme /ž/ as in *rouge* [ruːž] is not a descendant of any Old English phoneme, but is the result of a borrowing from French during the so-called Norman occupation (1066–1250), and still today occurs only in words of French origin.

One type of modern political situation which lends itself to large-scale borrowings even on the phonological level is the existence of the multinational state where more than one language may be recognized as official. In such situations, one of the official languages is usually the national means of intercommunication because of the political, social or numerical preponderance of its speakers. This language is then generally taught in all the schools, and generations of people grow up speaking both their native tongue and this national language. This is precisely the situation in a country like the Soviet Union, where numerous minority peoples in the member republics are allowed or encouraged to keep their own languages and develop their own literatures. At the same time, from a very early age, children begin the study of Russian as a second language, thus producing large numbers of bilinguals or near bilinguals. It should be obvious that large numbers of Russian loanwords enter the minority language, especially since Russian is not the only language of intercommunication among peoples of the Soviet Union, but it also forms the linguistic bridge with international scientific and cultural communities. These loanwords are often absorbed with the Russian pronunciation, which may contain sounds alien to the borrowing language.[6]

6 When a Russian word is borrowed into a minority language which uses the Cyrillic alphabet, Soviet custom requires that the word be written in

As an example consider the case of Kazakh, a Turkic language spoken in Soviet Central Asia. Kazakh has no native phoneme /f/, in the sense that there are no native Kazakh words with this sound. There are however, a number of borrowings which do contain /f/ in Russian and in speaking Kazakh, most speakers (since they know Russian) will tend to use the /f/ sound in borrowed words. Among such words are *flot* 'fleet' (← Russian *flot*), *filosof* 'philosopher' (← Russian *filosof*), *fizika* 'physics' (← Russian *fizika*). It is interesting to note that before there was extensive bilingualism in Kazakhstan, the native Kazakh phoneme /p/ was usually substituted for the /f/ in Russian borrowings. Thus, in the Kazakh of some forty years ago, the words given above would have been pronounced: /plot/, /pilosop/, and /pizika/.[7]

SYNTACTIC BORROWING

Perhaps even more unusual than phonological borrowing is the borrowing of syntactic forms or whole constructions. In English we have a few representatives of borrowed constructions, as in the legal terms *attorney general* and *court martial,* where the adjective follows the noun as it does in the source language, French. This served as a model for a few other titles such as *postmaster general.* This type of formation has remained more or less peripheral to English grammar.

One case of borrowing a very basic syntactic construction can be seen in the method of expressing "to have" in present-

Russian spelling, regardless of how it might be pronounced in the borrowing language. Many of the minority languages in the Soviet Union have had Cyrillic alphabets designed for them. Among these we might mention the Turkic language Kazakh, the Mongol language Buriat, and the Iranian language Tajik.

7 The same phenomenon can be seen in the living American Indian languages, which borrow extensively from English. In 1925 Bloomfield published some materials on Fox, an Algonquian language. In 1968, Voorhis gathered data on the same language at a Fox settlement in Iowa, and noted a number of changes which the language had undergone since Bloomfield's work. Among these was the fact that the English phonemes *f* and *v* had been borrowed into Fox via certain borrowed words as *fāmēha* 'farmer' and *tīvīhi* 'television set.'

day Russian. All the other Slavic languages usually use an
ordinary verb derived from the Common Slavic stem *ime-
'to have'. In Russian, however, while there is a verb *imet*ʸ
'to have', the ordinary way of expressing possession is by use
of the preposition *u* 'at, by' with the genitive. Thus,

u	menya	dengi.	
at	me (gen.)	money	'I have money'

In vain would we search the internal history of Russian or
its related languages to locate the origin of this construction.
In fact, its source is to be found outside Indo-European in
the Altaic or Finno-Ugric languages, where there is no verb
"to have," and possession is commonly expressed by a case
ending, such as the genitive, locative, or dative.

	van	nekem	egy	könyr.
Hungarian	there is	to me (dat.)	one	book.
				'I have a book'

	bende	para	var.	
Turkish	on me (loc.)	money	there is.	'I have money'

Another particularly striking example of syntactic borrowing involves the use of a particular Persian construction
(called the *izafet*) in Turkish. To link adjective and noun,
Turkish simply puts the adjective before the noun with no
sign of agreement or linking, as in:

akil   adam   'smart man'

Persian, however, has the reverse order; an adjective follows
a noun, and between the two is inserted the vowel *-e* (attached
to the noun). Thus,

Persian	ketab	-e	bozorg	
	book	-izafet	big	'big book'

```
Persian   mardan     -e      xub
          men       -izafet  good   'good men'
```

Because of a large number of Persian borrowings in Turkish during the Ottoman period, Turkish tended to adopt this construction (with -i replacing -e as the izafet marker), for use with Persian and Arabic loanwords. It was also used with native Turkish words, but this was frowned on by grammarians. However, its use was so common that Turkish words joined by an izafet became known as "the well-known mistakes." In other words, the izafet construction was part of Turkish grammar. Thus, it was perfectly possible to say in Turkish:

```
donanma    -i      hümayun
fleet      -izafet imperial  'the imperial fleet'
```

(*Donanma* 'fleet' is a native Turkish word, and should not be used in this construction.) The official language reformers of the twentieth century have attempted, with notable success, to remove the Persian izafet from Turkish as part of their general drive to "purge" the language of foreign elements.

FOR FURTHER STUDY

The most recent significant study of borrowing is Einar Haugen's "The Analysis of Linguistic Borrowing"; this is a rather complete article summing up previous knowledge as well as adding new facts and insights. Bloomfield distinguished three separate types of borrowing—intimate, cultural, and dialect; his discussion of these can be found in Chapters 25–27 of *Language*. Also worthwhile from the point of view of explanation and general theory is Chapter IX of Sapir's *Language*, "How Languages Influence Each Other." The most extensive general study of mutual influences of languages is Uriel Weinreich's *Languages in Contact*.

13

Social and Psychological Factors

In our study so far, we have attempted to look at language change as something basically internal to language systems. This approach, while extremely fruitful, still leaves certain problems. In many cases, the problems concern specific exceptions to the processes of linguistic change. We now seek other factors which should be taken into consideration when an attempt is made to account for all the facts connected with the history of a language.

DISCONTINUOUS TRANSMISSION

No matter how good our records are or how we try to formulate and reformulate our sound laws or other processes, there are some words in any language which stand out as exceptions. Among these are the so-called imitative or expressive words which speakers believe to imitate various natural sounds (also known as onomatopoetic words). Also part of the same group are interjections, including cries of anger, enjoyment, etc. It has long been recognized that these words were somehow resistant to the operation of sound laws. An example is the word for the cuckoo bird in Indo-European languages. Consider the Latin and Greek forms:

> Latin: cucu-lus
> Greek: kokku-ks

From Grimm's Law which was given previously (p. 110), the form we would expect in English and the other Germanic languages would be something like *huhu,* where there is the regular correspondence of Latin and Greek *k* to Germanic *h.* For some reason, this word has not undergone the normal sound change.

The solution to this problem lies in observing the way that languages are transmitted from one generation to the next. It involves what has been termed the *discontinuous transmission* of language. When a child learns his own language he is not presented with a grammar book from which he memorizes forms and explicit rules. Rather, he hears the people about him speaking and by some internal mechanism known as a *language acquisition device,* he abstracts from what he hears the rules of the grammar of his native language. The exact nature and complexity of the language acquisition device need not detain us here; it is currently a question of wide dispute and discussion among linguists, psychologists, and philosophers. Most of the words of a language then are transmitted over generations, with each generation perhaps adding variations which may modify the pronunciation of the words to a greater or lesser degree. The next generation then begins with these modifications and may extend them further.

This is the point at which the imitative and expressive words begin to differ from the rest of the lexicon. They are not as completely arbitrary as most of the words in the language. The signifiers are, in some sense, more closely tied to their signifieds. They are bound also by what we might call "appropriateness" and by the general structure of imitativeness or phonetic symbolism of the particular language.[1] Thus, these words have a value which does not reside exclusively in their being passed on from a previous generation; they are not entirely the products of history. In some way, we can say that they are created by each generation of speakers as the language itself is learned.

Thus, whatever the changes (gradual or abrupt) that Indo-European *k underwent in developing into English h, they have no effect on the word for "cuckoo" [kuku] simply be-

---

[1] Phonetic symbolism refers to the process whereby a given language selects certain phonemes or combinations of phonemes to carry specific expressive connotations. Thus, the cluster *fl-* in English is used in words expressing rapid movement, as in the words *flame, flicker, flash, flip,* etc. Note that phonetic symbolism is principally *language-specific;* it is not universal as we saw on p. 34, with our examples of dog barks in various languages.

cause each generation, on hearing the cuckoo bird, tried to imitate its call. Thus, while we know that the linguistic sign is arbitrary, it appears that at least for imitative words, it is somewhat less arbitrary. While different languages have different phonemes and groups of phonemes used for phonetic symbolism and imitativeness, no language has a dog that says anything like *miao* /miyau/, and so imitative words are *somewhat* constrained by the natural sounds they represent.

Another excellent example of this situation comes to us from Chinese. In Ancient Chinese (c. A.D. 600) there was a level tone in words beginning with both voiced and voiceless consonants. A sound shift later occurred in Chinese whereby the ancient level tone, whose exact phonetic properties need not concern us here, split into two tones in Modern Mandarin: the high (tone 1) and the rising (tone 2). This split was conditioned by the voicing of the initial consonant in the word. Where it was voiceless, the word acquired the modern high tone; where it was voiced, the word became the modern rising tone. Diagrammatically:

> tone 1 (from ancient voiceless initials)
> Ancient level tone
> tone 2 (from ancient voiced initials)

Still later, another sound change took place whereby the initial voiced stops and fricatives all became voiceless, but kept the developed tone. In formal terms the rules are as follows:

Ancient Chinese	Modern Mandarin
1. # C [− voice]	→ high tone (tone 1)
2. # C [+ voice]	→ rising tone (tone 2)
3. $\begin{bmatrix} \text{stops} \\ \text{fricatives} \\ + \text{voice} \end{bmatrix}$	→ [− voice]

Examples of these rules are:

tʰien		→	tʰien¹	'heaven'
dʰien → dʰien²		→	tʰien²	'field'
neng		→	neng²	'to be able'

Since there were no voiceless liquids or nasals in Ancient Chinese, we would not expect to find the first tone on modern words which begin with *m-, n-,* or *l-*. Words which began with *m-, n-,* and *l-* will have been affected by rule 2 and so gain the second tone. A check through any modern Chinese dictionary will show that it is true that there are very few words beginning with *m-, n-,* and *l-* in the first (high) tone.

Let us now make another observation. The tonal category of imitative words in modern Chinese is the first tone (tone 1). What this means is that, in some sense of phonetic symbolism, the modern Chinese first tone is the one which is formed on those words which "sound like" their referents. For example:

hou¹	'to snore'
śi¹	'to sob'
shən¹	'to groan'

Considering what we have said about transmission of imitative words, it is not surprising when we find that the only words beginning in *l-, m-,* and *n-* in the modern first tone are those which can be classified as imitative or expressive. Note the following examples of words which should be in the second tone according to the sound rule:

Ancient Chinese	Modern Chinese	
mau(r)	maur¹	'cat'
lie	lie¹	'sobbing of a child'
neng	neng¹	'babble'

In acquiring his native language every speaker of Chinese, over the last fourteen hundred years, re-created each of the imitative words in the first tone, regardless of the sound changes that might be occurring.

TABU

Another influence that may seem to interfere with our ideas of regular language change is that of social factors, the social attitude of the speech community toward particular linguistic forms. Most of the cases we will deal with can be subsumed under the headings of either *prestige* or *tabu*. Besides describing or classifying particular historical events, many times these factors provide a motivation or cause for the appearance, disappearance, and change of linguistic forms.

A linguistic *tabu* can be defined as the avoidance by a speech community of particular words for various social reasons. This avoidance usually has one of two results: the tabued word or an innocent homonym disappears entirely, or the tabued word or an innocent homonym is phonologically distorted. A word may be avoided for reasons connected with religion, superstition, personal respect, or societal attitudes towards bodily functions or other matters.

In human communities, a great, largely subconscious, importance is attached to the name of a thing, with the result that its mention might either offend someone or give the speaker power over the object named. Such practices are not limited exclusively to the so-called primitive societies, but are also present in our contemporary culture. A noted psychoanalyst recently pointed out that we often experience a spontaneous sense of relief when a physician is able to give our illness a name, whether or not a cure is readily available. By knowing the name of something, we have an unexplained feeling of somehow removing its mystery and thereby gaining control over it.

In another situation involving tabu, we tend to avoid pronouncing certain names as a sign of respect and substitute for them a title or euphemism. Thus, in our own society, one does not ordinarily speak of one's parents by name, but as "my mother" or "my father." This is done even when speaking with people of the parents' generation who would ordinarily call them by their given names. Also, in speaking to someone's son, say Alfred Newman, Jr., we do not ask about Alfred Newman, Sr., but rather refer to "your father." In Judeo-Christian culture, this tabu on the respected name is most strongly expressed in the second commandment: "Thou shalt not take the name of the Lord, thy God, in vain."

One of the most famous examples of lexical disappearance caused by tabu is the case of the Indo-European word for the *bear*. Consider the words for 'bear' in the following Indo-European languages:

Sanskrit	Greek	Latin	Old Church Slavonic	English
r̥kṣaḥ	arktos	ursus	medvedi	bear

We would be hard put to come up with phonological correspondence sets that would take into consideration all these forms. Indo-Europeanists generally posit the word *arktos* as the lexical item 'bear' in the parent language. This is the presumed ancestor of the Latin, Greek, and Sanskrit words. Our problem, then, is to explain the existence and origin of the Germanic and Slavic forms by looking outside the normal operation of sound laws, and turn our attention instead to the cultural situation of these two groups.

First, we note that geographically, these two branches of Indo-European are spoken in northern regions by people who were, at some point, hunters. So it appears likely that the name for the bear was tabued for fear of offending the beast or so that he might not hear his name and know he was being hunted. In its place another name was substituted which presumably the bear would not recognize. Germanic substitutes a word which originally meant simply "the brown one" (Common Germanic *ber- 'brown'; also Dutch *beer,* German *Bär*). In Slavic, a more descriptive title is provided, and a bear is spoken of as the "honey-eater" from the roots *medv-* (← Indo-European *madhu*) 'honey' and *ed-* (← Indo-European *ed-*) 'to eat'.

The idea of dropping an original name and substituting another one can be extended to a replacement by a complimentary or favorable appellation for the feared object. The sophisticated ancient Greeks called the Furies (Wreakers of Havoc) *eumenides* or 'well-minded ones' (← *eu-* 'good' + *menos* 'mind, spirit'). Undoubtedly this was done to placate them and somehow win their favor.

It is not always the case that a word under tabu will completely disappear from a language. As often as not it will be distorted in pronunciation to the extent that it can still be recognized, but does not carry the social disapproval of its original form. Thus, in 1948, an American writer wishing to use a common word, undoubtedly known by all his readers and often used by a majority of them, felt himself constrained to write *fug*. By voicing the last consonant of the spoken word in question he had achieved a sufficient likeness to insure understanding, and yet had achieved a sufficient difference to get past his censors.

If we look for the origin of the word *bunny* as in *bunny rabbit,* we will find an Old English word *coni*. Because of the similarity of the *coni* with an obscene word, the word meaning "rabbit" was distorted to *bunny*. (The substitution of /b/ for /k/ here is indeed unusual, and perhaps is to be explained by the proximity of the letters *b* and *c* in the normal order of the alphabet.) Our New English word *bunny* has completely lost all obscene connotations. One can only speculate on the future of the word *pussy,* as in *pussycat*.

One case of a tabu distortion resulting in a metathesis is found in the history of the Latin word *stercus* /sterkus/ 'ordure'. We know that this comes from an Indo-European root of the form **skat-* (e.g., Greek *skat-os,* English *shit* ← Old English **scit-*). Because of the unpleasant connotations of the word involved, Latin reversed the positions of the *t* and the *k*.

Bloomfield has remarked that when there are two homonyms, or near homonyms, in a language, and one of them becomes tabued, the tabued word will often live on in popular speech while the innocent homonym is distorted or dropped from the language, at least in certain situations. Thus, in Middle English there were two phonologically distinct words *arse* 'anus' and *ass* 'donkey'; in 1721, a new pronunciation for *arse* is noted, namely /ass/. Somewhat later, this form came to be the accepted pronunciation and still lives on with us unchanged.[2] The hapless new homonym, which was only the name of an animal, is now avoided (being generally replaced by *donkey*) unless we wish to be insulting or humorous. The tabued word lives on unchanged in popular speech.

Certain cultures have gone farther than others in the establishment of tabus. In many societies which are highly dependent on hunting and fishing, men may develop a particular code to be used during hunting or fishing expeditions which substitutes "harmless" expressions for the name of the quarry (presumably so as not to alert the beast to its hunters' intentions). Perhaps the most extreme case of tabu is that found in certain Australian languages, where a whole language is tabued in particular social situations. Thus, a language such as Dyirbal may be said to possess two lexicons, the "normal" language and the "mother-in-law" language. One uses the normal language in everyday communication except when speaking to or about one's mother-in-law, in which case a completely different vocabulary must be substituted.[3] In sum, then, tabu has two principle effects on the

[2] This is not necessarily true of all dialects of British English. In northern regions of England at least, the normal pronunciation of *arse* is [ars].

[3] Among certain peoples it is the custom to give as personal names the names of animals or natural objects. If this practice is accompanied by a tabu on names of the dead, it is obvious that changes in the vocabulary will be frequent and widespread. In *The Golden Bough*, Frazier cites several such cases, and an especially clear one may be quoted:

> A similar custom [of tabuing the names of the dead] used to be constantly transforming the language of the Abipones of Paraguay, amongst whom, however, a word once abolished seems never to have been revived. New words, says the missionary Dobrizhoffer, sprang up every year like mushrooms in a night, because all words that resembled the names of the dead were abolished by proclamation and others coined in their place. The mint of words was in the hands of the old women of the tribe, and whatever term they

processes of language change: disappearance and distortion, and these may affect either the tabued word itself or some harmless homonym.

PRESTIGE

The importance of social prestige in accounting for the acceptance and spread of new linguistic forms cannot be over-estimated. In the last analysis, people will tend to adopt linguistic habits different from their own only when they feel that in some way these other habits are "better." As with most human institutions, what constitutes a better item is defined by the higher social prestige of the individuals who use that item. Thus, the prestige factor might be looked upon primarily as a cause or reason for linguistic borrowing, whether across language or across dialect boundaries.

Across language boundaries, we see this quite clearly throughout history. For the past several centuries, the supposed superiority of French culture has led speakers of many other languages not only to learn French, but also to gild conversations in their native languages with French words and expressions. Even today, one can hear dialogues among the moderately educated studded with expressions such as *je ne sais quoi* or *joie de vivre*. In many of the world's cultures, nowadays, English has replaced French as the source of prestigious loanwords, which are reflections of the Anglo-

---

stamped with their approval and put in circulation was immediately accepted without a murmur by high and low alike, and spread like wildfire through every camp and settlement of the tribe. You would be astonished, says the same missionary, to see how meekly the whole nation acquiesces in the decision of a withered old hag, and how completely the old familiar words fall instantly out of use and are never repeated either through force of habit or forgetfulness. In the seven years that Dobrizhoffer spent among these Indians the native word for jaguar was changed thrice, and the words for crocodile, thorn, and the slaughter of cattle underwent similar though less varied vicissitudes. As a result of this habit, the vocabularies of the missionaries teemed with erasures, old words having constantly to be struck out as obsolete and new ones inserted in their place.

American technological, social and perhaps political achievements.

Within a given language area or speech community, there will almost invariably be some kind of social stratification, and if one wishes to identify with (and perhaps enter) a higher social class, one of the first requirements is to adopt its customs, including the manner of speaking. On the simplest and most obvious level, this will include the borrowing of words, as in the case of people who choose to call their *sofa* a *davenport* because they think that upper-class people use the word *davenport*. And the number of *ain'ts* lost on the ladder of social climbing is probably incalculable. The pronunciation of individual lexical items also can be affected by prestige factors. Thus, the pronunciation of words like *tomato* as /tomeyto/ or *vase* as /veys/ may be replaced by /tomato/ or /vaz/. In a similar vein, many might want to shift the pronunciation of *either* from /iðər/ to /ayðər/. Again, the reason for the replacement lies in the fact that the person who does change his pronunciation somehow feels that someone else's speech is more elegant.

A study made in 1933 showed that on Martha's Vineyard, in words like *right, might,* and *nice,* certain Islanders retained a feature of an older pronunciation in that they pronounced the diphthongs in these words [əy] as opposed to the general Eastern American [ay]. Essentially, this [əy] occurred only before voiceless dentals. Many upper-class people have summer homes on Martha's Vineyard, and one might expect that the Islanders' native dialect would be influenced by the standard Eastern pronunciation of these visitors, and that the [əy] would eventually disappear.

In fact, quite the reverse has taken place. Within this society, the prestige group was not identified with the upper crust easterners, but rather with the native island "Yankees." As a result, in a survey made some thirty years later, it was found that not only had the [əy] pronunciation not disappeared, but had in fact spread to other words which previously had [ay]. Thus words like *life,* and *wife* were now heard with [əy]. The [ə] had even replaced the [a] in the diphthong [aw] in *house* and *out,* which were now pronounced [hǝws] and [ǝwt]. In addition a great deal of fluctuation between [ǝy] ∼ [ay] and [ǝw] ∼ [aw] was noted in many words.

What this case shows is that the identification of the "prestige" group as far as linguistic change is concerned cannot be made without specific knowledge of societies. We need this purely sociological information in order to understand the direction of certain changes.

Another interesting case of the spread of a "prestige" pronunciation being resisted by some speakers is the case of the name of the Japanese city Nagoya. In the local dialect the name of the city is pronounced /nagóya/ with accent on the second syllable. In the Tokyo dialect, which is the standard language for the whole country, the city is called /nágoya/ with accent on the first syllable. As the Tokyo dialect spreads at the expense of the local dialects through the means of radio, TV, universal education, etc., speakers in the area surrounding Nagoya are giving up the local pronunciation for the prestige of the Tokyo one. However, in the city itself, the fierce pride of the local inhabitants has prevented them from adopting the standard pronunciation for the name of *their own* city. As a result this curious isogloss exists:

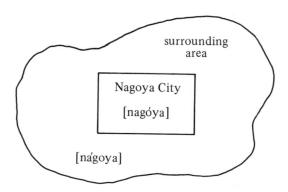

FOLK ETYMOLOGIES

As we have mentioned previously, the linguistic sign is arbitrary; there is no particular reason why a word should mean what it does (p. 33). In the first section of this chapter, we saw that imitative words were perhaps somewhat less arbitrary than others since they are constrained by the phonetic symbolism as well as by the natural sounds they try to imitate. In some real sense, compound words can also be considered to be somewhat motivated, to be less arbitrary than simple words. Take the example of the word *mailbox*. If asked why that word means what it does, one can reply that it is composed of the words *mail* and *box,* and it is a *box* where one puts *mail*. We have etymologized the word *mailbox* to known English roots and in some sense have explained the connection between the signified and the signifier.

Of course, if people ask the same question about the individual words *mail* and *box,* the situation is radically different. If we know nothing about language history, we can make no serious reply. If we are linguists, we can only answer that those words mean what they do to us because they meant certain things to people who spoke English before us and so on back throughout the history of the words *mail* and *box*. In both a scientific and a popular sense, this type of explanation is much less satisfying than that given for the compound word. In other words, these simple words are unmotivated, whereas some motivation can be found for the compound.

We noted in Chapter 2 (p. 25) that etymologizing has long been a trait of human beings who have reflected on language, and this is probably a manifestation of a simple human desire to know "why." Some etymologizing will take place on an unconscious level; longer words will be subject to being etymologized by connecting their parts with known words in the language. We have then a phenomenon known as *folk etymology*, whereby polysyllabic words are broken down into identifiable smaller parts which may or may not reflect their true history. The compound word is then restructured to show openly the parts of which it is felt to be composed. In Orr's formulation: ". . . words broken away from their etymological moorings and . . . which have become mere arbitrary, nonmotivated signs . . . become exposed to associative etymology."

Most obviously, this takes place with long borrowed words, whose component parts are unknown to the speakers of the borrowing language. For example, the Old English form of the word *mandrake* is *mandragora* (borrowed from Greek *mandragoras*). Because this longish word couldn't be understood as consisting of English roots and perhaps also because people saw a human form in the plant itself, the word was falsely etymologized to consist of the English roots *man* and *drake* and recompounded from these two words.

Note that the association between two words in a folk etymology is primarily phonological and no semantic connection is necessary. Thus the *pole-* in English *polecat* derives from the French word *poule* 'chicken' (because the animal in question kills chickens) and in Middle English was written *pulcat*. The syllable *pul-* had no identifiable meaning in this word and was replaced by *pole-*. The word *pole* has, of course, no semantic connection with the animal itself. The New English word *outrage* most of us would automatically etymologize to the two words *out* and *rage* 'fury'. In fact, its origin is in Old French *oultrage* 'excess, extravagance', which is compounded (ultimately) from Latin *ultrā* 'beyond' with the noun suffix *-agium*. An example from German is *Armbrust* 'crossbow' from late Latin *ar(cu)ballista*, but reanalyzed as *Arm* 'weapon' + *Brust* 'chest'.

The story is told of the hapless King Ethelred (ruler of England from 978 to 1016), who posthumously had an indifferent epithet folk-etymologized to one that was quite uncomplimentary. Because the king followed the probably praiseworthy course of seldom assembling his council, he acquired the nickname *rædleas* (← Old English *ræd* 'council' plus *leas* 'without'). Eventually the word *ræd* ceased to be used in English and was replaced by the French borrowing *council*. The morpheme *ræd* was associated with the word *ready*, and Ethelred is known to history as Ethelred the Unready.

One last type of folk etymology that we might mention is the occasional false division of phrases. In English this is seen in the surprising disappearance of the letter *n-* from the beginnings of certain words. For example:

Middle English	New English
nadder	adder
nauger	auger
napron	apron

This is due to a misinterpretation of the boundary between the indefinite article (*an* before vowels) and the following word.[4]

LEARNED ETYMOLOGIZING

Another cause of change in particular words which is somewhat different from folk etymologies is the case of learned false etymologizing. Basically, the difference between this latter process and the folk etymologies is that the folk etymologies originate in unconscious sound associations and appear first in the spoken language. Learned etymologies originate when a scribe or group of scribes consciously conclude that they have found a more correct way of *spelling* some particular word. "More correct" is based on what

[4] We have already seen a situation of false interpretation of boundaries across linguistic borders in the case of the Spanish article *al-* being incorporated in Arabic nouns as they are borrowed into Spanish (p. 187).

they know or think to be the history of the word or its previous spelling. Sometimes, these learned etymologies remain only as orthographic convention, but sometimes they also emerge into the spoken language.

One of the most famous examples is the "reformed" spelling of the New English word *delight*. This word was borrowed from Old French *deliter,* and up until the early sixteenth century was spelled *delite* in Middle English. Eventually, one or more scribes came to believe that this word was related to the native English word *light* (← Old English *lēoht*) and therefore should be spelled with a *-gh-*. Since the *-gh-* had already "become silent"[5] in English, this change in spelling had no effect on the pronunciation of the word.

A similar case is seen in the histories of the English words *doubt* and *debt*. These appear in Middle English as *douten* (borrowed from Old French *douter*) and *dette* (borrowed from Old French *dette*). The letter *-b-* was introduced into the spelling of these words by scribes who knew that the origin of the French forms were the Latin words *dubitum* and *debitum*. Again, this did not affect the pronunciation of the words in that the reintroduced *-b-* has remained "silent." This is probably due to the fact that the cluster *bt* is otherwise unknown in English. In New English orthography it is found only in these words and their derivatives such as *debtor* and *doubtless*.

The cases we have examined above were situations where a learned etymology entered the written language but had no effect on the spoken language. But it sometimes happens that after a learned spelling has become widespread among the populace, they tend to pronounce the word in accordance with the new spelling; we call this phenomenon of limited sound change a *spelling pronunciation*.

---

[5] "Become silent" or "be silent" are the popular terms which refer to the fact that a sound has ceased to be spoken either unconditionally or in a particular context and the spelling of the word has not caught up with the sound change and so reflects an obsolete pronunciation. The sound written *-gh-* as in *light, night, fight*, etc. was a voiceless velar fricative [x] and ceased to be pronounced in London English during the seventeenth century.

For example, in 1382, we find the word *autentick,* attested in English, which was in turn in a borrowing from Old French *autentique.* As knowledge of Greek increased, scribes became aware that the ultimate origin of the word was the Ancient Greek *authentikos,* and so in 1630 we find the spelling *authentique,* and in 1682 *authentick.* Needless to say, the pronunciation of the word changed and the normal reading of English *-th-* [θ] replaced the *t* [t] in this word. An almost identical case concerns the English word *throne.* Until the middle of the fourteenth century, this word was spelled *trone* (from Old French *trone*), and presumably pronounced with an initial [tr-]. By the end of the fourteenth century, scribes became aware of the original Greek spelling *thronos;* as this new spelling spread and became accepted, [t] was replaced eventually by [θ] in spoken English.

A relatively baffling case is presented by the spelling *author,* with a [θ] in the middle of the word. The word finds its immediate origin in Old French *autor,* which in turn comes from Latin *auctor.* And for awhile, some scribes knowing Latin wrote in the *c,* but we do not know whether or not this affected its pronunciation. Much more important and of definitely obscure origin was the appearance of the *-h-* in this word during the fifteenth and sixteenth centuries in both French and English, since the spelling with a *-th-* has no etymological justification at all. Nonetheless, the spelling with *-th-* became accepted in English, and thereupon followed the pronunciation with [θ].

FOR FURTHER STUDY

The fact that social factors influence linguistic change is fairly obvious. Perhaps the best attempt to integrate them solidly and scientifically into historical linguistic theory is the article by Weinreich, Labov, and Hertzog: "Empirical Foundations for a Theory of Language Change." Appended to this article is an excellent bibliography. The original study of the vowel change on Martha's Vineyard appeared in an article by Labov, "The Social Motivation of a Sound Change." Chapter 22 of Bloomfield's *Language,* "Fluctuations in Forms," attempts to classify items which look like exceptions of neogrammarian principles of sound change.

The influence of tabu on linguistic change is clearly limited to a small section of the language; nonetheless it is extremely interesting because it reflects the values of a particular speech community. The classic study of the animal name tabu is Meillet's "Quelques hypothèses sur des interdictions de vocabulaire dans les langues indo-européenes." A recent, precise study of how a tabued word caused "non-regular" developments in innocent homonyms is Stimson's "A Tabu Word in the Peking Dialect."

Perhaps the most extensive study of folk etymologies and back-formations is Houtzager's *Unconscious Sound- and Sense-Assimilations.* Drawing on data from four languages (English, French, Dutch, and German), Houtzager gives a wealth of examples of these processes.

14

Generative Grammar

The impact of generative grammar on linguistic research within the past decade or so cannot be underestimated. While most generative studies have been aimed at descriptive and theoretical models, some work has been done on the phenomena of language change. Generative grammar represents what is essentially "a new way" of looking at and describing languages. Its models were developed from intensive and detailed work on small parts of living languages. We could not hope to do justice to these in the small amount of space available here. In addition, there is a legitimate question of whether generative grammar adds anything to our understanding of language change and whether when we express historical facts in generative terms we are merely translating or reinterpreting things already known within a new framework. Since many students of linguistics are trained in generative grammar, it is only appropriate that we should point out some of the ways that facts of language change can be stated in generative terms.

There are several different schools of generative grammar in existence at any moment; most of them find their origin in the work of Noam Chomsky and his associates. We will try first to outline some of the generally accepted principles concerning the organization and structure of synchronic grammatical descriptions. In generative terms a grammar, or description of a language, consists of three principal components: phonology, syntax, and semantics. To these is added a fourth element, the lexicon or vocabulary of the language; the relationship of the lexicon to the other components of the grammar is somewhat obscure at the present moment. Diagrammatically, we might represent the structure of a generative grammar as follows:

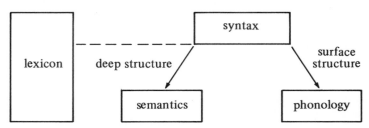

The central (= starting) component is the syntax. Here we begin with the symbol S (sentence or complete utterance) from which we derive all the acceptable sentences of a language. As the arrows show, the syntactic component has two outputs: the one that enters the semantic component is called the *deep structure* and contains all the information necessary for the semantic interpretation or understanding of the sentence; the output that enters the phonological component is called the *surface structure* and contains all lexical and grammatical elements arranged in proper order. Though their natures are not completely understood, each component is essentially a series of rules which characterize or describe the knowledge a speaker has of his own language.

The syntactic component is divided into two separate parts. One part, known as the *base,* produces deep-structure trees which show the meaning of a sentence, more specifically, the relations of one element of the sentence to another. The second part, known as the transformational section, contains rules which add, delete, and rearrange elements to produce grammatical sentences. A sample sentence will perhaps show how the processes of syntactic derivation work. Consider:

Carol read the book which Catherine bought.

We start off with the symbol S (sentence) and note that in English a sentence consists of a noun phrase followed by a verb phrase. In formal notation the rule is written:

$$S \rightarrow NP + VP$$

Furthermore, the verb phrase consists of a verb and its object (another noun phrase). Formally,

$$VP \rightarrow V + NP$$

We now have two noun phrases in the sentence; the first consists of a single noun (*Carol*) and the second contains an article (*the*), a noun (*book*) and a relative clause (*which Catherine bought*). It takes only a moment's thought to realize that the relative clause, in terms of its meaning, is actually a whole sentence, essentially equivalent to "Catherine bought the book." Now, we want to express this in our deep structure. We also want to express in our rules the fact that the definite article and sentences which become relative clauses are optional elements in a noun phrase. Essentially, this means that any given noun phrase may or may not have them and yet still be a complete noun phrase. We express optionality by the use of parentheses, and thus can draw up a rule for forming noun phrases:

$$NP \rightarrow (\text{article}) \ N \ (S)$$

Following these rules we can build a deep-structure tree:

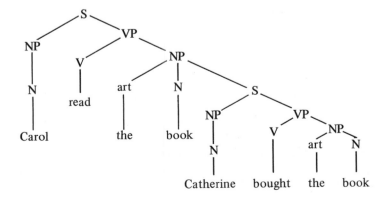

The derivation of the sentence is still not complete because we do not yet have the surface sentence. To achieve that level, we now turn to the transformational part of the grammar, which describes the difference between the deep and the surface structures. We note the following differences: in the relative clause the object of the verb has been moved to the front of the sentence and has been replaced by the relative pronoun *which*. We therefore need a transformational rule which will do precisely this. In formal terms, we describe the structure we start with (the deep structure) and then link this with an arrow to the structure which we end with (the surface structure). We can call this rule simply the relative transformation. For those familiar with the formal notation of generative grammar, the rule might be written as follows:

$$N_1 \, N_2 \, V \, art. \, N_3 \rightarrow N_1 \, which \, N_2 \, V$$

Conditions: 1. $N_2 \, V \, N_3$ form a sentence S_2.
2. N_1 and S_2 are part of the same noun phrase.
3. N_1 and N_3 have the same reference.

Putting our concrete example in the slots provided by the rule we have:

N_1	N_2	V	art.	N_3
book	Catherine	bought	the	book

The rule then transforms this into:

book which Catherine bought.

The phonological component of a generative grammar is also a set of rules. These rules operate on base forms of morphemes and produce a given phonetic output. Some of these rules (the morpheme structure rules) tell us the possible phonetic shape of morphemes in a particular language. Thus, English has a morpheme structure rule which says that a word may not begin with a stop consonant followed by a fricative;

in other words, the clusters *ts-* and *pf-* do not appear at the beginnings of English words. The other rules (morphophonemic rules) tell us exactly how certain phonemes are pronounced in particular environments. Thus, one rule would tell us that in a word like *dogs,* the plural morpheme (*-s*) is pronounced [z]. Another rule would tell us to voice the final consonant in the plural stems of words like *leaf* and *wife* (plurals *leav-es* and *wiv-es,* respectively). Diagrammatically we can look upon the phonological component as follows:

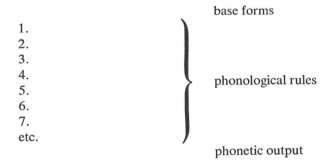

base forms

1.
2.
3.
4.
5.
6.
7.
etc.

phonological rules

phonetic output

The lexicon of a language is the list of all the morphemes in the language, together with information about the usage of each. Generative grammarians have tried to develop formal models of the exact type and form of this "information." Generally, it is said to consist of three parts:

1. Phonological information: the base form and marks relating to application of phonological rules. Ideally each morpheme of the language would be entered in the lexicon with a single base form. Thus, a word like *wife* would be written something like /wayf/; in addition this word would bear a marker which would tell us that a rule applies to this morpheme which voices the final consonant before the plural ending is added.

2. Semantic information: what the word means.

3. Syntactic information: how a word is used in forming sentences. This would consist of giving the part of speech, of

telling whether a particular word is a noun or a verb, etc. If it is a verb we would expect to find here some marker telling us whether it is transitive or intransitive. If it is a noun, we would expect to find information on whether it is a count noun or a mass noun, i.e., whether or not we can put a numeral in front of it. (Note the difference between the noun *table* (a count noun), for which we can say *one table, two tables,* etc., and the noun *water·* (a mass noun), for which such enumeration is not possible.)

Ideally, this information is contained in the form of marks or minimal contrasting units of the particular level of information, although the exact shape of these marks for all three parts of a lexical entry is by no means agreed upon, and in some instances, such as semantics, the nature of the marks has not been treated beyond a small section of the vocabulary, such as kinship systems.

After this brief sketch of synchronic generative grammar, we shall proceed to examine precisely the way the generative grammarian looks at language change. For the generative grammarian, the historical events which are of interest are changes in the grammar itself, and not changes in the surface forms.

Take the example we have already given of the loss of k between $\#$ and n in English (p. 191). In a more traditional view, the fact that k disappeared in this position is considered as being an historical event. For the generative grammarian, the significant event was the fact that a rule of the type $k \rightarrow \emptyset \: / \: \# \text{ ___ } n$ was at some point added to the history of English. This example illustrates clearly what the generative grammarian's point of view is and what type of information he is trying to extract from the data of language change. Essentially, he is trying to describe changes in the *grammar* of the language.

SIMPLE PHONOLOGICAL CHANGE

Within a generative framework, what we have previously called sound change is considered to be the result of addition, deletion, or reordering of rules in the phonological component of the grammar. There is one further possibility that should be taken in consideration, and that is the restructuring of a base form. Let us consider these processes one by one.

The simplest type of sound change involves the addition of a phonological rule. Thus, in Old High German, there were voiced stops at the ends of words; *Bad* 'bath' was pronounced [bad]. In Modern German there are no voiced stops before a word boundary on the phonetic level, though such voiced stops may be present in underlying (morphophonemic) representation.

In terms of generative theory, what has happened is that a new phonological rule has been added to the grammar of German, and this rule is of the form

$$\begin{bmatrix} - \text{ continuant} \\ + \text{ voice} \end{bmatrix} \rightarrow [- \text{ voice}] \ / \ \_\_ \ \#$$

In Modern German then, the word *Bad* has the same underlying representation that it had in Old High German, however it is pronounced [bat] due to the presence of the new rule.

When a phonological rule has been added to the grammar it alters the output (actual pronunciation) of items. Certain morphonemic alternations may preserve the original base form in the language. Thus, Turkish added to its grammar a rule similar to the German rule above. When this rule was added to the grammar of Turkish, a word like *ad* 'name' came to be pronounced *at*. However, as we can see in the contemporary paradigms given below, because of alternations in the paradigms the original base form of *ad* has not been changed.[1]

at	'horse'	at	'name'
at-ïn	'of the horse'	ad-ïn	'of the name'
at-ï	'his horse'	ad-ï	'his name'

[1] The phonetic symbol *ï* represents a high, back, unrounded vowel, i.e., a vowel pronounced in the same position as [u], but without a rounding of the lips. In normal Turkish orthography, it is written *ı* (i without a dot on it).

Obviously, in a description of contemporary Turkish we would want to set up our base forms as:

at   'horse'   ad   'name'

To these forms then the phonological rule given above would apply synchronically to yield the correct phonetic output.

When, however, there are no morphophonemic alternations which would in any way preserve the old base forms, there is a restructuring of the base form. When Grimm's Law took effect between Indo-European and Common Germanic

$$\begin{bmatrix} p \\ t \\ k \end{bmatrix} \rightarrow \begin{bmatrix} f \\ p \\ x \end{bmatrix}$$

words such as IE *ped- 'foot' became Common Germanic *fōt-. It would make no sense to say that the Common Germanic base form contained a p since the original sound is nowhere seen or preserved in alternations (as was true in the case of the Turkish paradigm given above). What has happened is that the base form of the word had been restructured. The optimal lexical (morphophonemic) representation of 'foot' in Common Germanic is *fōt-. In strictly generative terms, we would have to say that a rule (Grimm's Law) was added to the grammar of the Germanic languages. The forms that were affected by this rule were restructured. Lastly, the rule itself was deleted from the grammar because it no longer had any forms to apply to.

Another example of rule loss and restructuring would be the case of the Latin rhotacism which we have already seen (p. 131). We start off with the pre-Latin paradigm, where everything appears to be regular:

*honos
*honos-is
*honos-i

At some point in time a rule is added to the grammar of Latin:

$$s \rightarrow r\ /\ V \_\_ V$$

We can thus say that in the Old Latin period, the lexicon of Latin contains the underlying form *honos,* to which this rule is applied in the proper cases, thus yielding the Old Latin paradigm:

> honos
> honor-is
> honor-i

By the time of Classical Latin, we find that the form *honos* ceased to exist in Latin. *Honos* was replaced by the form *honor.* In addition, we can say that the rhotacism rule (at least so far as this word is concerned) has been dropped from the grammar. In generative terms, we say that the form *honos* has been *restructured* to *honor,* and the rule of rhotacism has been deleted since it no longer has a form to apply to. Thus, in the Classical Latin period we again have a "regular" paradigm to which no morphophonemic rules apply.

> honor
> honor-is
> honor-i

DISTINCTIVE FEATURES

It goes without saying that any of the phonetic symbols traditionally used would, in a generative study, be replaced by a rigidly defined system of distinctive features in an attempt to capture generalities in sound change. Distinctive feature theory is a contribution of the Prague School to general linguistic theory. According to this view, each phoneme of a language is made up of a bundle of particular traits or distinctive features. These features can be defined either in terms of articulation or in terms of acoustic properties which can be seen on a sound spectrogram. A phoneme is marked as either having (+) or not having (−) a particular feature. For example, two of the features generally posited are the vocalic feature and the consonantal feature. Vowels are [+ vocalic] and [− consonantal], most consonants are [− vocalic] and [+ consonantal]; the liquids (*l* and *r*) are [+ vocalic] and [+ consonantal]; and the glides (*w* and *y*) are [− vocalic] and [− consonantal]. One very important aspect of distinctive-feature theory is the fact that the phonemic systems of all the world's languages can be described using a remarkably small number of features, approximately fifteen. It should also be noted that the names and numbers of features will vary from linguist to linguist, though those of Jakobson and Halle used in our example below seem to be the most useful and durable.

The use of distinctive features often does make certain odd-looking changes emerge as a simple shift of a single feature. Thus, from Latin to Rumanian we have a shift $k \to p,$ before *t* or *s,* as can be seen from the following words:

Latin	Rumanian	
lactum	lapte	'milk'
coxa [koksa]	coapsa	'hip'
factum	fapt	'done'
noctem	noapte	'night'

In the traditional understanding of sound change, the shift from *k* to *p* presented certain difficulty. How, after all, could a sound made at the velum change to one which is articulated at the other end of the mouth? If it were a case of gradual movement from one position to the other, why did not this wandering *k* bump into and become confused with *t* somewhere on its journey?

For the generative grammarian's answer, let us assume a feature system such as in Jakobson and Halle where the oppositions *grave/acute* and *compact/diffuse* are distinctive for consonants.[2]

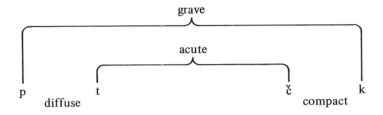

Which results in the following (partial) distinctive feature chart:[3]

	p	t	k
continuant	—	—	—
voiced	—	—	—
grave	+	—	+
compact	—	—	+

The shift, then, from *k* to *p* is seen not as some sort of wandering across the roof of the mouth from back to front,

[2] In articulatory terms, the features grave-acute can be read as central vs. peripheral, and compact-diffuse can be read as back vs. front. Thus, given the four points of articulation as they are located in the mouth, we have in the order (front-to-back):

| labial | dental | palatal | velar |

Labials and velars form the class of grave consonants since they are articulated at the two extremes of the possible positions; dentals and palatals are acute in that they are formed at the central positions. From the point of view of relative front-back position in the mouth, we have a different classification. Here the palatals and velars go together as forming the class of back (compact) consonants, while the front (noncompact or diffuse) class consists of the labials and dentals.

[3] For purposes of this chart, we have chosen, perhaps arbitrarily, the features grave and compact to designate the oppositions in question. Thus [− grave] is equivalent to [+ acute], and [− compact] equals [+ diffuse].

but is instead a simple change of one feature in a particular environment:

$$\begin{bmatrix} - \text{ continuant} \\ - \text{ voiced} \\ + \text{ compact} \end{bmatrix} \rightarrow [- \text{ compact}] \; / \; \_\_ \begin{bmatrix} - \text{ compact} \\ + \text{ acute} \end{bmatrix}$$

The other features including noncontinuance, voicing, gravity, etc., are not affected.

SIMPLIFICATION AND ANALOGY

Within the framework of generative grammar, most of what we have spoken of as being due to analogy can be subsumed under the rubric of grammar simplification. Simplification basically involves deletions, either of marks on particular items in the lexicon and/or of rules in the phonological component. The fewer exceptions or irregular forms that exist in a language, the fewer marks and rules will be needed to account for them. The grammar with fewer rules and special marks is in some vaguely defined, intuitive sense "simpler." Let us see how this would operate on our example of the Old English plurals (pp. 132–135). First of all, in the synchronic grammar of Old English, nouns would have to be divided into "classes," and we would need a series of rules to account for the different plural formations:

1. pl. → -*a* in class X nouns
2. pl. → -*an* in class Y nouns
3. pl. → ϕ in class Z nouns

In addition, each noun would have to be marked in the lexicon as to which class it belonged. Thus, *hand* 'hand' plural *handa* would be marked [+ class X], *eage* 'eye' plural *eagan* would be marked [+ class Y], and *gear* 'year' plural *gear* would be marked [+ class Z]. These marks of particular classes would be used to trigger the appropriate plural formation rule 1, 2, or 3. Since the nouns which formed their plural in *-as* (later *-es, -s*) formed the largest class in the language we assume that these formed an unmarked class. In other words, in Old English where there is no class marker to trigger a specific rule, the general rule, {pl} → *-as,* would apply. The rules which apply to words not otherwise marked are called *major rules;* those which require a specific mark on a lexical item to trigger their operation are called *minor rules.* In many senses, the notions "major" and "minor" concerning rules may be considered to be equivalent to what has been traditionally termed "productive" and "nonproductive" processes (p. 138).

It is also true that according to our present understanding of complexity in a grammar, the more highly marked a lexicon must be, the more complex it is. Therefore, in this sense at least, the reduction of marks on lexical items would be a simplification of the grammar. This is exactly what we have in the case of the evolution of the modern English plurals.

As the plural *-as* (and its descendants) spread in the speech of English speakers, what was the exact change in the grammatical rules and in the lexicon? Consider first the lexicon. The nouns which previously had to bear a mark as belonging to a specific class lost this mark. Thus, *hand* lost its mark [+ class X], and *eage* lost its mark [+ class Y], since the plural of both nouns could now be predicted from the general or major rule.

With regard to the morphophonemics, when all nouns requiring a particular plural formation had lost the given mark, then the rule was deleted from the grammar. Thus, in New English, there are no nouns which form a plural in *-a,* so we can assume that the rule has been deleted from the grammar. (We are ignoring the case of the borrowings from Latin and Greek, such as Latin *datum,* plural *data,* Greek *phenomenon,* plural *phenomena.* In the grammar of educated speakers, these words would be marked as [+ Latin] or

[+ Greek] and would be accompanied by the original Latin and Greek rules of plural formation.)

A rule might remain for some time as a very minor rule affecting only a few items. This would be the case of rule 2, which now is restricted to one lexical item, namely *ox,* plural *oxen.* (The New English plurals *children* and *brethren* would be created by a different rule.)

So we see now that our grammar has been simplified by the loss of special marks on individual items in the lexicon and the loss of rules. Such an explanation as we have given for the spread of the English plural could be applied to numerous other cases in which we see the spread of the regular form and the restriction or disappearance of irregular items.

SYNTAX

Generative studies in syntactic change, or change in the syntactic component of a grammar are not extensive. Certain schools of transformational grammar tend towards the notion that a great deal of syntax is universal and therefore would not be subject to any kind of change. Such a presumed universality would exist primarily in the base component of the syntax, the part that gives the primary structures and the grammatical relationships between the words of a sentence.

Nonetheless, certain very obvious observations about syntactic change can be made, and some of those developments which we considered before under analogy or change cf grammatical systems can be reinterpreted within the framework of a generative grammar. As a first example, consider the case of the position of the verb in subordinate clauses in the history of English (p. 147). We saw that in Old English the verb in a subordinate clause came at the end of that clause as in the example:

þæt	synd	þā	ðe	þæt	word	gehȳra	ð
these	are	those	that	that	word	heard	

Since the presence of the verb at the end of the clause is purely automatic and carries no specific meaning, we would assign this sentence an intermediate structure something like:

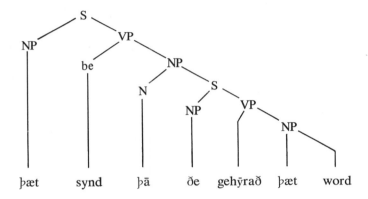

Then there would be the operation of a transformational rule of the following type (where X and Y are variables and V is the verb):

$$[\ X \ V \ Y \ ]_s \rightarrow X \ Y \ V$$

Condition: This sentence is embedded in a higher sentence.

If we accept this to be the synchronic situation in Old English, then the change to New English can be described very simply: the transformational rule which shifts a verb to the end of a subordinate clause has been deleted from the grammar of English.

Another example of rule loss can be found in those languages which have lost inflectional cases and are now dependant on word order to indicate grammatical relationships. We saw previously (p. 152) the shift from Latin to Italian. In Latin it might be said that there was a trans-

formational rule of *scrambling,* which allowed one to put the
subject, verb, and object in different positions in order to
achieve certain stylistic or emphatic effects. With the loss of
case endings, that rule has been deleted from the grammar.
Lest anyone think that this means that everything in the
language is now simpler, consider what has replaced the
scrambling rule for indication of emphasis. Where one can
no longer emphasize a particular word by its position in
a sentence, one now uses much more sophisticated and less
obvious devices, such as phonological stress in English or
the French habit of "drawing out" or pronouncing slowly
and carefully each syllable of the emphasized word.

Another case of the deletion of a rule from the syntactic
component would be the deletion of the agreement rules,
whereby adjectives agree with the nouns they modify. In
Old English, we had the phrases:

mid godcunde gyfe	'with a divine gift'
godcundra hāda	'of divine offices'

Presumably at an intermediate level we had simply the forms:

mid godcund- gyfe	(fem. dat. sing.)
godcund- hāda	(masc. gen. pl.)

To these structures was applied a transformational rule which
added the proper endings to the adjectives. In formal terms,
the rule would be something like:[4]

$$\text{Adj.} \rightarrow \text{Adj.} + \text{ending} / \underline{\quad} \text{N}$$
$$\begin{bmatrix} \alpha \text{ gen} \\ \beta \text{ num} \\ \gamma \text{ case} \end{bmatrix} \begin{bmatrix} \alpha \text{ gen} \\ \beta \text{ num} \\ \gamma \text{ case} \end{bmatrix}$$

[4] Greek letters (α alpha, β beta, and γ gamma) are used to indicate
variables in a rule of this type. Quite simply, the rule says that an adjective
acquires an ending which has the same number, gender, and case as the
noun it modifies.

Though the categories of grammatical gender and case are no longer with us, number is still a very important distinction in English. Yet our adjectives do not in any way change their form to "agree" with following nouns. The agreement rule has been completely deleted from the grammar of English.

One clear case where a rule has been added to a grammar is the case of Evenki, which is almost alone among the Altaic languages in having adjectives which agree with nouns in number and case.[5] It is fairly certain that in the Common Altaic language no such rule of agreement existed. Perhaps because of contact with speakers of Uralic languages at some point in history, Evenki acquired such a rule, so that in contemporary Evenki one finds phenomena as exemplified in the following sentence:

kolkos-tulā	u nä	ayadig-il -wa	xawamnī-l -wa
Kolkhoz-to	they sent	best -pl. -acc.	worker -pl. -acc.

'They sent the best workers to the Kolkhoz.'

In generative terms, we would say simply that the rule of the following type has been added to the grammar of Evenki:

$$\text{Adj.} \rightarrow \text{Adj.} + \begin{array}{c}\text{ending} \\ \left[\begin{array}{c}\alpha \text{ number} \\ \beta \text{ case}\end{array}\right]\end{array} \quad / \underline{\quad} \quad \begin{array}{c}\text{N} \\ \left[\begin{array}{c}\alpha \text{ number} \\ \beta \text{ case}\end{array}\right]\end{array}$$

FOR FURTHER STUDY

Generative studies in historical linguistics essentially began with Halle's article "Phonology in a Generative Grammar." At the end of that paper, Halle considered the implications of his synchronic theories and structures for historical change by discussing the relative chronologies of Grimm's and Verner's laws. Perhaps the high point in historical studies from the generative point of view was Paul Kiparsky's thesis,

---

[5] There is no grammatical gender in the Altaic languages.

"Phonological Change," which unfortunately has not been published. A later paper by Kiparsky, "Linguistic Universals and Language Change," contains a certain amount of the same information and examples with a slightly different emphasis. Klima's thesis "Studies in Diachronic Transformational Syntax" (also unpublished) was the first attempt to deal with syntactic aspects of language change within the framework of transformational grammar. A short article by Klima, "Relatedness Between Grammatical Systems," covers certain principles of how syntactic systems might change.

Scattered studies are still available. There is Closs-Traugott's "Diachronic Syntax and Generative Grammar." The second part of Postal's book, *Aspects of Phonological Theory,* is entitled "On the So-called Mentalistic Character of Sound Change." There is one entire book devoted to this topic: King's *Historical Linguistics and Generative Grammar.* Since this work is biased towards extolling the "power" of generative explanations, it should be read with this prejudice in mind. More balanced examinations and evaluations of the role of generative grammar vis-à-vis historical linguistics can be found in two reviews of the King book: Campbell's in *Language* and Jasanoff's in *Romance Philology.*

Finally, mention should be made of a collection of short studies edited by Mária Tsiapera under the title *Generative Studies in Historical Linguistics.*

15

Language and History

History, in its broadest sense, is the study of the development of human institutions. Thus, we speak of cultural or intellectual history, which traces the evolution of human thought and the great thinkers, how they influenced one another, or how the same ideas often arose independently in different cultures. There is also political history, which tells us of the dealings of great statesmen and the rise and fall of the world's great empires and nations. Economic history deals with the commercial aspects of society and how the various economic systems developed and changed, often in conjunction with great political movements. In these fields, as well as in others where people call themselves historians, the goal is often to find a pattern, to show how causes X and Y will produce result Z in perhaps widely varying cultures.[1]

Thus, historical linguistics deserves to be classified with the disciplines of history. It is the science which studies the development of a particular human institution, language, and the internal and the external forces which influence or cause language change. And where causality is not found, we seek at least the general directions or tendencies of that change. Or, we may wish to identify and name a previously unknown change. In many senses, historical linguistics is the most highly developed and the most "scientific" of the historical disciplines, just as general linguistics is often considered the most "scientific" of the social sciences. In no other area of historical studies do we have concepts approaching the rigidity of the

[1] Our discussion of the discipline of history here is admittedly limited to history considered as a "social science." Many historians would not consider their work to be a search for patterns or trends, but rather a search for explanation of particular historical events. These might be found in particular political or economic situations or in the psychology of important historical personages.

sound laws, or even the "general tendencies" observable and classifiable in morphologic, syntactic, and semantic change.

WRITTEN RECORDS

One very curious distinction between historical linguistics and other historical studies involves the value one can place on written documents from which one draws initial facts. The documents on which the political historian relies are very much subject to personal biases, inadequate information, and even deliberate falsification. The writer of chronicles may let his own view of the world get in the way of recording what actually happened, or he may be subject to the current prejudices of his government. For example, in writing the dynastic histories of China, the official court historians were certainly not free to include any material which might reflect poorly on the reigning family. Likewise, in our own day, we have seen that Soviet histories vary in their enumeration and evaluation of the deeds of Josef Stalin, depending on the shifting judgment of the ruling powers.

Linguistic data drawn from written texts is, however, much more reliable. We assume that whatever was written was set down in order to be read by others who knew the same language, and therefore the language which was recorded was something in use, perhaps only as a literary style. Also, if people tended to use an archaic form of their language in certain documents, especially those of a juridical or religious nature, these often eventually came to be provided with translations or glosses into the idiom current at the time the documents were written or recopied. Thus, we are given two stages of a language.

Perhaps the most obvious way of obtaining historical data of various cultural aspects is by the examination of the borrowings in a particular language. For example, if all of the histories of music were somehow destroyed, we would have no difficulty establishing the fact that the Italians had an enormous influence on Western music. We need merely look at almost any piece of music, by a composer of any nationality, or work on music written in whatever language, and we will observe many Italian words, such as *andante, allegro,* and *moderato.*

In a similar vein, we could determine the French influence on English (and American) political and judicial structures due to the presence of titles such as attorney general (cf. p. 193), or when we hear the Supreme Court open with the cry of *oyez,* 'hear!' In this last case we can even date the time of borrowing back to the Anglo-Norman period because *oyez* is not the form of this word in Modern French.

PREHISTORY

The prehistoric period is taken to mean the time between the emergence of man and the invention or adaptation of writing systems which enabled people to record in a lasting linguistic form the events of their own or previous times. Thus, the end of the prehistoric period and the beginning of recorded history will be different for different parts of the world. In Mesopotamia, Egypt, and China, prehistory ends and history begins at a very early time, perhaps in the third millennium B.C. Among peoples who neither developed nor adopted a writing system, the historic period begins with the arrival of foreigners who record their history. This observation is not intended to downgrade the value of oral traditions, which may contain much that is reliable, and often critical philological examination can extract valuable historical information.

In general, though, when one wishes to deal with human events in periods before the invention of writing, one turns first to the archeologist. The archeologist unearths the physical remnants of human cultures in the forms of pots and tools and jewelry and various artifacts. He examines the structures and sites of dwellings and temples. From these he tries to reconstruct and describe the civilization of the people who manufactured and used the objects. By finding the same artifact in several different areas dating from several different periods, he may be able to tell us something about the movement of cultural items; where they originated and in what directions they spread. Thus, waves of cultural diffusion can be established.

The linguist can also contribute something to our understanding of the prehistoric period—by examining the historical implications and interpretations involved in family tree diagrams and the status of reconstructed languages.

In what may appear as a truism, Meillet has remarked that the indispensable condition for the existence of a language is the existence of a speech community which uses that language as its chief means of communication. Now, we are not merely building castles in the air with our reconstructed languages as some kind of intellectual exercise—the evidence of recurring correspondence points to the fact that we are not. We must assume that there was, at some point in space and time, a community which spoke that language. A reconstructed language is, as Mary Haas has remarked, "a glorious artifact, one which is far more precious than anything an archeologist can ever hope to unearth."

A further observation by Meillet that common language implies common civilization is also worthy of mention here. What this means is that all the people who speak a particular language share certain elements of a material and nonmaterial nature as parts of their culture. Thus, the speakers of French share certain habits of cooking, attitudes towards law and love, etc., which we lump together as French culture, the variation among these being perhaps similar to the variation among French dialects.

A contradictory statement made by Sapir in Chapter 10 of his book *Language* to the effect that speakers of the same language may have widely different cultures is shown to be untenable by Sapir's own example. Sapir referred to the distribution of the Athabascan languages, and pointed out that speakers of Athabascan ranged from those with forest cultures in the west of Canada, such as the Beaver Indians, to desert dwellers such as the Navaho in the southwestern United States. The simple fact here is that while these cultures are different, so are the languages, even though they might be genetically related. The degree of separation in time and space which led to the divergence of the cultures did the same to the languages.

The reverse of this is not necessarily true; i.e., a common civilization does not imply a common language. Thus, we might speak of the inhabitants of Syria, Turkey, and Iran as sharing a common Middle Eastern Islamic civilization, yet their languages are vastly different and belong to three separate families: Arabic to the Semitic, Turkish to the Altaic, and Persian to the Indo-European. So then, it is starting off with the assumption that the speakers of a single proto-language shared a relatively uniform culture that we approach the task of extracting information from that language.

The use of a reconstructed language for reconstructing a culture might be compared to a hypothetical situation involving written documents. Suppose we were to discover in one of the world's great libraries a handwritten vocabulary of an otherwise unknown language written by some traveler or missionary. Unfortunately, we find that the introduction has been lost or destroyed, so that we are unable to tell where this language was spoken or what was the culture of the people who spoke it. How could we begin to satisfy our curiosity on these questions? The way is to examine the vocabulary to see what items are mentioned. Thus, if we found words for 'polar bear', 'snow house', and 'iceberg', we could be reasonably certain that this language was one spoken in the Arctic regions. On the other hand, if this vocabulary included words glossed as 'palm tree', 'mango', and 'parrot', we would become quite sure that our language was one spoken in the tropics. Elements of the material culture could be gleaned from the presence of words like 'boot' or 'saddle' or 'stool'. We would also learn a great deal about the nonmaterial culture if we found words glossed as 'family', 'king', 'judge', or 'priest'.

With the discovery of the Indo-European family, great interest was generated in finding out everything possible about the people who spoke this language. The German word coined by Schleicher for proto-language was *Ursprache* 'original language', and of course the people who spoke this were called the *Urvolk* 'original people'. Furthermore, it was assumed that they must have lived in a place called the *Urheimat* 'original homeland'.

Determining the *Urheimat* is a particularly difficult task as regards the Indo-Europeans because man has so changed the Eurasian land mass that it is extremely difficult to determine its natural state some four thousand years ago. The search for it has occupied linguists, ethnographers, archeologists and others for long periods of time. Some of these studies are of value, and others involve nothing more than the most fanciful speculation. As a particularly striking example of the latter, we might mention Ihering's pronouncement that the date of the departure of the Proto-Germanic peoples (and others) from the *Urheimat* was March the first!

Leaving aside for the moment the question of the *Urheimat,* there is a great deal of information to be gleaned about the Indo-Europeans by examining the vocabulary of the reconstructed language. For example, from the presence in the reconstructed Indo-European language of roots such as *$g^w ou$-* 'cow, bull', *$o\u{u}i$-* 'sheep', *$ag^w hno$-* 'lamb', *aig-* 'goat', and *su-* 'swine' we can tell that the Indo-Europeans were familiar with these animals, and therefore that stock breeding and animal husbandry were among their occupations. That certain grains were also known to this people is shown by the existence of the roots *$grano$-* 'corn', *$i\underline{e}\u{u}o$-* 'wheat', *$\u{u}rughi\u{o}$-* 'rye', *$bhares$-* 'barley'. Some information about domestic occupations and perhaps clothing is yielded by the verbs *$sn\bar{e}$-* 'to spin wool', *$s\u{i}u$-* 'to sew' and the noun *$\u{u}ln$-* 'wool'.

We have already noted the fact that the words *$m\bar{a}ter$* and *$p\partial ter$* designated particular positions in the social order (p. 182). We can also find terms like *$snusos$* 'daughter in law', *$dai\u{u}er$-* 'husband's brother', and *$gal\bar{o}$* 'husband's sister'. The fact that we do not find terms for 'son-in-law' or 'wife's brother' or 'wife's sister' seems to indicate that these relationships were not important in Indo-European society. The further conclusion we reach is that among the Indo-Europeans a woman moved into the household of her husband at the time of marriage, and there was probably very little contact with her own family. This need for kinship terms to refer to her husband's relatives is reflected in the many words collected, but corresponding terms referring to the wife's relatives are not found.

We can then picture Indo-European society as consisting of a nuclear family headed by a *pǝter and a *māter. This nuclear family was in turn part of a larger, extended family which was called a *gen- and the household itself was called a *dom-. This household was headed by a patriarch of some kind who bore the title *dems-pot- (from the roots *dem-, e-grade of *dom-, and *pot- 'to be able, power', i.e., 'he who holds the power of the *dom-).

Of course a great deal more is known about the Indo-Europeans than what we have presented here. Specialists in related disciplines such as archeology or comparative mythology and religion continue to work with linguists in advancing and improving knowledge of our linguistic ancestors. Some of these more extensive studies are noted in the bibilography for this chapter.

In contrast to the difficulties of locating the Indo-European *Urheimat,* we have an excellent example of how this type of work can yield fruitful results. I refer to Siebert's recent researches in trying to locate the original home of the Proto-Algonquian people. Siebert divides the words he is to use into four classes: birds, mammals, fish, and trees. He points out that birds usually migrate over large distances in search of seasonal homes and food. Thus, reconstructed bird names are a less reliable source than trees, which are limited to particular areas by climate, soil, and moisture. Siebert also emphasizes the necessity of discovering the *original* state of natural affairs by determining and discounting what is known of relatively recent climatic changes as well as human intervention, such as stocking lakes and streams with fish that are not native to a particular body of water. He is also aware of the danger that words may be applied to new, similar species when a speech community migrates from one area to another.

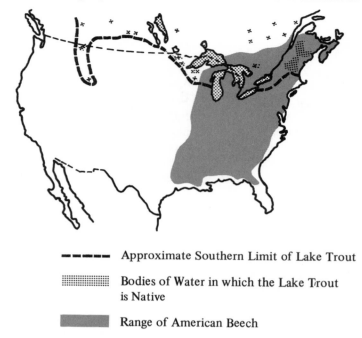

───── Approximate Southern Limit of Lake Trout

░░░░░ Bodies of Water in which the Lake Trout is Native

▓▓▓▓▓ Range of American Beech

For example, consider the case of a group that lived in an area where moose were the only large edible animals. If they then migrated to a place where the only large edible animals were deer, they might well apply the term for "moose" to the deer.

Siebert has collected over fifty words which can be used to plot the location of the original homeland and has reconstructed them with reasonable accuracy as to both phonological and semantic value. Thus, he has reconstructed the Proto-Algonquian words:

*wešawe•minšya	'American beech'
*name•kwa	'lake trout'

The American beech was found throughout the eastern United States and the southern part of eastern Canada. The range of the lake trout extends down from the north as far as the Great Lakes region. The original locations of both of these items were plotted on a map (see Fig. 15-1). By looking at the map we can conclude that if the Proto-Algonquian peo-

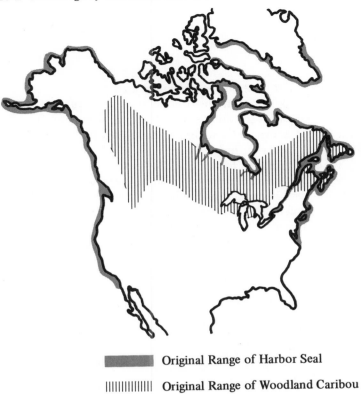

█████████ Original Range of Harbor Seal

||||||||||||| Original Range of Woodland Caribou

ple knew both the lake trout and the beech tree, their original homeland must have been no further west than the Great Lakes region, no further north than approximately the same area, but also no further south than the 43rd parallel which (approximately) marks the southern limit of the Lake Trout. Confirming evidence for this location is found when we examine the habitats of two other natural items whose names can be reconstructed:

*a·çkikwa²	'harbor seal'
*atehkwa	'woodland caribou'

---

² The ç in this word is a purely algebraic symbol used by Algonquianists to indicate the first member of this cluster whose phonetic reality cannot be more precisely determined. In the attested Algonquian languages, the reflexes of ç are usually either *h* or *s*.

Again, we find that our geographical area of the harbor seal and the woodland caribou overlap with our previous items (the American beech and the lake trout) in what is the northern United States and southern Canada (see Fig. 15-2) from the Great Lakes to the east.

By comparing the location of the items to which these and other names refer, Siebert was able to postulate both a compact original homeland and a later expanded area, still presumably inhabited by a unified people speaking a relatively uniform language (see Fig. 15-3).

Data obtained from researching language history can probably be applied in limitless ways to the study of mankind's history in general. So long as assumptions are made explicit and research proceeds according to a tightly controlled methodology, we may be sure that the results are of scientific validity. Investigating phonological systems and writing rules for sound changes may not appear to be the most exciting and interesting occupation; in fact, it can be readily admitted that for many people a discussion of the nonlinguistic implications and applications remains the most engrossing part of language history.

Nonetheless, it remains true that unless the painstaking and time-consuming work of setting up correspondences and tracing detailed developments is done, our conclusions about the relatedness of languages, peoples, and cultures will be of no serious value. Those conclusions which do not stand on a solidly researched basis can be subject to prejudice or political perversion to serve any end. In the 1930s the pseudo-scientific "popular" work on Indo-Europeans (Aryans) formed one of the bases of Nazi policy, while the exquisitely scientific and well-founded studies of Meillet were banned.

FOR FURTHER STUDY

As is true with most areas of historical linguistics, the most advanced studies in linguistic archeology have been done in Indo-European. Recently, Benveniste published a masterly

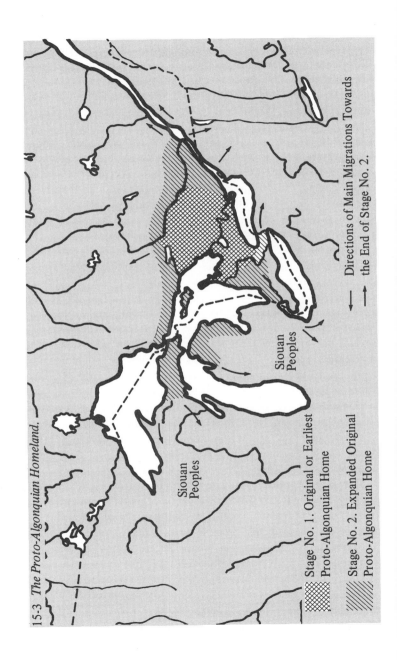

15-3 *The Proto-Algonquian Homeland.*

Siouan Peoples

Siouan Peoples

→ Directions of Main Migrations Towards
⇢ the End of Stage No. 2.

▨ Stage No. 1. Original or Earliest
   Proto-Algonquian Home

▨ Stage No. 2. Expanded Original
   Proto-Algonquian Home

two-volume work about the nonmaterial culture of the Indo-Europeans which could be recovered or reconstructed from linguistic data. The entire work is entitled *Le vocabulaire des institutions indo-européennes;* the first volume deals with economics, kinship, and society; the second includes political power, law, and religion. An excellent brief survey of Indo-European culture is found in Calvert Watkins's article "Indo-European and the Indo-Europeans," which is appended to the *American Heritage Dictionary.* The book edited by Cardona et al., *Indo-European and Indo-Europeans,* is a collection of papers by linguists, ethnographers, and archeologists and should probably be considered the last word on our knowledge of certain aspects of Indo-European culture.

Recently, a collection of articles dating from 1892 to 1963 and dealing with the original homeland of the Indo-Europeans was edited by Scherer and published under the title of *Die Urheimat der Indogermanen.* The review article by Marija Giboutas, "The Indo-Europeans: Archeological Problems," shows how archeological evidence can be used to substantiate or call into question linguistic conclusions on prehistory. For a complete study by a linguist of a limited geographical area from linguistic, archeological, and historical points of view, there is Ernst Pulgram's *The Tongues of Italy.*

A theoretical approach can be found in Swadesh's article "Linguistics as an Instrument of Prehistory." A more extensive treatment of the same subject is Hans Krahe's book *Sprache und Vorzeit,* which contains both general and Indo-European information.

For purely antiquarian interest or for amusement one can look at Ihering's *The Evolution of the Aryan.* This work may be taken as typical of nineteenth-century pseudo-scientific attempts to discover all possible knowledge about the Indo-Europeans. The philological, historical, and linguistic scholarship may look impressive at first glance, but in fact the book is simply a collection of wild speculations.

The article by Siebert dealing with the home of the Proto-Algonquians is found in Bulletin 214 of the National Museum of Canada. Here one can find all the words Siebert used in his work as well as additional maps and discussion of his conclusions.

The interesting developments regarding the historical relationships between languages and the rise of the modern nation states is discussed lucidly in Chapter 6, "Language and Nation," in von Wartburg's *Problems and Methods in Linguistics*. Finally, as a general statement of changes in language and changes in culture, mention should be made of Hoijer's article, "Linguistic and Cultural Change."

Appendix 1: Basic Elements of Phonetics

This appendix is intended for students who have had no previous training in phonetics or phonology. It provides only the basic concepts and symbols necessary for understanding the phonological sections of this book and is certainly not a substitute for a course in general phonetics and phonology. Those who would like further information about general phonetics are advised to consult Chapter 6 of Bloomfield's *Language* or Chapter 15 of Gleason's *Introduction*.

Our first task is to determine the elements of sound which languages string together to form words. Most often, this is done in terms of *articulatory phonetics,* i.e., by describing the positions of the various speech organs at the time a particular sound is produced. The different sounds used in all the world's languages are indeed numerous, and in this brief sketch, we are limiting ourselves specifically to explaining only those items which we have used in this book.

For some languages, like Turkish, the writing system is remarkably close to the spoken word; in others, such as English, the orthography is notoriously deviant from what is actually said. For this and other reasons linguists have devised various series of symbols, known as *phonetic alphabets,* which are intended to set down in visual form the pronunciations of words. The alphabet we will present here is that generally used by American linguists. When it is necessary to indicate that something is being written in phonetic script as opposed to normal orthography, the script is enclosed in square brackets, i.e., [ ].

Before proceeding any further it will be necessary to describe the organs which are used in the production of human speech. A simple diagram of the vocal tract is necessary:

The Vocal Tract

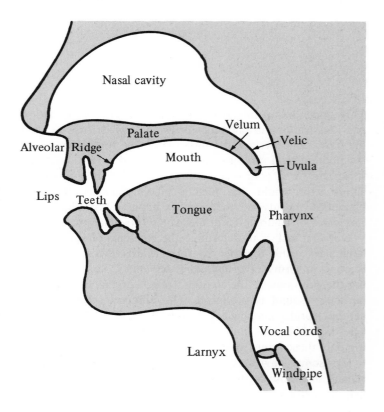

When we speak, air is forced out of the lungs and through the vocal tract. Various modifications at different points in the vocal tract are what produces the different sounds of human language. For the most part, these are unconscious muscular movements on the part of adult speakers, but children learn them very slowly as do adults who attempt to learn new sounds of foreign languages.

When the air leaves the lungs, it passes through the larynx, the visible part of which is known as the Adam's apple. The larynx consists of a tube-like opening (the glottis) which can be closed by two pieces of muscle, the vocal cords. The vocal cords may be closed either tightly, in which case no air may pass through, or they may be closed loosely, in which case the air passing through causes them to vibrate. The vibrating vocal cords produce the noise which is known as voice.

CONSONANTS

In a most general definition, *consonants* are sounds produced when there is an obstruction somewhere in the vocal tract. The obstruction may be complete or partial, and it may take place at a number of points in the passage through which the air must pass. Most consonants can be defined by describing three aspects of their articulation:

1. The point of articulation—where in the vocal tract the obstruction is located.

2. The manner of articulation—whether the obstruction is complete or only partial.

3. Voicing—whether the vocal cords are completely open, so that the air flows through freely, or whether they are lightly closed so that the air vibrates as the air passes through.

Consider first the manner of articulation. When the obstruction is a complete closure, we have the class of consonants which are known as *stops* (or plosives). The air from the lungs is completely shut off, and pressure builds up behind the point of closure. When the air is released we hear the stop consonant (e.g., *p, t,* or *k*). All other consonants are continuants.

When the air leaves the lungs, the first place where it may be impeded is at the glottis itself. By tightly closing the vocal cords, and then releasing them quickly with a vowel sound, a speaker can produce the glottal stop, for which the phonetic symbol is ? (a question mark without the period under it). The glottal stop is the sound heard in certain English interjections such as *uh oh.*

Let us now turn to consider the other points of articulation with regard to the formation of stops. For our purposes we need only distinguish four principal locations where the flow of air may be obstructed. From front to back in the mouth these are the lips, the teeth (or the region directly behind the teeth, the alveolar ridge), the palate, and the velum. Obstructions at these points produce consonants which are known as labials, dentals, palatals, and velars, respectively.

We can now proceed to define some of the consonants. When there is a complete closure at the lips and the vocal cords are open (i.e., air passing through, but no vibration) we have the sound *p* as in *pet*. In technical terms, a *p* is called a voiceless labial stop. If we keep the same point and manner of articulation, but lightly close the vocal cords so that they vibrate as the air moves through, we produce a *b*, which is a voiced labial stop.

Moving back one point in the mouth, we can effect a complete closure by raising the tip of the tongue to a point immediately behind the teeth. This will produce the voiceless dental stop *t* and the voiced dental stop *d*. Palatal stops have certain peculiarities and we will return to them later.

Further back in the mouth, we find that we can raise the back of the tongue so that it meets the velum and we can produce a complete closure. Stopping the air at this point results in either the voiceless velar stop *k* or the voiced velar stop *g* (as in *good*). The production of velar stops can be readily observed by standing in front of a mirror, with mouth wide open, and saying *ka* or *ga*.

We mentioned above that all consonants which are not stops are continuants. Continuants are divided into several classes. Among these are fricatives, nasals, liquids, and glides. *Fricatives* are produced when the air is forced through a narrowed passageway in the vocal tract and produces a clearly audible sound of friction. These may be further distinguished by the shape of the passageway, i.e., whether it is a slit or a groove.

For our purposes we need note two pairs of slit fricatives: those produced at the lips, and those produced at the teeth. When the lower lip is brought back and makes contact with the upper teeth, it is possible to force the air out through a narrow slit in the center. This produces the voiceless labial fricative *f* and the voiced labial fricative *v*. When the tongue is raised to the upper teeth, it is again possible to force the air out through a narrow slit and so produce dental slit fricatives. In English both of these are written *th*. Linguists generally used the symbol θ (theta) to indicate the voiceless dental slit fricative—*th* as in *thin*;[1] the symbol ð (eth) stands for the voiced dental slit fricative—*th* as in *then*.

Finally, in the velar region it is also possible to produce slit fricatives, though these do not occur in English. The voiceless velar slit fricative is usually written with the letter *x*; it occurs in many languages, such as German, where it is the last sound in *Bach*. The voiced velar slit fricative is written with the symbol γ (gamma); this sound occurs today in North German *sagan*.

Groove fricatives, also known as sibilants, or hushing sounds, are found in the dental and palatal regions. They are formed similarly to the slit fricatives, except that the opening through which the air is forced resembles more a rounded groove than a straight slit. Immediately behind the teeth the tongue forms the voiceless dental groove fricative *s* (as in *sit*) and its voiced counterpart *z* (as in *zebra*). In the palatal region we find two more groove fricatives: the voiceless one is written *š* and sounds like the *sh* in *ship*. The voiced palatal groove fricative is represented by the symbol *ž* and is pronounced like the *z* in *azure* or the *s* in *measure*.

Stops formed in the palatal region generally are different from other stops in that they are affricated, i.e., they are immediately followed by the fricative which is produced at the same point of articulation. We write the voiceless palatal stop as *č* (like the *ch* in *cheese*) and the voiced palatal stop as *ǰ* (like the *g* in *gem*). The fact that these stops are affricated leads some authors to write them as [tš] and [dž]. This phonetic peculiarity of palatal stops is generally not very important, and we may consider them to be normal stops.

[1] In writing the phonetics of the Germanic languages, it is traditional to use the symbol þ (thorn) in place of θ (theta) to represent the voiceless dental slit fricative.

The next group of continuant consonants we will consider are the *glides*. Their primary point of articulation is in the glottis and they are modified at two points in the vocal tract: the lips and the palate. The labial glide *w* (as in *well*) is formed by rounding the lips tightly and forcing the air out through this narrow opening. The palatal glide *y* (as in *yet*) is produced when the tongue is raised to the palate, creating a slit through which air is passed.

There is one last set of continuant consonants which must be considered and this consists of the *liquids: r* and *l*. Both of these are generally voiced. *l* is called the lateral liquid since it is produced by forcing the air over the sides of the tongue, which is raised to a point just behind the teeth. The production of *r*-sounds varies greatly from language to language. For English we may define it simply as a retroflex liquid, which is produced by the movement of air over the tongue which has been curled up and back to the hard palate.

All of the consonants which we have dealt with so far are oral consonants; that is, we are dealing with a situation where the air from the lungs passes out of the body through the oral cavity (the mouth). In producing oral consonants, the velic has been raised to completely cut off the passage of air through the nose. However, it is also possible to stop the flow of air at some point in the mouth, lower the velic, and allow the air to flow through the nasal cavity and out through the nose. It is precisely such a situation that produces the *nasal consonants*.

In the production of a nasal the air may be stopped at the previously mentioned points of articulation. The labial nasal is *m*, the dental nasal is *n*. The palatal nasal, written *ñ*, does not occur in English, but may be heard in Spanish words like *señor*. The velar nasal is represented by the symbol ŋ (angma) and is the sound we hear at the end of words such as *sing* or *ring*. If you listen to your own pronunciation of these words you will hear quite clearly that there is no *g* at all, merely a nasal sound produced in the same region of the mouth as *g* (the velar region).

The sound [h], as in the English word *hat*, has been defined in various articulatory ways. For our purposes, we shall consider it to be a voiceless glottal fricative, i.e., a sound produced by narrowing the opening of the glottis so that the air passing through creates an audible friction.

SECONDARY ARTICULATIONS

A secondary articulation involves additional modification in the vocal tract while an individual sound is being produced elsewhere. For our purposes, we need consider only three of these: palatalization, labialization, and aspiration.

Palatalization consists of raising the tongue to the hard palate simultaneously with the production of a particular sound. This produces an audible *y*-like effect which seems to follow immediately after. We indicate a palatalized sound by writing a superscript *y* next to that sound. Thus, t^y is palatalized *t* and k^y is palatalized *k*. The overall effect of a palatalized consonant is somewhat similar to that found in English words like *cute* which can be written [k^{y}ut] phonetically.

When the lips are rounded throughout the articulation of a particular sound, we say that that sound is *labialized*. This is indicated by a superscript *w* following the consonant in question. In Indo-European, for example, we assume that in addition to the set of normal velars there existed a set of velar stops produced while the lips were rounded, thus yielding a set of labio-velars: k^w, g^w, etc. Such sounds are found in modern spoken languages—Igbo, for example. We can produce the acoustic effect of labio-velars by rounding our lips before producing the first sound, as we do when we pronounce *queen.*

When a consonant is immediately followed by a slight puff of breath we say that that sound is *aspirated*. Aspiration is indicated by a superscript *h* immediately following the sound in question, for example, p^h, t^h, g^h. In English we automatically aspirate every voiceless consonant which begins a word. To hear aspiration, compare the *p* in *pit* [p^{h}ɪt] and the *p* in *spit* [spɪt]. In the production of the first word, you will definitely hear a puff of breath following the *p;* this is not found in the second word. In transcribing certain languages, such as

Principal Consonant Sounds

POINT OF ARTICULATION

MANNER OF ARTICULATION	LABIAL	DENTAL	PALATAL	VELAR	GLOTTAL
STOPS					
voiceless	p *pet*	t *to*	č *cheese*	k *key*	ʔ *uh oh*
voiced	b *bet*	d *do*	ǰ *jam*	g *go*	
FRICATIVES					
Slit					
voiceless	f *fat*	θ *thin*		x German: *Bach*	h *how*

voiced	v *vat*	ð *then*		γ N. German: *sagan*
Groove				
voiceless		s *so*	š *show*	
voiced		z *zoo*	ž *measure*	
GLIDES	w *wet*		y *yet*	
LIQUIDS		l *led*	r *red*	
NASALS	m *met*	n *net*	ñ Spanish: *señor*	ŋ *sing*

Sanskrit, Greek, or reconstructed Indo-European, it is traditional to write the *h* which indicates aspiration not as a superscript, but on the same line as the regular consonant. Thus, Sanskrit or Indo-European *bh, dh, gh,* are equivalent to [bʰ], [dʰ], and [gʰ], respectively.

VOWELS

Vowels are distinguished from consonants primarily by the fact that the production of vowels does not involve any obstruction in the vocal tract. The articulation of vowels consists of the passage of air through the lightly closed vocal cords (thus producing voice) and then freely through the oral cavity. The different vowels are formed by modifying the shape of the oral cavity by the use of various organs; the principle one of these is the tongue. The tongue is visualized as moving along two axes: top to bottom and front to back, thus giving different shapes to the oral cavity.

Vowels are defined by describing the position of the tongue at the time of articulation. In other words, to define a vowel, we tell where the tongue is with regard to relative height in the mouth and with regard to its relative backness or frontness. We can imagine there being some sort of "box" in the mouth which is divided into various squares that locate the position of the tongue in the production of the various vowels.[2]

Starting in the upper left-hand corner, we find that when the tongue is high and pushed forward, we produce the vowel [i], which is pronounced like the *ee* in *beet*. Keeping the tongue high, but retracting it slightly to a position slightly further back we have the vowel [ɨ], which has the sound of *i* in the word *bit*. Pulling the tongue still further back, we produce the vowel [u], the sound of *oo* in *boot*. We have now defined three high vowels. Technically, [i] is known as a high

---

[2] The pronunciation of the words used to exemplify different sounds varies from dialect to dialect, especially with regard to the vowels. The examples chosen here represent the author's speech, which might be described as northeastern American (New York–Boston).

Principal Vowel Sounds

	FRONT	CENTRAL	BACK
HIGH	i *beet*	ɨ *bit*	u *boot*
MID	e *bait*	ə *but*	o *boat*
LOW	æ *bat*	a *hot*	ɔ *horse, law*

front vowel; [ɨ] is a high central vowel; and [u] is a high back vowel.

Lowering the tongue slightly and using the same front–back points of location, we produce the mid vowels. [e] is a mid front vowel and sounds like the *ai* in *bait*. [ə], known as schwa, is the mid central vowel and is pronounced like the *a* in *about* or the *u* in *but;* the mid back vowel is [o], and this is the sound of the *oa* in *boat*.

At the bottom of the mouth we can again produce three vowels. In the front in the vowel [æ] which is pronounced like the *a* in *bat*. The low central vowel is [a] and is the sound of the vowel *o* in a word like *hot*. In the low back position we find a vowel written [ɔ], which has the sound of the *o* in *horse* or the *aw* in *law*.

ADDITIONAL REMARKS ON VOWELS

The nine principal vowels which appear in our chart above by no means exhaust the list of possible vowel sounds. For example, the vowel [ɛ], like the *e* in *bet,* does not appear there. [ɛ] can be described as being a lower mid front vowel; in a more complete vowel chart, [ɛ] would appear between [e] and [æ] among the front vowels.

One additional feature of vowels that our chart above does not show is the feature of *rounding,* i.e., whether or not the vowel is produced with rounded lips. In English, all the front vowels are unrounded and all the back vowels are rounded. This is not the case for many of the world's languages, where we may find front rounded vowels or back unrounded vowels. A front rounded vowel is written phonetically by placing two dots (an umlaut) over the corresponding back rounded vowel. For our purposes we need note only two of these, [ü] and [ö]. [ü] is pronounced with the tongue in the same position as [i], but with the lips rounded. [ö] is pronounced with the tongue in the same position as [e], but with the lips rounded. The [ü] sound can be found in French *tu* 'you' or German *für* 'for'. The [ö] sound is found in the same two languages; for example, French *feu* 'fire' or German *schön* 'pretty'.

The sounds which have traditionally been called *diphthongs* consist of a vowel either preceded or followed by one of the glides (*y* or *w*). We should note two of these: the diphthong [aw] occurs in words such as *cow* [kʰaw], and the diphthong [ay] is the sound of the *i* in *bite* [bayt].

Appendix 2: Writing Rules

The formal rules which the linguist writes are intended to express, in a shorthand way, significant facts about the operation of languages. The rules which are operative at a given point in time are known as *synchronic rules;* those which express changes in particular languages over time are known as *diachronic rules.* We, of course, are primarily interested in the latter.

The simplest form of the diachronic rule consists of the earlier and later forms linked by an arrow. Thus, if sound X at one stage of a language changes into sound Y at a later stage, we write the rule:

$$X \rightarrow Y$$

If a particular change takes place only in a specific environment, this environment is written following a single slash (/). The slash is read "in the environment." The location of the changing sound vis-à-vis the conditioning environment is indicated by a low dash (__). Some examples of rules, with their expression in words, are as follows:

$X \rightarrow Y / \_\_ Z$	'X becomes Y when it occurs in the environment before Z.'
$X \rightarrow Y / Z \_\_$	'X becomes Y when it occurs in the environment after Z.'
$X \rightarrow Y / Z \_\_ Q$	'X becomes Y when it occurs in the environment between Z and Q.'

Elements that are optional, i.e., whose presence or absence does not affect the operation of a rule, are placed in parentheses. Thus, if a particular change takes place before Z, and this change takes place whether or not Z is preceded by Q, the rule is written:

$$X \rightarrow Y / \underline{\quad} (Q)Z \quad \text{'X becomes Y before Z, and Z may be preceded by Q.'}$$

When an environment consists of an either/or situation, braces are used. Thus:

$$X \rightarrow Y / \underline{\quad} \begin{Bmatrix} Z \\ Q \end{Bmatrix} \quad \text{'X becomes Y before either Z or Q.'}$$

Since sounds tend to change in groups of natural classes, or environments often consist of groups of similar sounds, we try to express these facts in our rules. We do this by naming the class of sounds (in articulatory terms) usually within square brackets [ ]. Thus if some language has the three voiceless stops *p, t,* and *k* and these change to *f, θ,* and *x,* respectively, we can write the rule:

$$[\text{voiceless stops}] \rightarrow [\text{fricatives}]$$

In a similar way environments can be expressed. Take, for example, a situation where *u* becomes *i, o* becomes *e,* and *ɔ* becomes *æ* after *č, ǰ, š,* and *ž.* All these changes and the environment can be expressed simply as:

$$[\text{back vowels}] \rightarrow [\text{front}] / [\text{palatal stops and fricatives}] \underline{\quad}$$

Two generally accepted cover symbols used in writing rules are C (for consonant) and V (for vowel). For example, if we are dealing with a situation where all consonants become voiced when they occur between vowels, we can simply write:

$$C \rightarrow [\text{voiced}] / V\underline{\quad}V.$$

Bibliography

Allen, W. Sidney. *Vox Latina*. Cambridge: Cambridge University Press, 1965.

Benveniste, Émile. *Problèmes de linguistique générale*, Paris: Gallimard, 1966.
"La classification des langues," pp. 99–118.
"Problèmes sémantiques de la reconstruction," pp. 289–307.

———. "Mutations of Linguistic Categories." In Lehmann, W., and Malkiel, Y., eds., *Directions for Historical Linguistics*, pp. 83–94. Austin: University of Texas Press, 1968.

———. *Le vocabulaire des institutions indo-européenes*, 2 vols. Paris: Les Éditions de Minuit, 1969.

Bloomfield, Leonard. *Language*. New York: Holt, Rinehart, and Winston, 1933 and later editions. Chapters 17–27 reprinted as *Language History*, 1965.

———. "Algonquian." In Osgood, C., ed., *Linguistic Structures of Native America*, pp. 85–129. New York: The Viking Fund, 1946.

Bourciez, Édouard. *Éléments de linguistique romane*. Revised edition. Paris: E. Klincksieck, 1946.

Bréal, Michel. *Semantics*, trans., Cust. New York: Dover, 1964.

Brugmann, Karl. *Grundriss der vergleichenden Grammatik der indogermanischen Sprachen*. Strassburg: K. J. Trübner, 1886–1900. Second Edition, 1897–1916. English translation by Wright, J., *Elements of the Comparative Grammar of the Indo-Germanic Languages*. New York: Westermann, 1888–1895.

Buck, Carl Darling. *Comparative Grammar of Greek and Latin*. Chicago: University of Chicago Press, 1933.

———. *A Dictionary of Selected Synonyms in the Principal Indo-European Languages*. Chicago: University of Chicago Press, 1965.

Campbell, Lyle. "Review of King, *Historical Linguistics and Generative Grammar.*" *Language* 47 (1971): 191–209.

Cardona, George; Hoenigswald, Henry; and Senn, Alfred, eds. *Indo-European and Indo-Europeans.* Philadelphia: University of Pennsylvania Press, 1970.

Chadwick, John. *The Decipherment of Linear B.* Cambridge: Cambridge University Press, 1958.

Closs Traugott, Elizabeth. "Diachronic Syntax and Generative Grammar." *Language* 41 (1965): 402–415. Reprinted (with corrections) in Lass, R., ed., *Approaches to English Historical Linguistics,* pp. 311–324. New York: Holt, Rinehart, and Winston, 1969.

Cowan, William. *Workbook in Comparative Reconstruction.* New York: Holt, Rinehart, and Winston, 1971.

Diringer, David. *Writing.* London: Thames and Hudson, 1962.

Frazer, (Sir) James George. *The Golden Bough.* New York: Macmillan, 1925.

Gelb, Ignace, J. *A Study of Writing.* Chicago: University of Chicago Press, 1952.

Gimboutas, Marija. "The Indo-Europeans: Archeological Problems." *American Anthropologist* 65 (1963): 815–836.

Gleason, H. A. *An Introduction to Descriptive Linguistics,* Revised edition. New York: Holt, Rinehart, and Winston, 1961.

Goddard, Ives. "Philological Approaches to the Study of Native North American Languages: Documents and Documentation." In Sebeok, T., ed., *Current Trends in Linguistics,* Vol. 10, *Linguistics in North America.* The Hague: Mouton, forthcoming.

Greenberg, Joseph H. "A Quantitative Approach to the Morphological Typology of Language." *International Journal of American Linguistics* 26 (1960): 178–194.

————. *The Languages of Africa.* Bloomington: Indiana University, 1963.

Haas, Mary. "Historical Linguistics and the Genetic Relationship of Languages." In Sebeok, T., ed., *Current Trends in Linguistics,* Vol. 3, pp. 113–153. The Hague: Mouton, 1966. Reprinted, with additions and corrections, as *The Prehistory of Languages.* The Hague: Mouton, 1969.

Halle, Morris. "Phonology in Generative Grammar." *Word* 18 (1962): 54–72. Reprinted in Fodor, J., and Katz, J., eds.,

The Structure of Language, pp. 334–352. Englewood Cliffs, New Jersey: Prentice-Hall, 1964.

Haugen, Einar. "The Analysis of Linguistic Borrowing." *Language* 26 (1950): 210–231. Reprinted in Lass, R., ed., *Approaches to English Historical Linguistics,* pp. 58–82. New York: Holt, Rinehart, and Winston, 1969.

Hill, Archibald. "Phonetic and Phonemic Change." *Language* 12 (1936): 15–22. Reprinted in Joos, M., ed., *Readings in Linguistics,* pp. 81–84. New York: American Council of Learned Societies, 1963.

Hockett, Charles. "Implications of Bloomfield's Algonquian Studies." *Language* 24 (1948): 117–131. Reprinted in Joos, M., ed., *Readings in Linguistics,* pp. 281–289. New York: American Council of Learned Societies, 1963.

———. "Sound Change." *Language* 41 (1965): 185–204.

Hoijer, Harry. "Linguistic and Cultural Change." *Language* 24 (1948): 335–345. Reprinted in Hymes, D., ed., *Language in Culture and Society,* pp. 455–463. New York: Harper and Row, 1964.

Houtzager, Maria Elizabeth. *Unconscious Sound and Sense Assimilations.* Amsterdam: H. J. Paris, 1935.

Ihering, Rudolph von. *The Evolution of the Aryan,* trans., Drucker. New York: Holt, 1897.

Jakobson, Roman. *Selected Writings,* Vol. 1. The Hague: Mouton, 1962.
"The Concept of Sound Law and the Teleological Criterion," pp. 1–2.
"Principes de phonologie historique," pp. 202–220.

Jakobson, Roman, and Halle, Morris. "Phonology and Phonetics." In *Fundamentals of Language,* pp. 3–51. The Hague: Mouton, 1956. Also in Roman Jakobson, *Selected Writings,* Vol. 1, pp. 464–504. The Hague: Mouton, 1962.

Jasanoff, Jay. "Review of King, *Historical Linguistics and Generative Grammar." Romance Philology* 25 (1971).

King, Robert D. *Historical Linguistics and Generative Grammar.* Englewood Cliffs, New Jersey: Prentice-Hall, 1969.

Kiparsky, Paul. "Phonological Change." Unpublished doctoral dissertation. Cambridge: Massachusetts Institute of Technology, 1965.

———. "Linguistic Universals and Linguistic Change." In Bach, E., and Harms, T., eds., *Universals in Linguistic Theory,* pp. 170–202. New York: Holt, Rinehart, and Winston, 1968.

Klima, Edward. "Relatedness Between Grammatical Systems." *Language* 40 (1964): 1–20. Reprinted in Reibel, D., and Schane, S., eds., *Modern Studies in English*, pp. 227–246. Englewood Cliffs, New Jersey: Prentice-Hall, 1969.

————. "Studies in Diachronic Transformational Syntax." Unpublished doctoral dissertation. Cambridge: Harvard University, 1965.

Krahe, Hans. *Sprache und Vorzeit*. Heidelberg: Winter Universitäts Verlag, n. d.

Kuryłowicz, Jerzy. "La nature des procès dits 'analogiques'." *Acta Linguistica* 5 (1945–1949): 121–138. Reprinted in Hamp, E.; Householder, F.; Austerlitz, R., eds., *Readings in Linguistics II*, pp. 158–174. Chicago: University of Chicago Press, 1966.

————. *L'apophonie en indo-européen*. Wroclow, Poland: Wydawnictwo Polskiej Akademii Nauk, 1956.

————. *Akzent und Ablaut*. Vol. 2 of *Indogermanische Grammatik*. Heidelberg: Carl Winter, 1969.

Labov, William. "The Social Motivation of a Sound Change." *Word* 19 (1963): 273–309.

Lehmann, Winfred P. *Historical Linguistics: An Introduction*. New York: Holt, Rinehart and Winston, 1962.

————. *A Reader in Nineteenth-Century Historical Indo-European Linguistics*. Bloomington: Indiana University Press, 1967.

Mańczak, Witold. "Tendences générales des changements analogiques." *Lingua* 7 (1958): 298–325; 387–420.

Martinet, André. *Économie des changements phonétiques*. Berne: Francke, 1955.

Meillet, Antoine. *Introduction à l'étude comparative des langues indo-européennes*. Paris: Hachette, 1903 and later editions. Edition of 1937 reprinted by University of Alabama Press, 1964.

————. *La méthode comparative en linguistique historique*. Oslo: Aschehoug, 1925 and later editions. English translation by Ford, *The Comparative Method in Historical Linguistics*. Paris: Honoré Champion, 1967.

————. "À propos de οἰστός." *Festschrift für Paul Kretschmer*, pp. 140–141. Wien: Deutscher Verlag für Jugend und Volk, 1926.

————. *Linguistique historique et linguistique générale,* 2 vols. Paris: Champion, 1921, 1938, and later editions.
"Le problème de la parenté des langues," Vol. 1, pp. 76–101.
"Les parentés de langues," Vol. 1, pp. 102–109.
"L'évolution des formes grammaticales," Vol. 1, pp. 130–148.
"Le renouvellement des conjonctions," Vol. 1, pp. 159–174.
"Comment les mots changent de sens," Vol. 1, pp. 230–271.
"Quelques hypothèses sur des interdictions de vocabulaire dans les langues indo-européennes," Vol. 1, pp. 281–291.
"Sur le sens linguistique de l'unité latine," Vol. 1, pp. 310–322.
"Le vocabulaire dans la question des parentés de langues," Vol. 2, pp. 44–46.
"Introduction à la classification des langues," Vol. 2, pp. 53–69.

Meillet, Antoine, and Cohen, Marcel, eds. *Les langues du monde.* Paris: Centre national de la recherche scientifique, 1952.

Morris, William, ed. *The American Heritage Dictionary of the English Language.* New York: American Heritage, 1969.

Muller, Siegfried H. *The World's Living Languages.* New York: Frederick Ungar, 1964.

Oswalt, Robert. "The Case of the Broken Bottle." *International Journal of American Linguistics* 37 (1971): 48–49.

Paul, Hermann. *Principles of the History of Language,* trans., Strong. London and New York: Longmans, Green, 1891.

Pedersen, Holger. *The Discovery of Language: Linguistic Science in the Nineteenth Century,* trans., Spargo. Fourth printing. Bloomington: Indiana University Press, 1967.

Pike, Kenneth L. *Axioms and Procedures for Reconstructions in Comparative Linguistics.* Revised edition. Santa Ana, California: Summer Institute of Linguistics, 1967.

Pokorny, Julius. *Indogermanisches Etymologisches Wörterbuch.* Bern: Francke, 1959.

Poppe, Nikolaus. *Verleichende Grammatik der altaischen Sprachen.* Wiesbaden: Harassowitz, 1960.

Postal, Paul. *Aspects of Phonological Theory.* New York: Harper and Row, 1968.

Powell, J. W. "Indian Linguistic Families of America North of Mexico." *Seventh Annual Report,* Bureau of American Ethnology, Washington, D.C.: Government Printing Office, 1891. Reprinted by University of Nebraska Press, 1966.

Prokosch, E. *A Comparative Germanic Grammar.* Philadelphia: Linguistic Society of America and the University of Pennsylvania, 1939.

Pulgram, Ernst. *The Tongues of Italy.* Cambridge: Harvard University Press, 1958.

Samarin, William J. *Field Linguistics: A Guide to Linguistic Field Work.* New York: Holt, Rinehart, and Winston, 1967.

Sapir, Edward. *Language.* New York: Harcourt, Brace, and World, 1921 and later editions.

Scherer, Anton, ed. *Die Urheimat der Indogermanen.* Darmstadt, Germany: Wissenschaftliche Buchgesellschaft, 1968.

Siebert, Frank T., Jr. "The Original Home of the Proto-Algonquian People." *National Museum of Canada Bulletin* 214 (1967): 13–47.

Stimson, Hugh. "A Tabu Word in the Peking Dialect." *Language* 42 (1966): 285–294.

Swadesh, Morris. "Linguistics as an Instrument of Prehistory." *Southwestern Journal of Anthropology* 15 (1959): 20–35. Reprinted in Hymes, D., ed., *Language in Culture and Society,* pp. 575–583. New York: Harper and Row, 1964.

Thieme, Paul. "The Comparative Method for Reconstruction in Linguistics." In Hymes, D., ed., *Language in Culture and Society,* pp. 585–598. New York: Harper and Row, 1964.

Thomsen, Vilhelm. *Inscriptions de l'Orkhon déchifrées.* Helsingfors, Finland: Impr. de la Société de littérature finnoise, 1896.

Tsiapera, Mária, ed. *Generative Studies in Historical Linguistics.* Edmonton, Alberta, and Champaign, Illinois: Linguistic Research, 1971.

Ullmann, Stephen. *The Principles of Semantics.* Second edition. Glasgow: Jackson, 1959.

Voorhis, Paul H. "New Notes on the Fox Language." *International Journal of American Linguistics* 37 (1971): 63–75.

Wartburg, Walter von. *Problems and Methods in Linguistics,* trans., Reid. Oxford: Blackwell, 1969.

Watkins, Calvert. "Review of Kuryłowicz, *L'apophonie en indo-européen.*" *Language* 34 (1958): 381–389.

———. *Indo-European Origins of the Celtic Verb.* Dublin: Dublin Institute for Advanced Studies, 1962.

————. "Preliminaries to a Historical and Comparative Analysis of the Syntax of the Old Irish Verb." *Celtica* 6 (1963): 1–49.

————. "Italo-Celtic Revisited." In Birnbaum, H., and Puhvel, J., eds., *Ancient Indo-European Dialects.* Berkeley and Los Angeles: University of California Press, 1966.

————. *Geschichte der Indogermanischen Verbalflexion,* Vol. 3, Part I of Kuryłowicz, J., ed., *Indogermanische Grammatik.* Heidelberg: Carl Winter, 1969.

Weinreich, Uriel. *Languages in Contact.* The Hague: Mouton, 1963.

Weinreich, Uriel; Labov, William; and Herzog, Marvin. "Empirical Foundations for a Theory of Language Change." In Lehmann, W., and Malkiel, Y., eds., *Directions for Historical Linguistics* (pp. 95–180). Austin: University of Texas Press, 1968.

Index

Albanian, 104, 105
Algic language family, 60
Algonquian language family, 58,
  60
Algonquians
  studied through language, 237–
  40, 242–43
Altaic language family, 48, 102
  syntax described by generative
  grammar, 229
Analogy, 130, 149
  in affixes, 132–35
  differs from grammaticalization, 159–60
  in generative grammar, 224–
  26
  implications in for reconstruction, 142–45
  Kuryłowicz's laws of, 135–42
  references for, 147–48
  in stems, 130–32
  in word order, 145–47
Anatolian, 104
Apocope, *80*
Apophony, *110, 119*–24, 173–74
  lengthened grade, *124*–28
Armenian, 103, 105
Assimilation, *81*
  lenition, *83*–84
  progressive, *81,* 82
  regressive, *81*–82
  vowel harmony in, *85*–86
Athabascan language family, 58,
  234–35

Australian language family, 55
  tabu in, 203–04

Back-formation, *138,* 212
  see also Etymology
Balto-Slavic, 104, 109
Basic form, *138*
Basque language family, 48, 50
Benveniste, Émile, 44, 127, 149,
  151, 164, 183, 240, 260
Bibliography, *21,* 260–67
Borrowing, *38,* 40, 172, 167–68,
  178–79, *184,* 204, 232–33
  lexical, 184–88
  loan translations in, *189*–91
  phonological, 191–93
  references for, 195
  syntactic, 193–95
Bréal, Michel, 166, 183, 260
Brugmann, Karl, 103–04, 116,
  128, 260

Calquing, *189*–91
Celtic, 104, 105–06
  lenition in, 83
  loss of phonemes in, 78
  paradigm restructuring in, 154–
  55, 157–58
  see also Irish
Chinese
  calquing in, 190–91
  discontinuous transmission in,
  198–200
  interrogative particle in, 161